My First Fun Questions and Answers

My First Fun

Questions and Answers

Catherine Chambers and Chris Oxlade

Miles Kelly

First published in 2014 by Miles Kelly Publishing Ltd
Harding's Barn, Bardfield End Green, Thaxted, Essex, CM6 3PX, UK

This material was previously published in 2007 as part of *My First Question and Answer Book*

2 4 6 8 10 9 7 5 3 1

Publishing Director Belinda Gallagher

Creative Director Jo Cowan

Editorial Assistant Carly Blake

Cover Designer Simon Lee

Designers Jo Brewer, Venita Kidwai,
Sophie Pelham, Elaine Wilkinson, Candice Bekir

Production Manager Elizabeth Collins

Reprographics Stephan Davis, Jennifer Cozens, Thom Allaway,
Liberty Newton, Anthony Cambray

The publisher would like to thank iStockphoto.com for the use of the image on page 147

ISBN 978-1-78209-574-3

Printed in China

British Library Cataloguing-in-Publication Data
A catalogue record for this book is available from the British Library

Made with paper from a sustainable forest

www.mileskelly.net
info@mileskelly.net

Contents

Questions about...

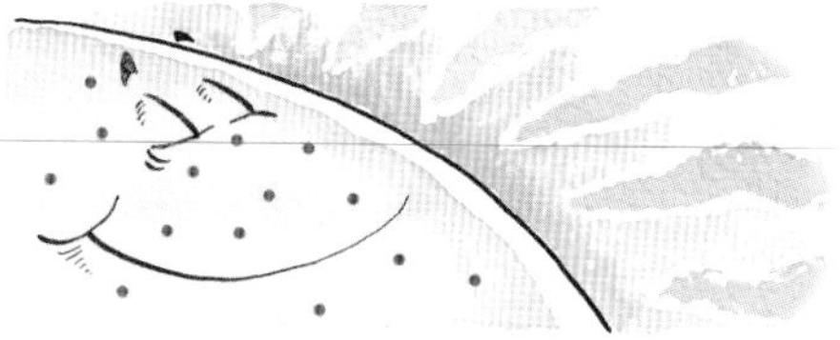

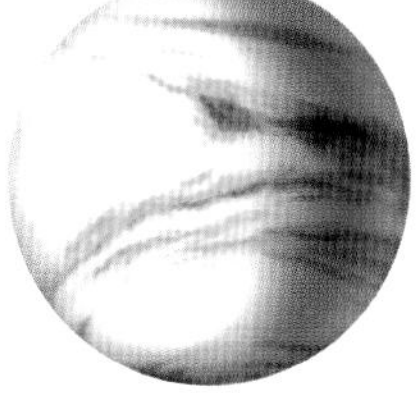

Space

Which star keeps us warm?

The Sun does. It is a star like all the others in the night sky, but it is much closer to Earth. The Sun is a giant ball of hot, glowing gas and it gives off heat that keeps the Earth warm. It also gives us light.

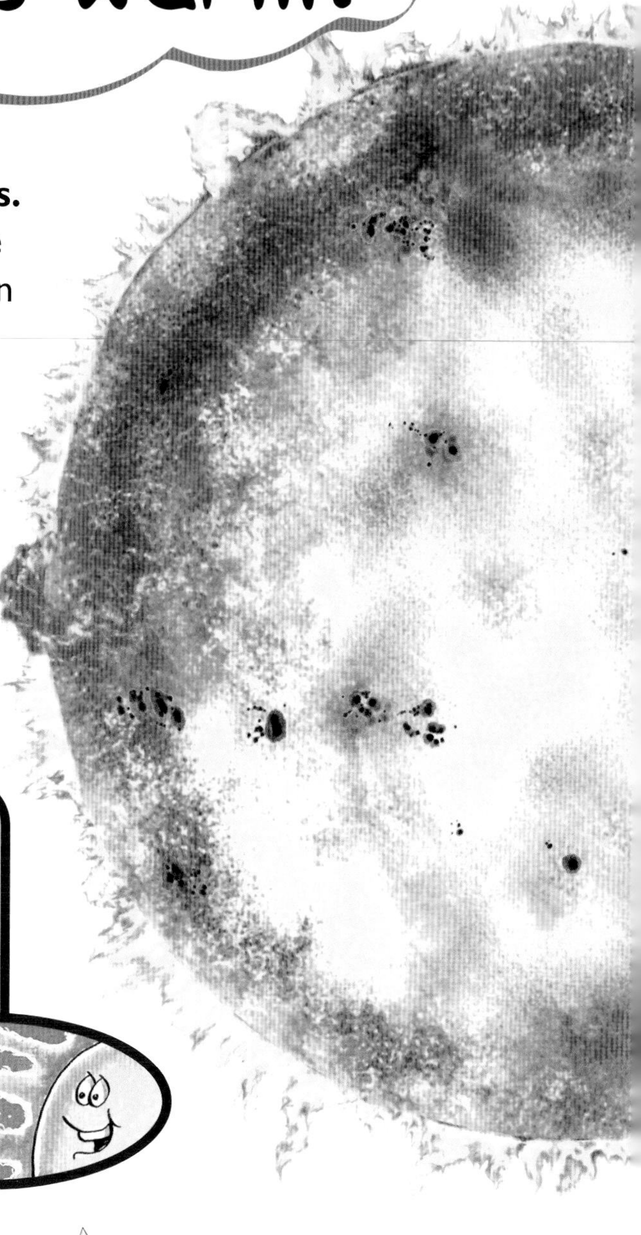

Hot hot hot!

The Sun's surface is so hot that it would melt a metal spacecraft flying near it! It is 15 times hotter than boiling water.

When is it night time during the day?

Sometimes the Sun, the Earth and the Moon all line up in space. When this happens, the Moon's shadow falls on the Earth, making it dark even if it's daytime. This is called an eclipse.

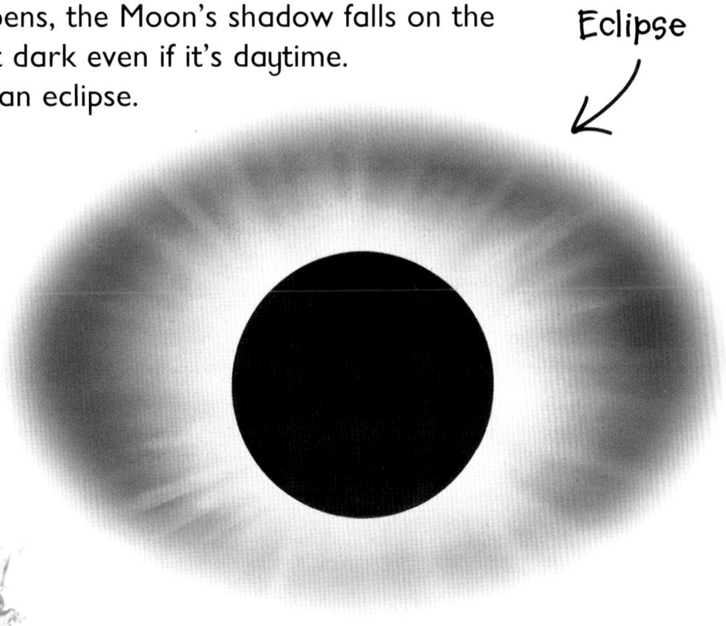

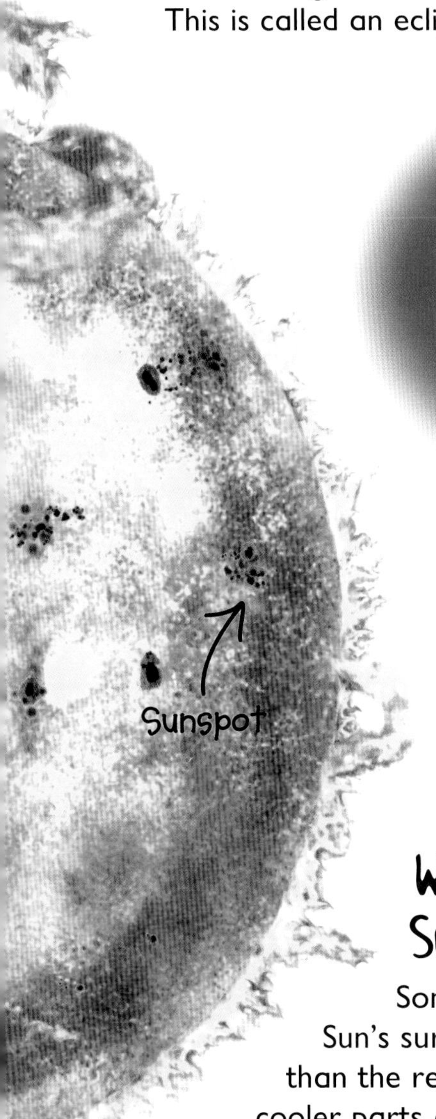

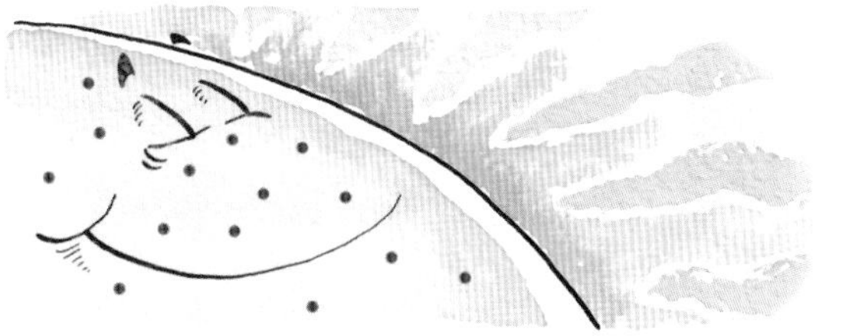

Why is the Sun spotty?

Some parts of the Sun's surface are cooler than the rest of it. These cooler parts appear darker than the rest of the Sun, like spots on its surface. They are called sunspots.

Remember

Never look straight at the Sun. Your eyes could be badly damaged.

Is Earth the only planet near the Sun?

No, there are other planets near the Sun. Mercury and Venus are nearer to the Sun than the Earth is. The other planets are further away. All the planets move around the Sun in huge circles. The Sun and its family of planets is called the Solar System.

Draw

Can you draw a picture of all the planets? You could copy the pictures on this page.

Do other planets have moons?

Earth is not the only planet with a moon. Mars has two moons. Jupiter and Saturn have more than 30 moons each. Venus and Mercury are the only planets with no moons.

What are the other planets like?

Mercury, Venus and Mars are rocky planets, like the Earth. They have solid surfaces. Jupiter, Saturn, Uranus and Neptune are balls of gas and liquid. They are much bigger than the rocky planets. Pluto is a dwarf planet.

One big, happy family!

There are millions of smaller members in the Sun's family. Tiny specks of dust speed between the planets along with chunks of rock called asteroids.

What is inside the Earth?

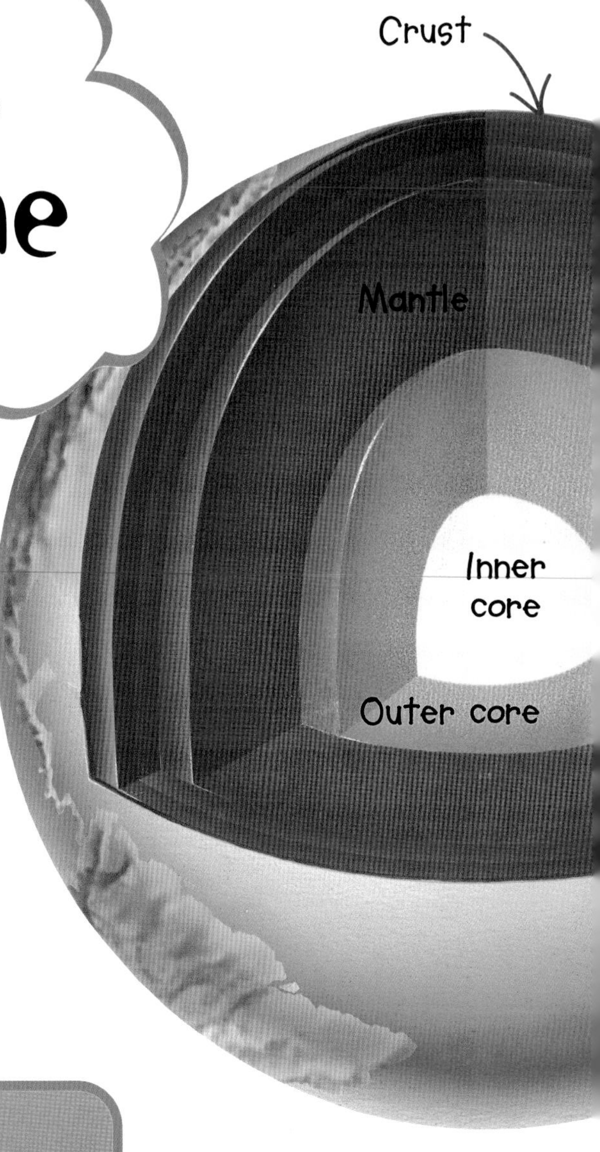

There are layers of hot rock inside the Earth. We live on the Earth's surface where the rock is solid. Beneath the surface, the rock is hot. In some places, it has melted. This melted rock may leak from a volcano.

Living it up!

Earth is the only planet with water on its surface. This means that people, plants and animals can live here. No life has yet been found on other planets.

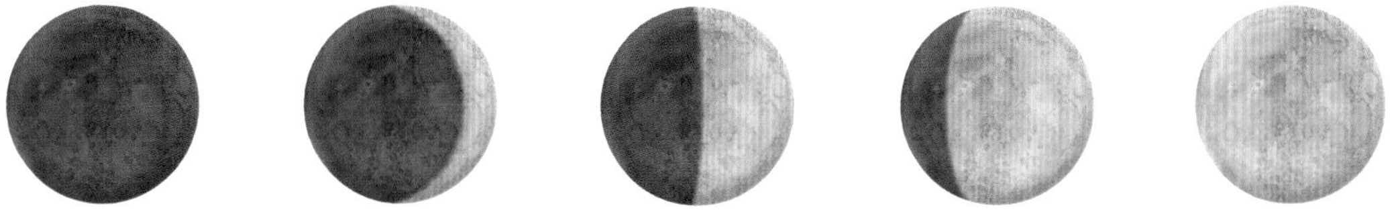

New Moon | Crescent Moon | First quarter Moon | Gibbous Moon | Full Moon

Why does the Moon change shape?

The Sun lights up one side of the Moon. The other side is dark. As the Moon circles the Earth, we see different parts of the lit side. This is why the Moon seems to change shape.

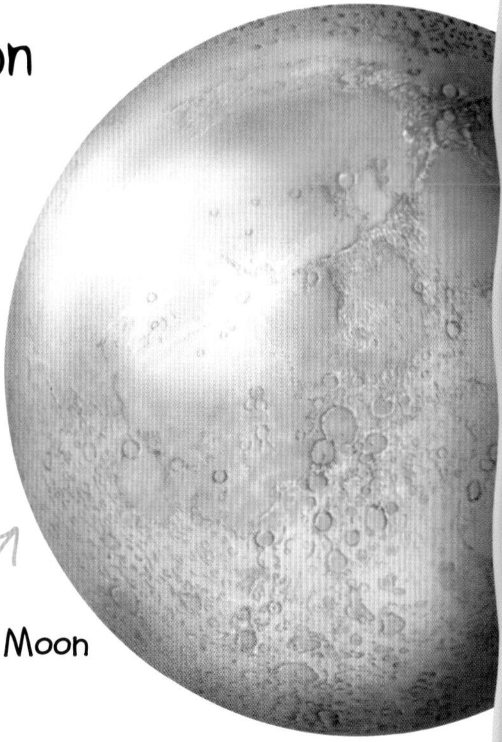

The Moon

Why do we have day and night?

The Earth spins round once every day. When the part you live on faces the Sun, it is daytime. When this part faces away from the Sun, the sunlight can't reach you. Then it is night time.

Look

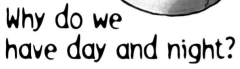

Look at the picture of the Moon. The circles are called craters. They were made by lumps of rock smashing into the Moon's surface.

What is the hottest planet?

Venus is the hottest planet in the Solar System. Its surface is hotter than the inside of an oven. Venus is covered in a blanket of thick, yellow gas. The gases trap heat from the Sun but don't let it escape. This means that Venus can't cool down.

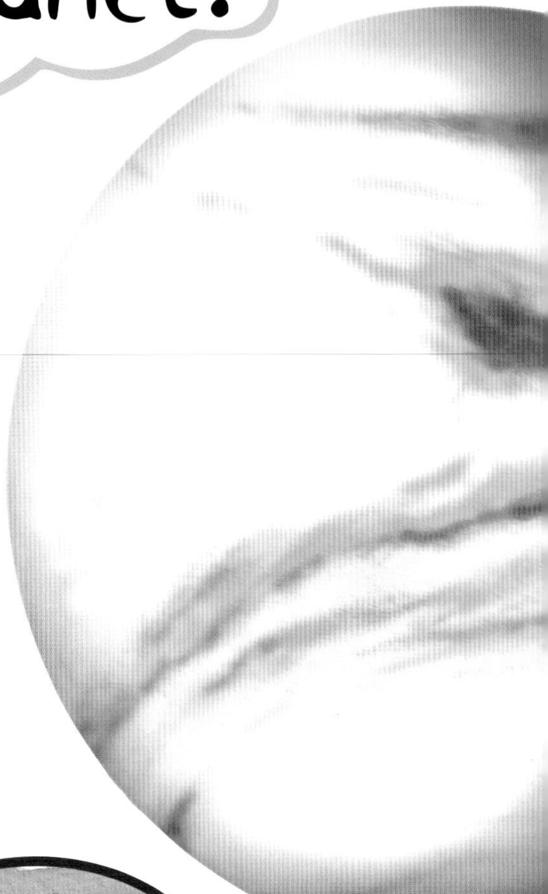

Venus

Back in a year!

Nobody has ever been to Mars. It is so far away that it would take a spacecraft six months to get there. It would take another six months to get home again!

Why is Mars called the red planet?

Mars looks red because it is covered with red rocks and red dust, the colour of rust. Sometimes, winds pick up the dust and make swirling dust storms. In 1971 dust storms covered the whole planet. The surface completely disappeared from view!

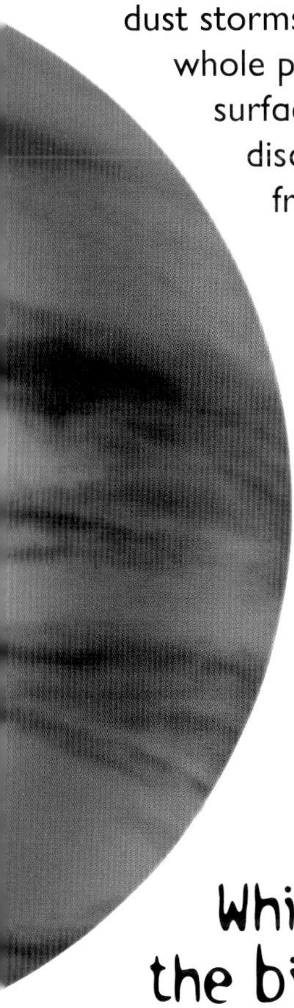

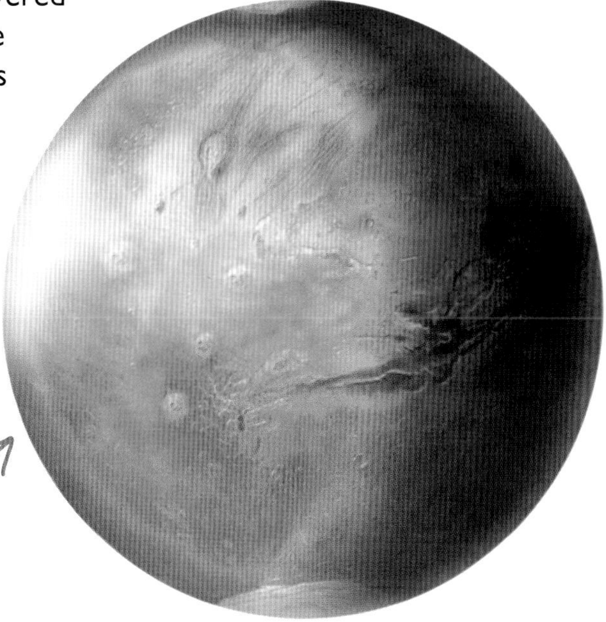

Mars

Which planet has the biggest volcano?

Mars has the biggest volcano. It is called Olympus Mons and it is three times higher than Mount Everest, the highest mountain on Earth. Olympus Mons has gently sloping sides, like an upside-down plate. Mars has many other volcanoes, too. There are also giant canyons and craters.

Discover

Try looking for Venus in the night sky. It looks like a bright star in the early morning or evening.

Does Pluto have its own moon?

Yes, it does. Pluto, a dwarf planet, has its own moon called Charon. Charon is half the size of Pluto and was discovered by scientists in 1978. It takes Charon six and a half Earth days to orbit around Pluto.

Why does Mercury look like the Moon?

Mercury looks a bit like our Moon. It is covered in dents called craters. These were made when rocks crashed into the surface. There is no wind or rain on Mercury, or the Moon, to wear away the craters.

Sun trap!

Mercury is very close to the Sun. It gets much hotter there than on Earth. If you travelled to Mercury, you would need a special spacesuit and shoes to protect you from the heat.

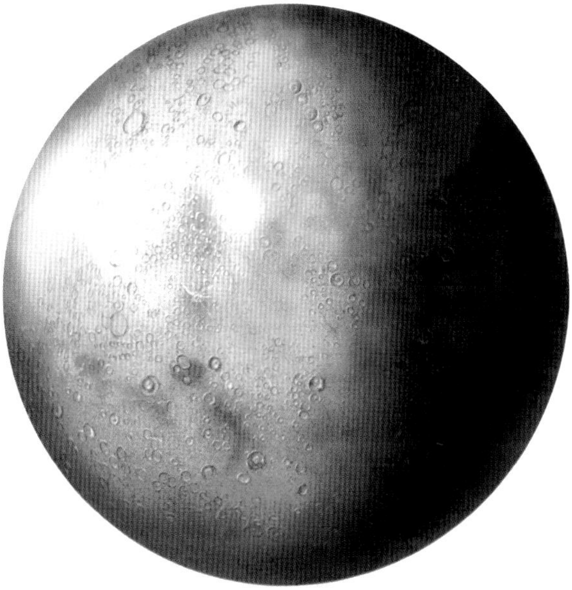

Mercury

Think

Pluto is really cold. Can you think why?

Which planet is baking hot and freezing cold?

Mercury is hot and cold. It spins very slowly. The side that faces the Sun is baked until it is hotter than the inside of an oven. When this side faces away from the Sun, it cools down until it is colder than a freezer.

What is the biggest planet?

Jupiter is the biggest planet. It is 11 times as wide as the Earth. All the other planets in the Solar System would fit inside it! Jupiter is covered in swirls of red and orange gas. These are giant storms.

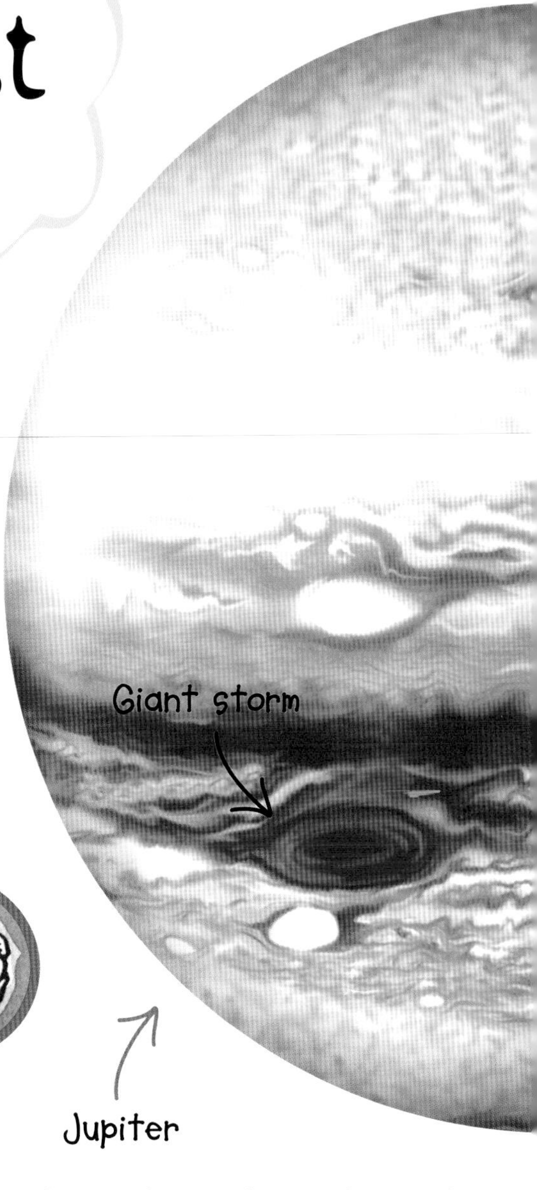

Moon pizza!

Io is one of Jupiter's moons. It is covered in yellow and orange blotches. Io looks like a pizza in space! The blotches are made by hot liquid that comes out of volcanoes.

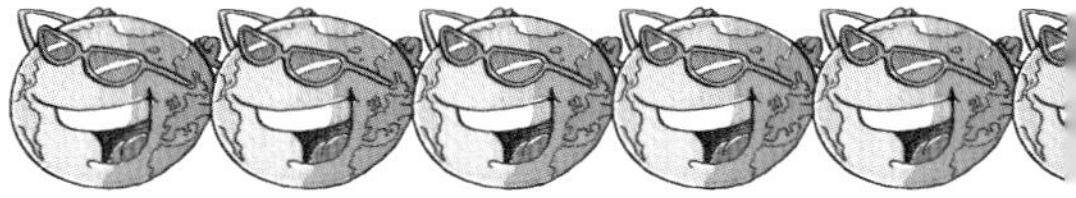

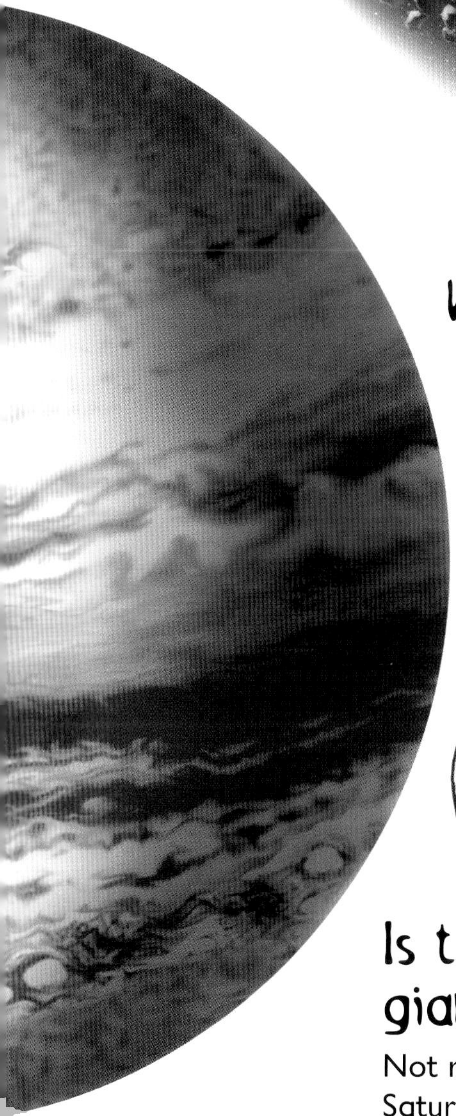

Which planet has rings?

Saturn is surrounded by rings that shine brightly in the sunlight. The rings are made from millions and millions of lumps of ice. Some lumps are the size of ice cubes. Others are as big as cars!

Count

Can you count how many planet Earths there are on these pages?

Is there a giant made of gas?

Not really! However, Jupiter and Saturn are called gas giants. This is because they don't have solid surfaces like the Earth. They have a thick layer of gas and then liquid. You couldn't land on them in a spacecraft.

Which planet rolls around?

Uranus is different to the other planets. Most planets are almost upright. They spin as they move around the Sun. Uranus is tipped right over on its side. This planet spins, too, but it looks as though it is rolling around!

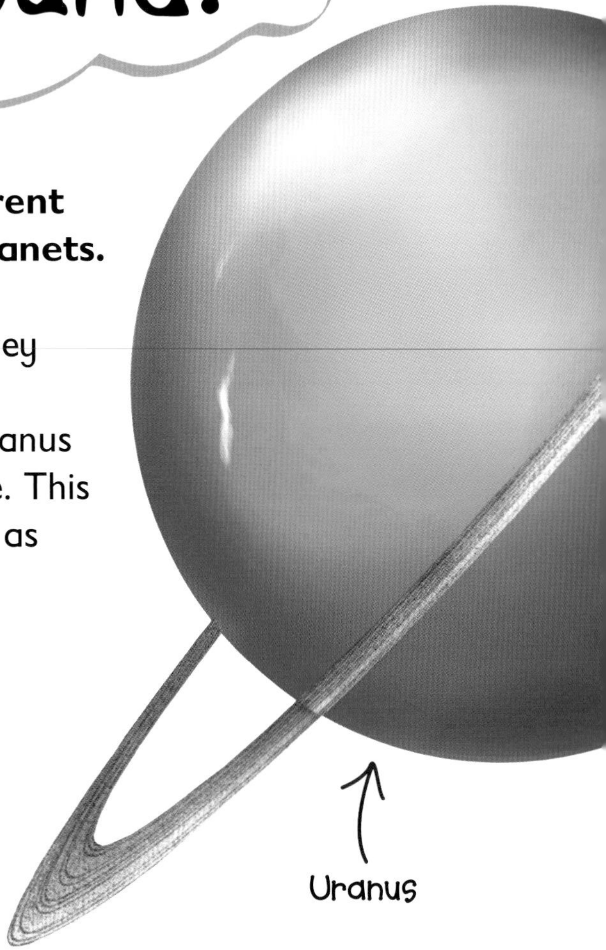

New new moons!

Astronomers (scientists that study space) keep finding new moons around Uranus. They have found 27 so far. There are four big moons and lots of small ones. But there may be more!

Why does Neptune look so blue?

Neptune is covered in bright blue clouds. Sometimes there are streaky, icy white clouds, too. One white cloud is called The Scooter because it scoots around Neptune at high speed. There is also a giant storm called the Great Dark Spot.

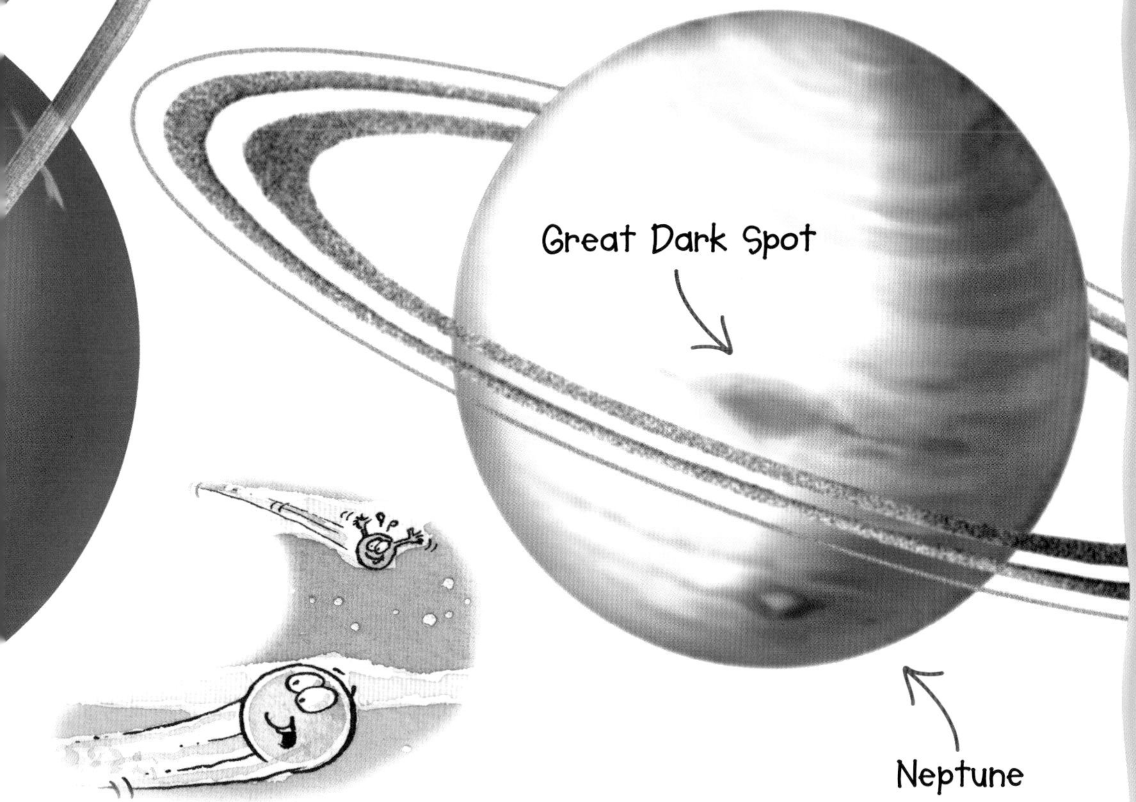

Why do Neptune and Pluto swap places?

Most of the planets move around the Sun in huge circles. Pluto's circle is a bit squashed. This means that it is sometimes closer to the Sun than Neptune. Then it is Neptune's turn to be the planet that is furthest from the Sun!

Remember

Uranus and Neptune have rings. Which other two planets have rings, too?

Are there snowballs in space?

Not really! However, comets are a bit like giant snowballs. They are made up of dust and ice mixed together. When a comet gets close to the Sun, the ice begins to melt. Then dust and gas stream away from the comet. They form a long, bright tail.

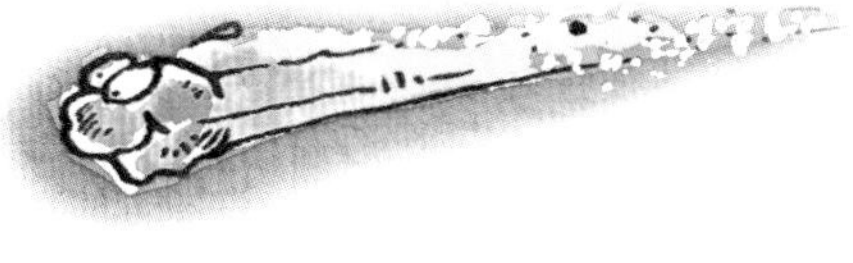

What is a shooting star?

A shooting star is a bright streak across the night sky. It is not really a star. It is made when a small lump of rock shoots into the air above the Earth. Because the rock is going so fast, it burns brightly.

Rocky road!

There are millions of asteroids in the Solar System. Some asteroids are tiny, but some are as big as mountains.

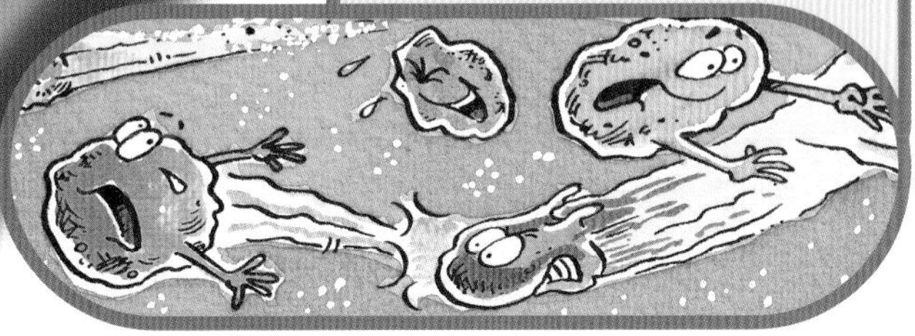

Does the Sun have a belt?

The Sun has a belt made up of lumps of rock called asteroids. We call this the asteroid belt. The asteroids move around the Sun between Mars and Jupiter. The biggest asteroids are round, but most are shaped like giant potatoes.

Discover

Can you find out the name of a famous comet?

How are stars made?

Stars are made from huge clouds of dust and gas. Gradually the cloud shrinks and all the gas and dust clump together. The centre of the cloud gets hotter and hotter and a new star begins to shine. The star gives off heat and light.

Shine on!

Stars can shine for thousands of millions of years! The Sun started shining five thousand million years ago. It will stop shining in another five thousand million years.

What is a group of stars called?

A group of stars is called a star cluster. A star cluster is made from a giant cloud of gas and dust. Some clusters contain just a few stars. Others contain hundreds of stars and they look like a big ball of light.

Star cluster

2. The cloud begins to spin

Are all stars white?

Only the most giant stars shine with a bright white light. This is because they are extremely hot. Smaller stars, such as our Sun, are not so hot. They look yellow instead. Very small stars are cooler still. They look red or brown.

Draw

Can you paint white, yellow and red stars on a sheet of black paper?

What is the Milky Way?

The stars in space are in huge groups called galaxies. Our galaxy is called the Milky Way. All the stars in the night sky are in the Milky Way. There are so many that you couldn't count them all in your whole lifetime!

Can galaxies crash?

Sometimes two galaxies crash into each other. But there is no giant bump. This is because galaxies are mostly made of empty space! The stars just go past each other. Galaxies can pull each other out of shape.

Count

Look at the pictures on these pages. How many different shapes of galaxies can you find?

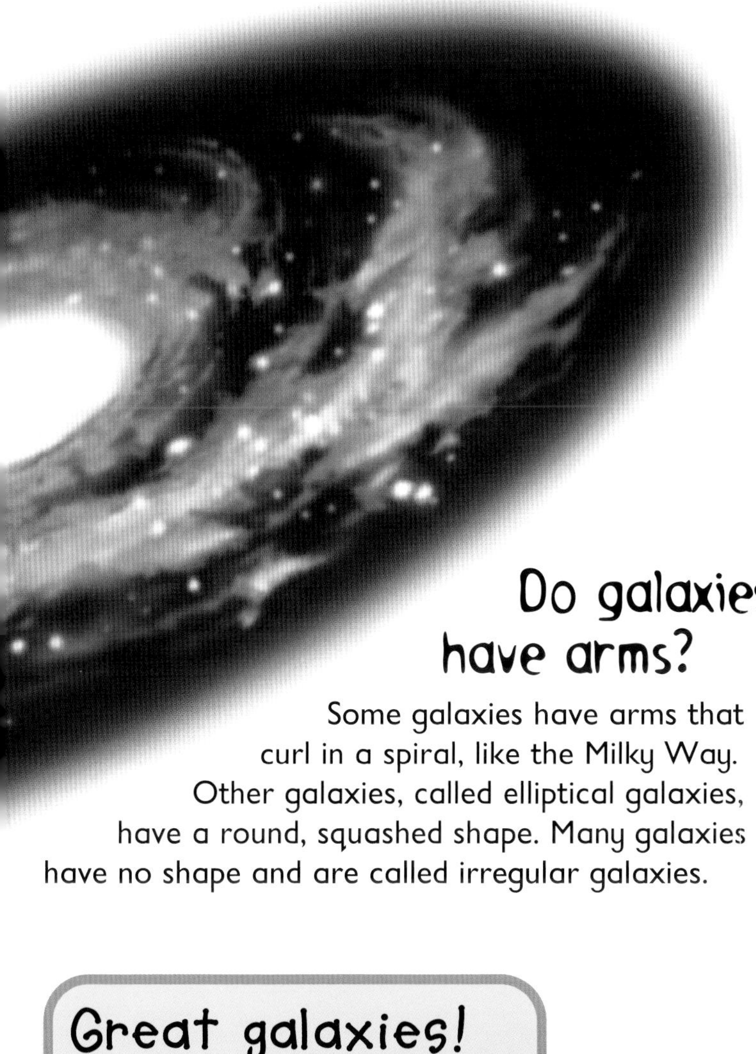

The Milky Way

Do galaxies have arms?

Some galaxies have arms that curl in a spiral, like the Milky Way. Other galaxies, called elliptical galaxies, have a round, squashed shape. Many galaxies have no shape and are called irregular galaxies.

Elliptical galaxy

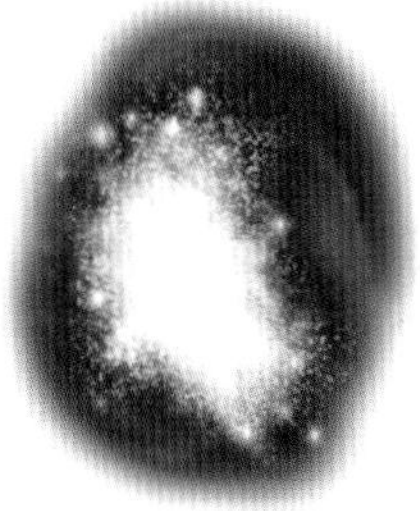

Irregular galaxy

Spiral galaxy

Great galaxies!

There are thousands of millions of galaxies in space. Some are much smaller than the Milky Way. Others are much larger. They all contain too many stars to count!

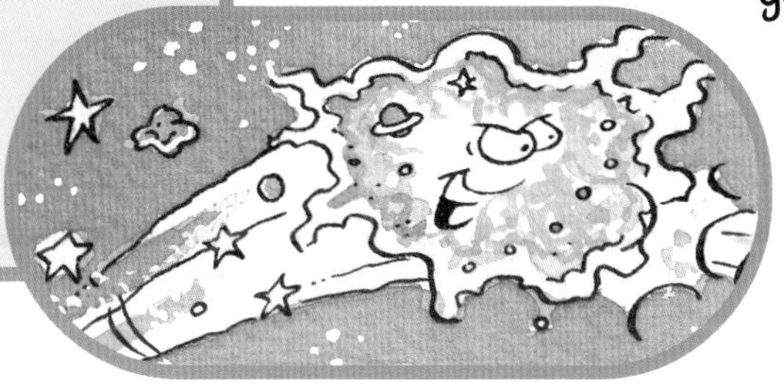

How does a shuttle get into space?

A shuttle blasts into space like a big rocket. It has rocket motors in its tail. They get fuel from a giant fuel tank. There are two booster rockets, too. The fuel tank and the booster rockets fall off before the shuttle reaches space.

Rocket power!

Rockets are filled with fuel. The fuel burns in the rocket motor to make hot gases. The gases rush out of the motor and push the rocket upwards.

How fast do rockets go?

Very, very fast indeed! After blasting off, a rocket goes faster and faster and higher and higher. When it reaches space, it is going 30 times faster than a jumbo jet. If a rocket went slower than this it would fall back to Earth.

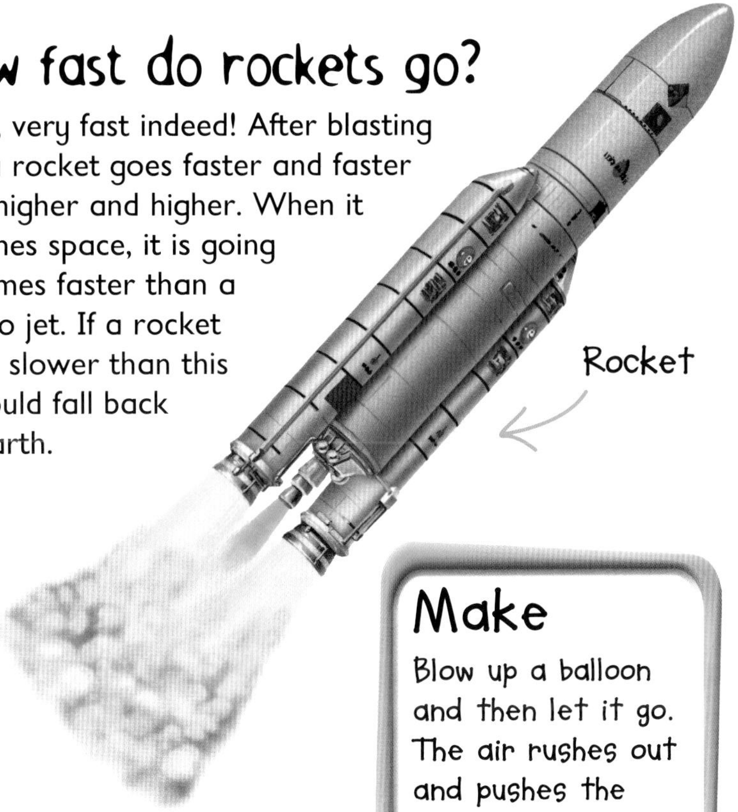

Make

Blow up a balloon and then let it go. The air rushes out and pushes the balloon along, like a simple rocket.

When is a shuttle like a glider?

When a shuttle travels back to Earth it slows down. Then it begins to fall. It does not use its motors to fly down. Instead, it flies like a giant glider. The shuttle lands on a long runway and uses a parachute to slow to a stop.

Why do astronauts float in space?

When things are in space they don't have any weight. This means everything floats. So do astronauts! This makes them feel sick, too. In a spacecraft everything is fixed down to stop it floating away. Astronauts have footholds and handholds to grab onto.

All packed?

Astronauts must take everything they need into space. In space there is no air, water or food. All of these things have to be packed into the spacecraft and taken into space.

Astronaut

Sleeping bag

Where do astronauts go to sleep?

Astronauts sleep in sleeping bags. The bags are fixed to the wall inside a spacecraft. They keep astronauts warm and stop them floating about while they sleep! A special shower lets the astronauts wash without drops of water floating everywhere.

Why do astronauts wear spacesuits?

Space is a dangerous place. Spacesuits protect astronauts when they go outside their spacecraft. There is no air in space. So a spacesuit has a supply of air for the astronaut to breathe. The suit also stops an astronaut from getting too hot or too cold.

Remember

Can you remember why astronauts have to carry air with them in space?

Are there robots in space?

There are robot spacecraft, called probes, in space. They have visited all the planets. Some probes travel around the planets. They send photographs and other information back to Earth. Other probes land on a planet to take a closer look.

Snap happy!

A probe called *Voyager 2* was the first to visit Uranus and Neptune. It took photographs of the planets and sent them back to Earth.

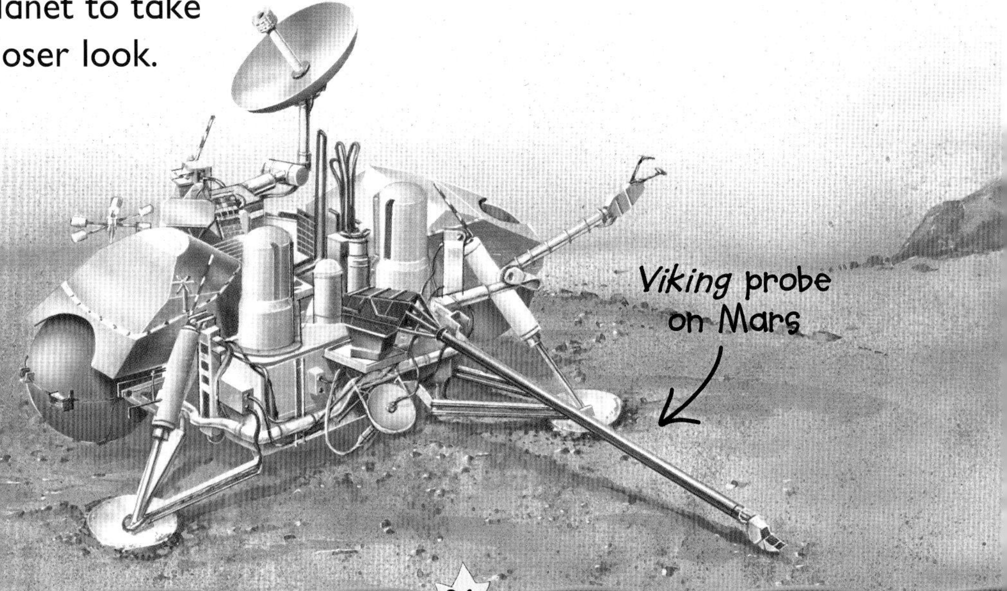

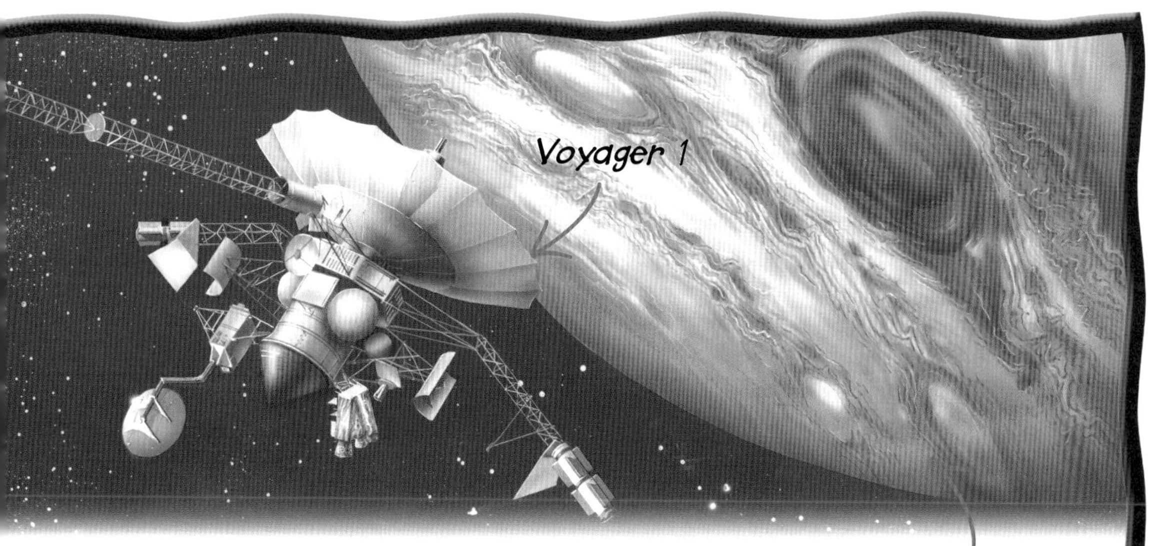

Which probe has travelled the furthest?

A probe called *Voyager 1* was launched from Earth in 1977. It visited Jupiter in 1979 and then Saturn in 1980. Then it kept going, out of the Solar System. *Voyager 1* is now 14 thousand million kilometres from Earth!

Draw

Try designing your own robot explorer. You can take some ideas from these pages.

Have probes been to Mars?

More probes have been to Mars than any other planet. In 1997 a probe called Pathfinder landed on Mars. Inside Pathfinder was a tiny robot vehicle, called *Sojourner*. Scientists steered it using remote control. It investigated the soil and rocks on Mars.

Quiz time

Do you remember what you have read about space?
Here are some questions to test your memory. The pictures will help you. If you get stuck, read the pages again.

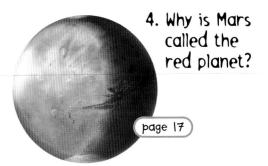

1. Which star keeps us warm?

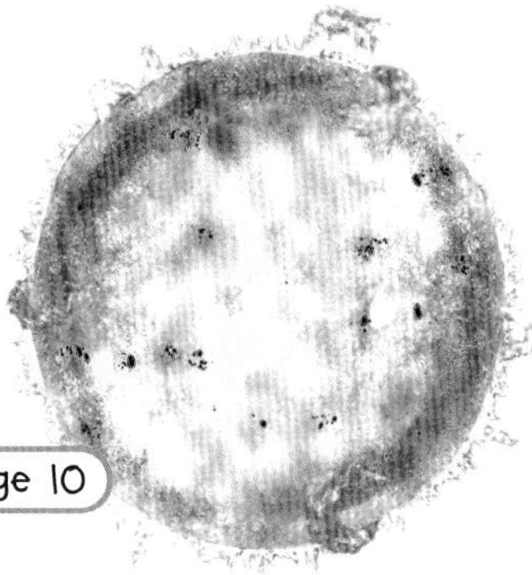

page 10

2. Why is the Sun spotty?

page 11

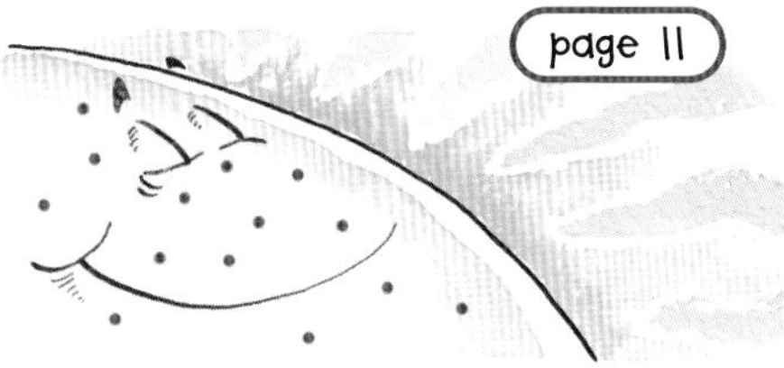

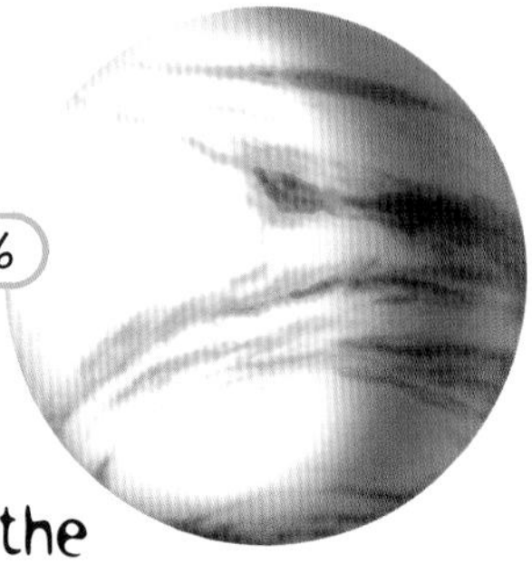

page 16

3. What is the hottest planet?

4. Why is Mars called the red planet?

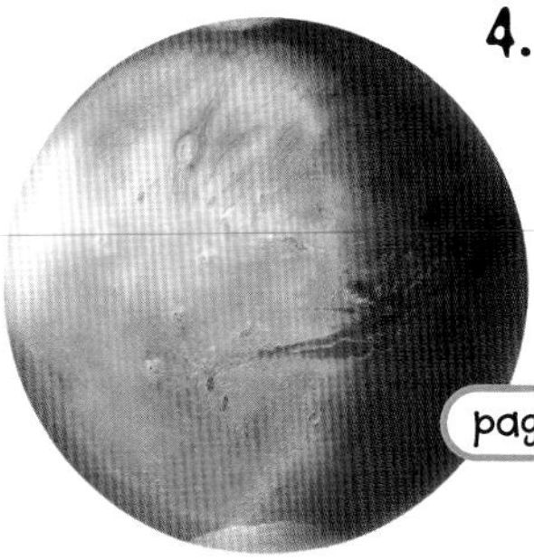

page 17

page 18

5. What is Charon?

page 24

6. What is a shooting star?

7. Does the Sun have a belt?

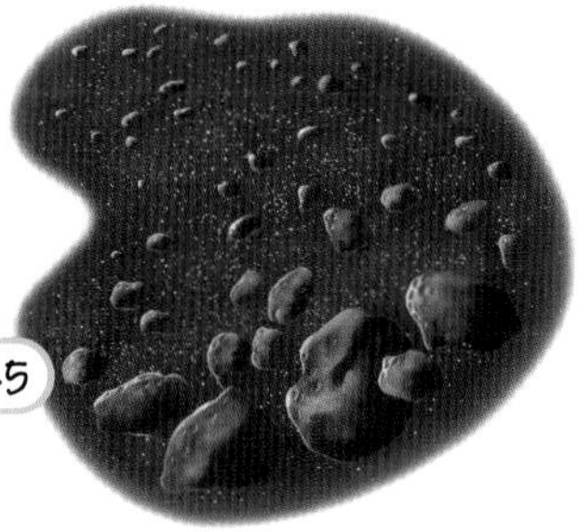

page 25

11. How does a shuttle get into space?

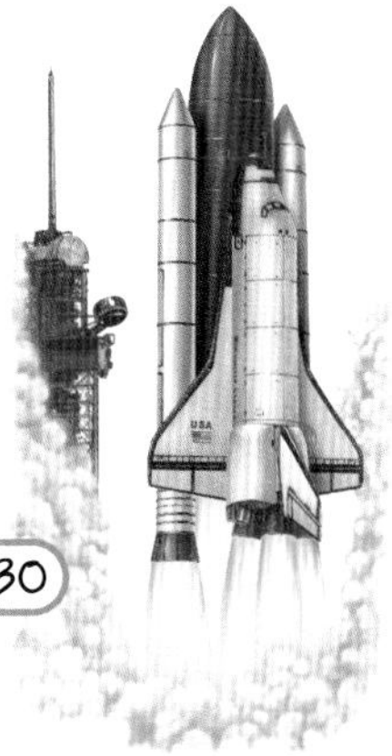

page 30

8. What is a group of stars called?

page 27

12. When is a shuttle like a glider?

page 31

13. Why do astronauts float in space?

page 32

9. What is the Milky Way?

page 28

10. Can galaxies crash?

page 28

Answers

1. The Sun
2. Cooler parts look darker, like spots
3. Venus
4. It is covered with red rocks and dust
5. Pluto's moon
6. A lump of rock burning in the sky
7. Yes, the asteroid belt
8. Star cluster
9. A huge group of stars
10. Yes
11. Like a giant rocket does
12. When it travels back to Earth
13. Because they have no weight in space

Questions about...

Planet Earth

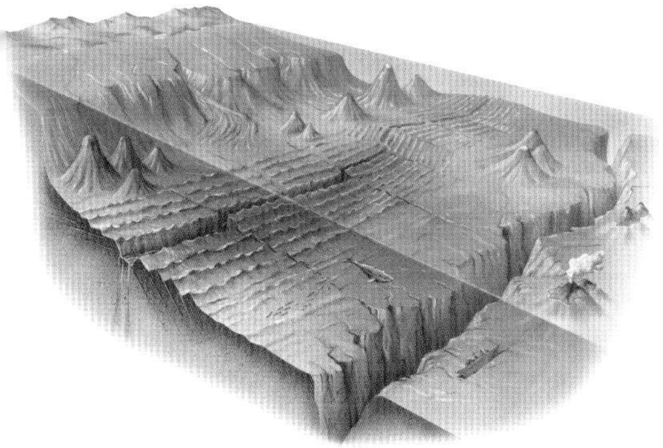

Where did the Earth come from?

The Earth came from a cloud of dust. The dust whizzed around the Sun at speed and and began to stick together to form lumps of rock. The rocks crashed into each other to make the planets. The Earth is one of these planets.

Why does the Moon look lumpy?

Big rocks from space, called meteorites, have crashed into the Moon and made dents on its surface. These dents are called craters and they give the Moon a lumpy appearance.

Look

At night, use some binoculars to look at the Moon. Can you see craters on its surface?

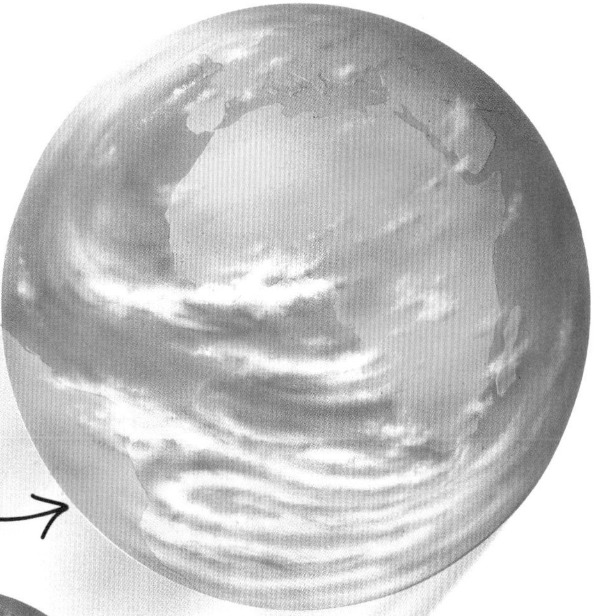
The Earth was formed from the lumps of rock

What is the Earth made of?

The Earth is a huge ball-shaped lump of rock. Most of the Earth's surface is covered by water – this makes the seas and oceans. Rock that is not covered by water makes the land.

Face the Moon!

The Moon travels around the Earth. As the Moon doesn't spin, we only ever see one side of its surface.

Why does the Earth spin?

The Earth is always spinning. This is because it was made from a spinning cloud of gas and dust. As it spins, the Earth leans a little to one side. It takes the Earth 24 hours to spin around once. This period of time is called a day.

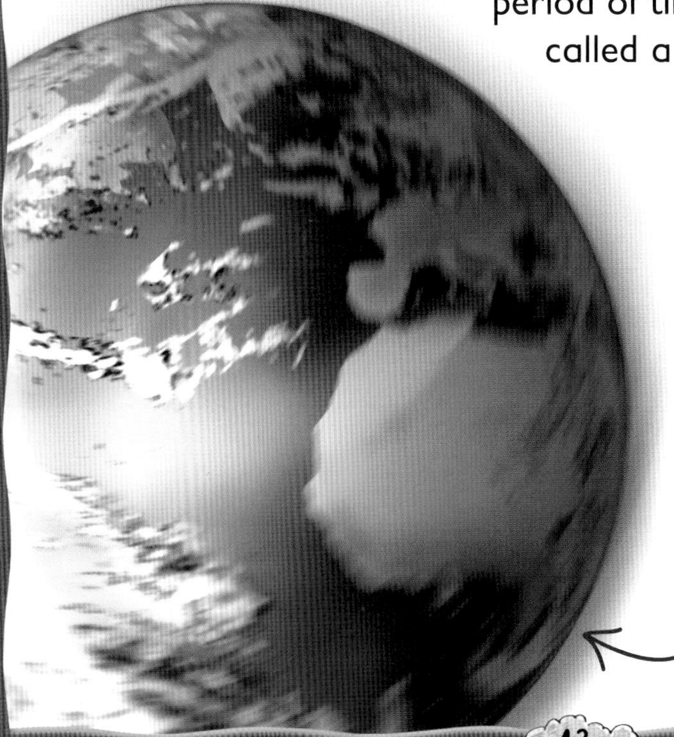
Spinning Earth

Discover

There are 24 hours in a day. How many minutes are there in one hour?

Hot and cold!

In the Caribbean, the sea can be as warm as a bath. In the Arctic, it is so cold, that the sea freezes over.

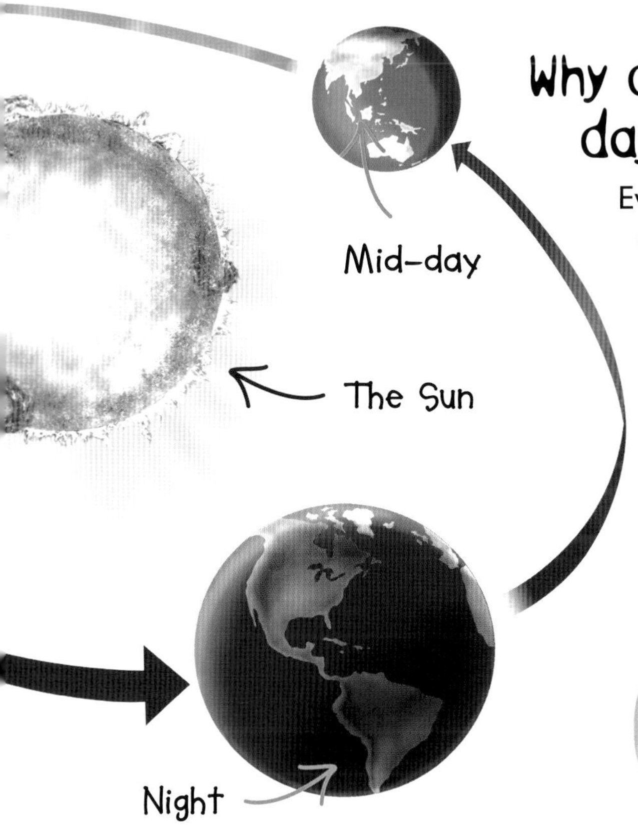

Why do we have day and night?

Every day, each part of the Earth spins towards the Sun, and then away from it. When a part of the Earth is facing the Sun, it is daytime there. When that part is facing away from Earth, it is night time.

Do people live on the Moon?

No they don't. There is no air on the Moon so people cannot live there. Astronauts have visited the Moon in space rockets. They wear special equipment to help them breathe.

What is inside the Earth?

There are different layers inside the Earth. There is a thin, rocky crust, a solid area called the mantle and a centre called the core. The outer part of the core is made of hot, liquid metal. The inner core is made of solid metal.

Natural magnet!

Near the centre of the Earth is hot, liquid iron. As the Earth spins, the iron behaves like a magnet. This is why a compass needle points to North and South.

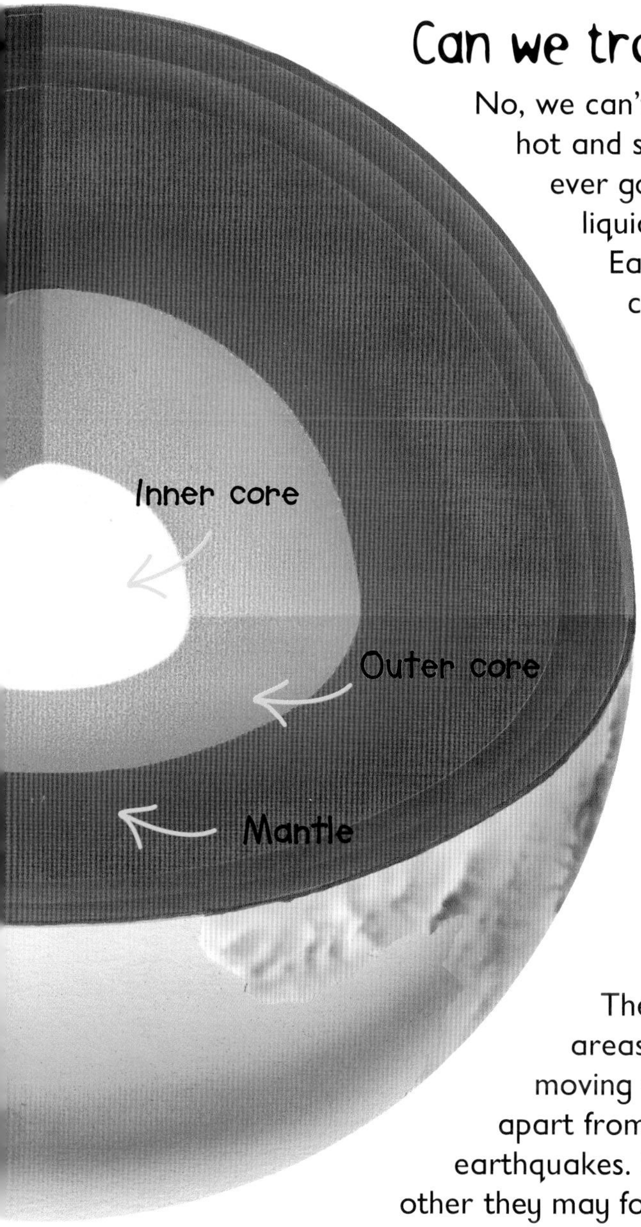

Can we travel into the Earth?

No, we can't. The Earth's core is incredibly hot and so far down that no one could ever go there. Sometimes, boiling-hot liquid rock bursts up through the Earth's surface from mountains called volcanoes.

Which way?

Use a compass to find out which direction is North. Move around holding your compass, does the needle move?

Does the ground move?

The Earth's crust is split into huge areas called plates. Each plate is moving very slowly. If the plates move apart from each other they may cause earthquakes. If they move towards each other they may form volcanoes or mountains.

What is a fossil?

A trilobite was an ancient sea creature

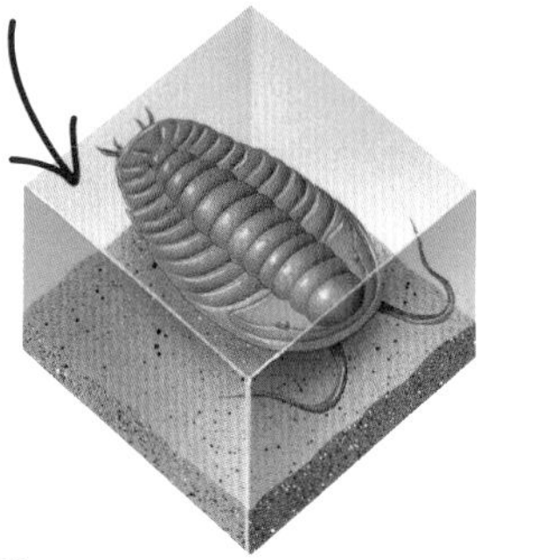

A fossil was once a living thing that has now turned to stone. By studying fossils, scientists can learn more about the past and how animals, such as dinosaurs, used to live.

Scientists digging up and studying fossils

How is a fossil made?

It takes millions of years to make a fossil. When an animal dies, it may be buried by sand. The soft parts of its body rot away, leaving just bones, teeth or shells. These slowly turn to rock and a fossil has formed.

Find

Look for rocks in your garden. They may be so old dinosaurs could have trodden on them.

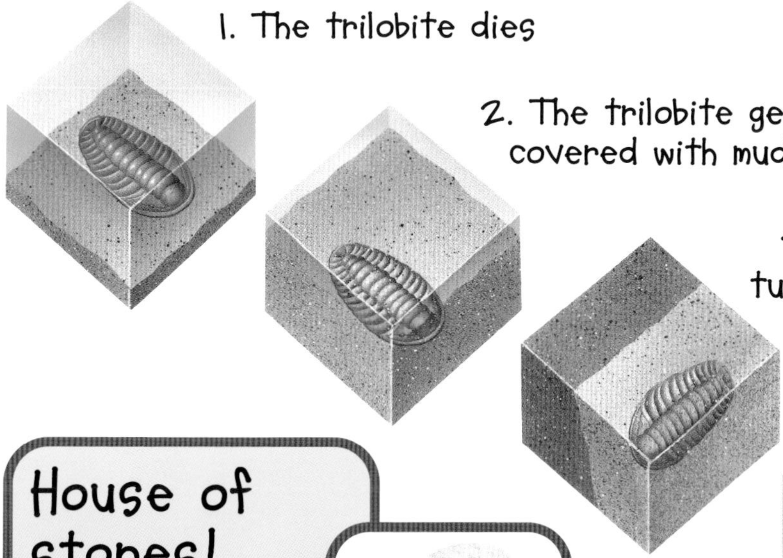

1. The trilobite dies
2. The trilobite gets covered with mud
3. The mud turns to stone
4. The fossil forms inside the stone

House of stones!

In Turkey, some people live in caves. These huge cone-shaped rocks stay very cool in the hot weather.

Why do rocks crumble?

When a rock is warmed up by the Sun it gets a little bigger. When it cools down, the rock shrinks to its original size. If this process happens to a rock too often, it starts to crumble away.

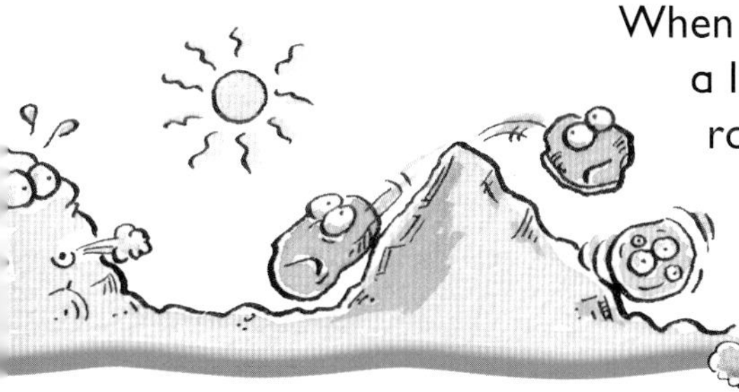

What is a volcano?

A volcano is a mountain that sometimes shoots hot, liquid rock out of its top. Deep inside a volcano is an area called a magma chamber. This is filled with liquid rock. If pressure builds up in the chamber, the volcano may explode, and liquid rock will shoot out of the top.

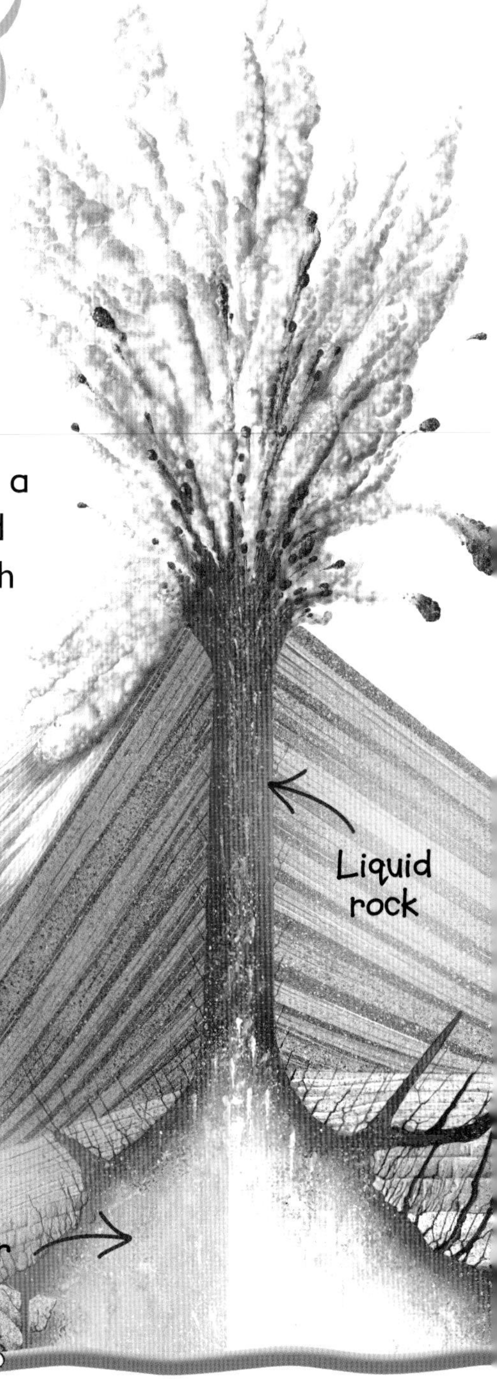

Colour

Draw a picture of a volcano erupting. Remember to colour the lava bright red.

What is a range?

A range is the name for a group of mountains. The biggest ranges are the Alps in Europe, the Andes in South America, the Rockies in North America and the highest of all – the Himalayas in Asia.

How are mountains made?

One way that mountains are formed is when the Earth's plates crash together. The crust at the edge of the plates slowly crumples and folds. Over millions of years this pushes up mountains. The Himalayan Mountains in Asia were made this way.

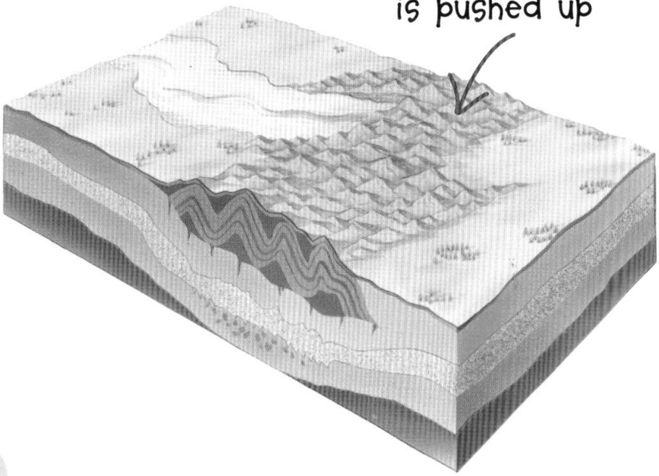
Mountain range is pushed up

Layer on layer

When a volcano erupts, the hot lava cools and forms a rocky layer. With each new eruption, another layer is added and the volcano gets bigger.

Why are there earthquakes?

Earthquakes happen when the plates in the Earth's crust move apart suddenly, or rub together. They start deep underground in an area called the focus. The land above the focus is shaken violently. The worst part of the earthquake happens above the focus, in an area called the epicentre.

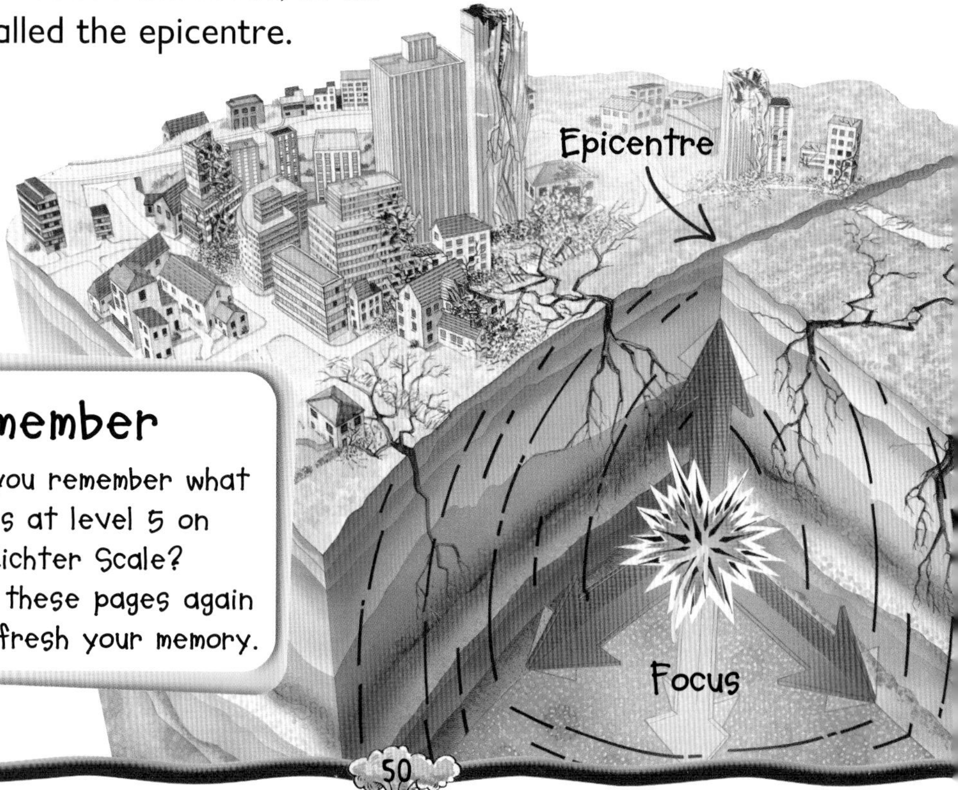

Remember

Can you remember what breaks at level 5 on the Richter Scale? Read these pages again to refresh your memory.

Lights swing at level 3

Windows break at level 5

Bridges and buildings collapse at level 7

What is The Richter Scale?

The Richter Scale measures the strength of an earthquake. It starts at zero and goes up to number ten. The higher the number, the more powerful and destructive the earthquake.

Super senses!

Some people believe that animals can sense when an earthquake is about to happen!

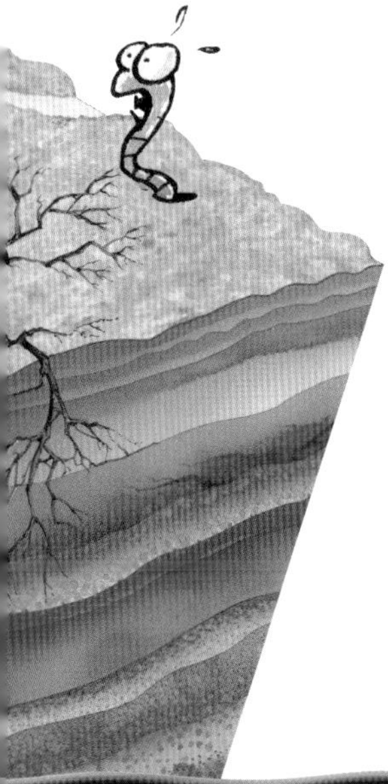

Can earthquakes start fires?

Yes, a powerful earthquake can cause fires. In 1906, a huge earthquake in San Francisco, USA caused lots of fires. The fires burnt down most of the city and the people who lived there became homeless.

What is a glacier?

Glaciers are huge rivers of ice found near the tops of mountains. Snow falls on the mountain and becomes squashed to make ice. The ice forms a glacier that slowly moves down the mountainside until it melts.

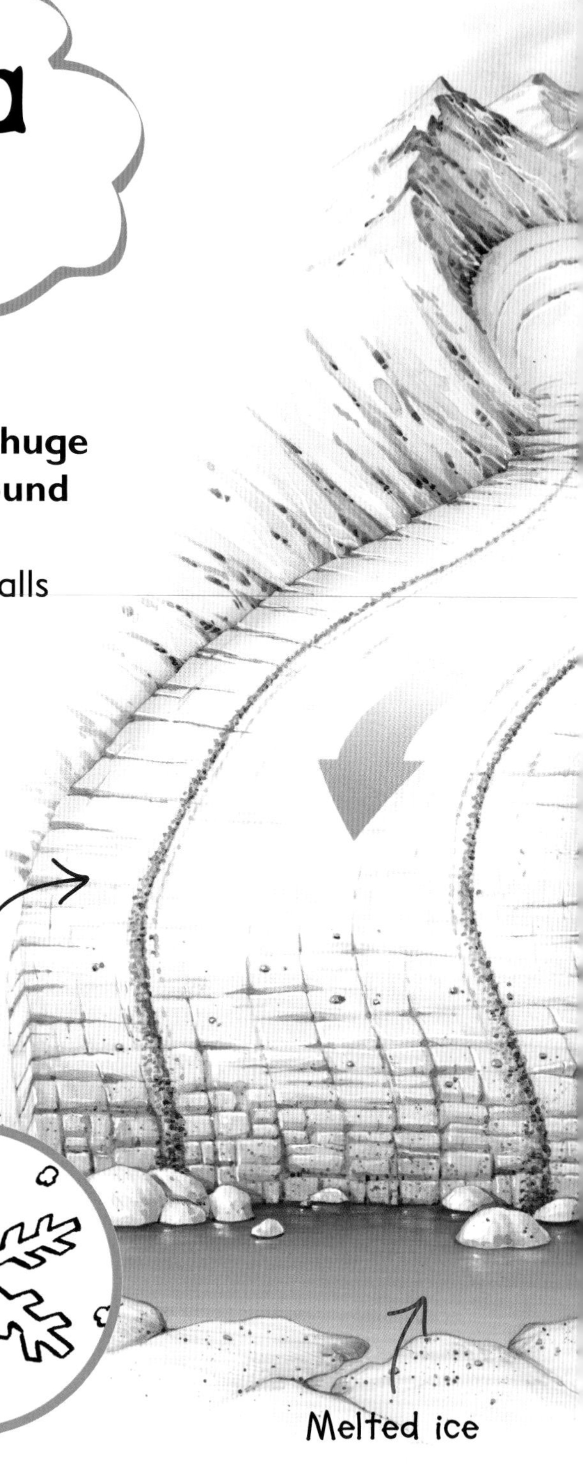

Fancy flakes!

Snowflakes are made of millions of tiny crystals. No two snowflakes are the same because the crystals make millions of different shapes.

Can ice be fun?

Yes, it can! Many people go ice skating and they wear special boots with blades on them called ice skates. Figure skaters are skilled athletes who compete to win prizes.

What is an iceberg?

Icebergs are big chunks of ice that have broken off glaciers and drifted into the sea. Only a small part of the iceberg can be seen above the water. The main part of the iceberg is hidden under the water.

Look

Next time it snows, put some gloves on and let the snowflakes fall into your hand. Can you see crystals?

Where do rivers flow to?

Rivers flow to the sea or into lakes. They start off as small streams in hills and mountains. The streams flow downhill, getting bigger and wider. The place where a river meets the sea, or flows into a lake, is called the river mouth.

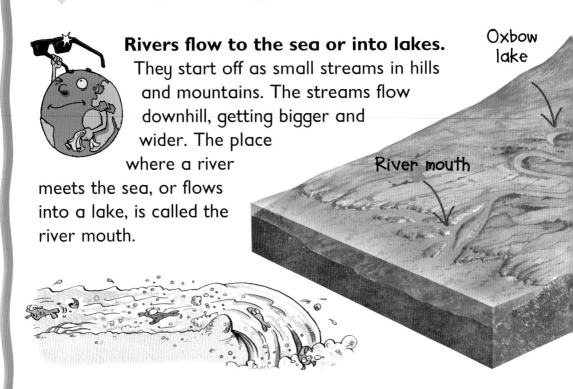

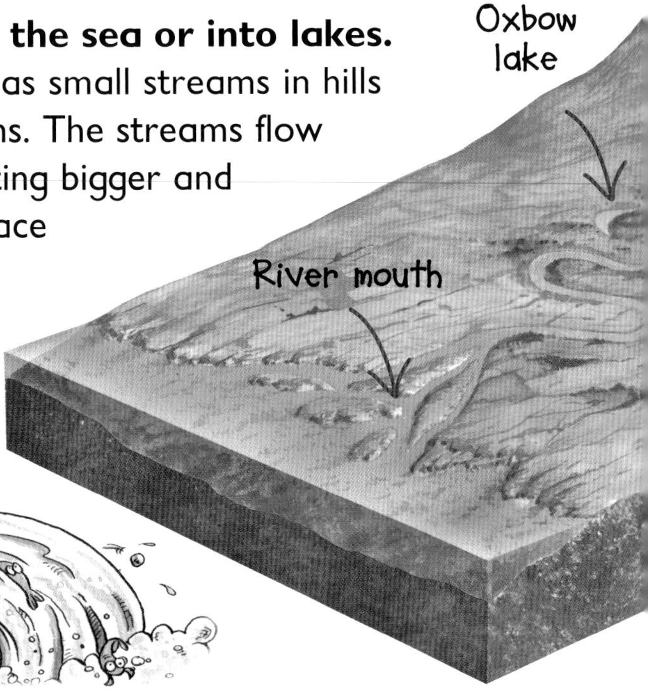

Why are there waterfalls?

Waterfalls are made when water wears down rocks to make a cliff face. The water then falls over the edge into a deep pool called a plunge pool. Waterfalls may only be a few centimetres high, or several hundred metres high!

Discover

Try to find out the name of the highest waterfall in the world. Where is it?

Risky business!

Salmon are a type of fish. Every year, fishermen try to catch them as they swim back to the river they were born in to have their babies.

What is a lake?

A lake is a big area of water that is surrounded by land. Some lakes are so big that they are called inland seas. Most lake water is fresh rather than salty. The biggest lake in the world is the Caspian Sea in Asia.

Are there mountains under the sea?

Yes there are. Mountains lie hidden in very deep oceans. The ocean floor is very flat and is called a plain. Large mountain ranges may rise across the plain. Some oceans even have underwater volcanoes.

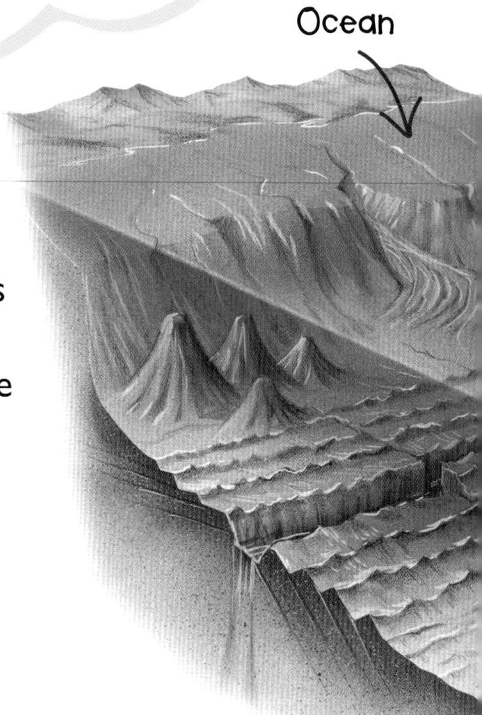

Exploring underwater!

Scientists can learn more about life underwater by exploring the ocean in submarines. They can be underwater for months at a time.

Why do coasts change?

The coast is where the land meets the sea, and it is always changing. In many places, waves crash onto land and rocks, slowly breaking them up. This can change the shape of the coastline.

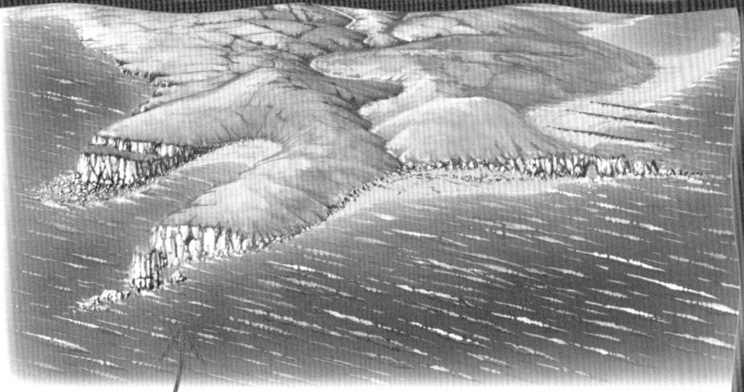

Find out

Have a look in an atlas to find out which ocean you live closest to.

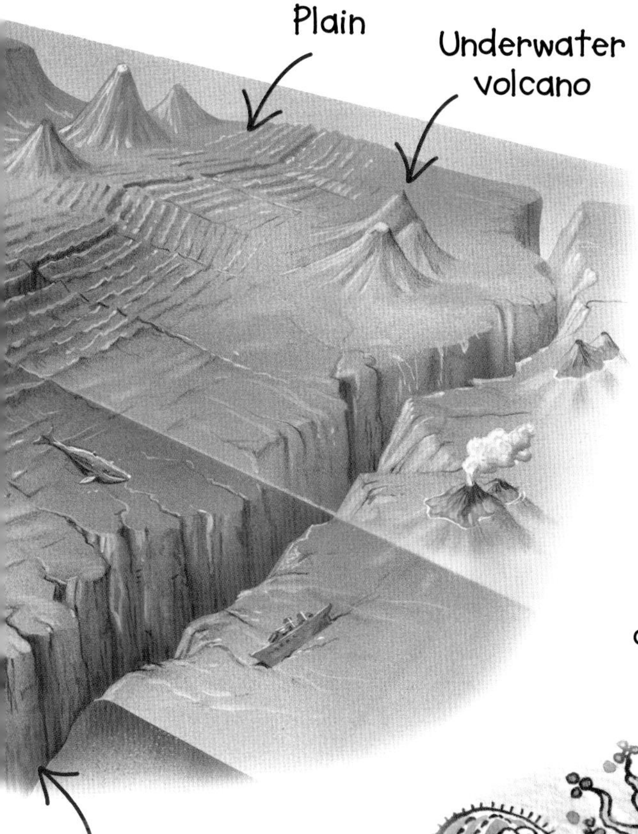

What is coral?

Coral is made from polyps. These are tiny creatures the size of pin heads that live in warm, shallow waters. The polyps join together in large groups and create rocky homes. These are called coral reefs.

How are caves made?

When rain falls on rock, it can make caves. Rainwater mixes with a gas in the air called carbon dioxide. This makes a strong acid. This acid can attack the rock and make it disappear. Underground, the rainwater makes caves in which streams and lakes can be found.

Remember

Stalactites hold on tight, stalagmites might reach the top!

Can lava make caves?

When a volcano erupts and lava flows through the mountain, it can carve out a cave. A long time after the eruption, when the volcano is no longer active, people can walk through this lava cave without having to bend down.

What is a stalactite?

Rocky spikes that hang from cave ceilings are called stalactites. When water drips from the cave ceiling, it leaves tiny amounts of a rocky substance behind. Very slowly, over a long period of time, this grows into a stalactite.

Super spiky!

Stalagmites grow up from the cave floor. Dripping water leaves a rocky substance that grows into a rocky spike.

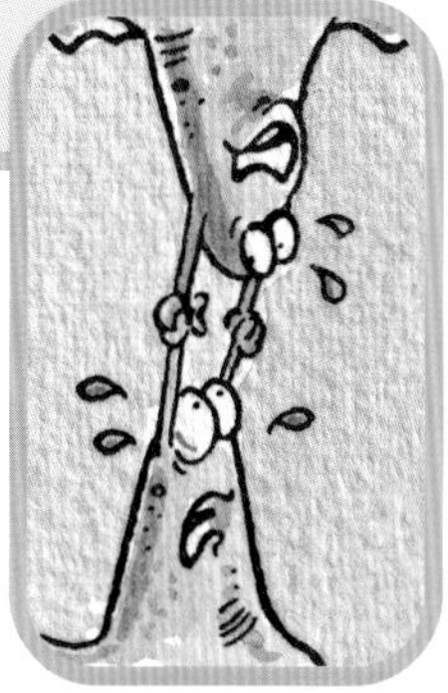

Is there water in the desert?

Yes there is. Deserts sometimes get rain. This rainwater seeps into the sand and collects in rock. The water then builds up and forms a pool called an oasis. Plants grow around the oasis and animals visit the pool to drink.

What are grasslands?

Grasslands are found when there is too much rain for a desert but not enough rain for a forest. Large numbers of animals can be found living and feeding on grasslands, including zebras, antelopes and lions.

Draw

Create a picture of a camel crossing a desert – don't forget to include its wide feet!

Big feet!

Camels have wide feet that stop them sinking into the sand. They can also store water in their bodies for a long time.

What is a rainforest?

In hot places, such as South America, grow areas of thick, green forest. These are rainforests, and they are home to many amazing plants and animals. Rainforests have rainy weather all year round.

Where does rain come from?

Rain comes from the ocean! Water moves between the ocean, air and land in a water cycle. A fine mist of water rises into the air from the ocean and from plants. This fine mist then forms clouds. Water can fall from the clouds as rain.

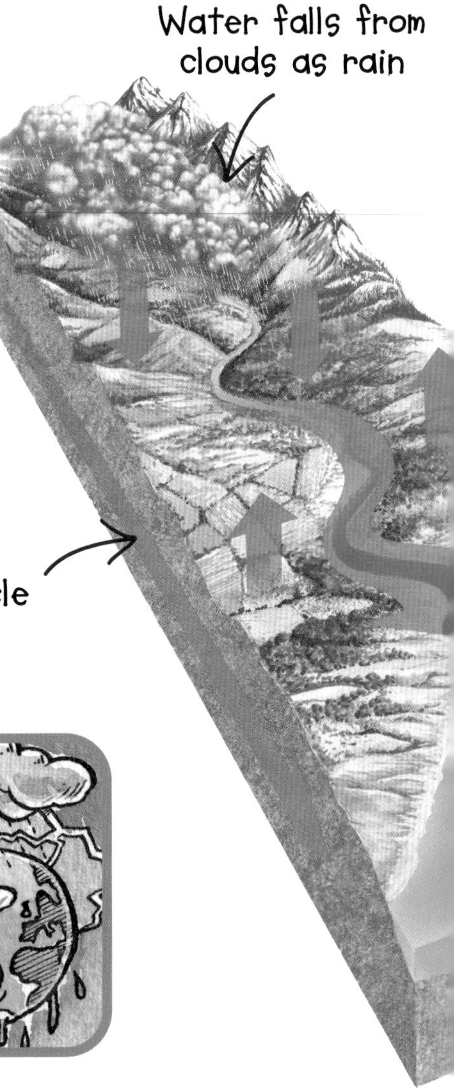

Stormy weather!

Every day there are more than 45,000 thunderstorms on the Earth! Thunderstorms are most common in tropical places, such as Indonesia.

Pretend

Spin around as fast as you can and pretend to be a tornado – watch out! You will get very dizzy!

How does a tornado start?

A tornado is the fastest wind on Earth. Tornadoes start over very hot ground. Here, warm air rises quickly and makes a spinning funnel. This funnel acts like a vacuum cleaner, destroying buildings and lifting cars and lorries off the ground.

A fine mist of water rises from the ocean

Do storms have eyes?

Yes, storms do have eyes! A hurricane is a very dangerous storm. The centre of a hurricane is called the eye and here it is completely still. However, the rest of the storm can reach speeds of up to 300 kilometres an hour.

How do we damage the Earth?

Some of the things that people do can damage the Earth. Factories pump chemicals into the air and water. Forests are being cut down, killing the wildlife that lives there, and fumes from cars are clogging up the air. Scientists are trying to find new ways to protect the Earth before it is too late.

Help

Save all of your empty drinks cans and bottles and take them to your recycling centre.

Save the planet!

Large areas of land have been made into national parks where wildlife is protected. People can go there to learn about both plants and animals.

1. Old bottles are collected from bottle banks

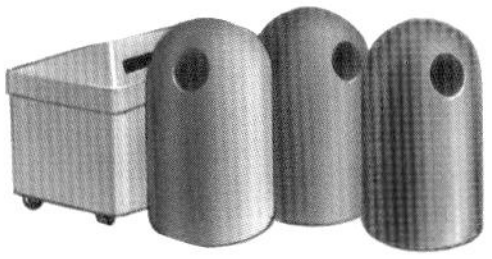

What is recycling?

Recycling is when people collect waste materials such as paper and plastic. The waste is then taken to a recycling centre and changed back into useful materials to make many of the things we use today.

2. The glass or plastic are re-cycled to make raw materials

3. The raw materials are re-used to make new bottles

Trees are cut down

How can we protect the Earth?

There are lots of things we can do to protect our planet. Recycling, picking up litter, switching lights off and walking to the shops all help to make a difference.

Quiz time

Do you remember what you have read about planet Earth?

These questions will test your memory. The pictures will help you. If you get stuck, read the pages again.

page 40

1. Why does the Moon look lumpy?

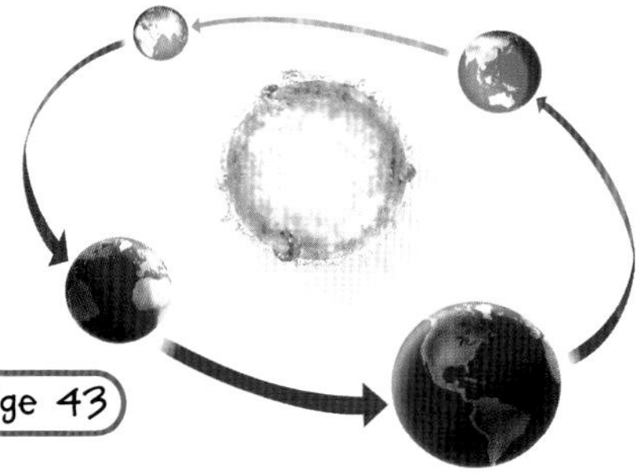

page 43

2. Why do we have day and night?

3. What is inside the Earth?

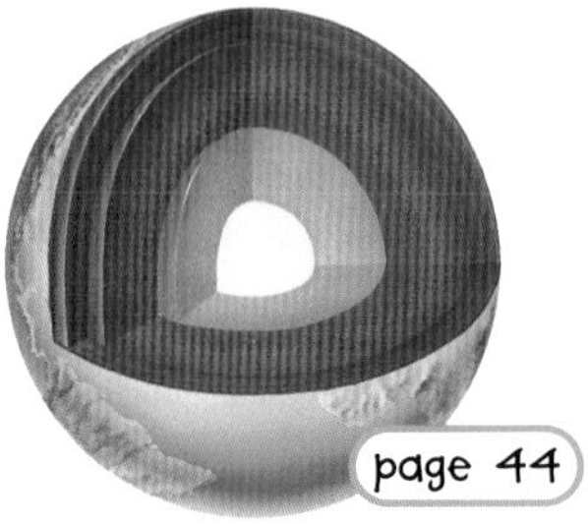

page 44

4. What is a fossil?

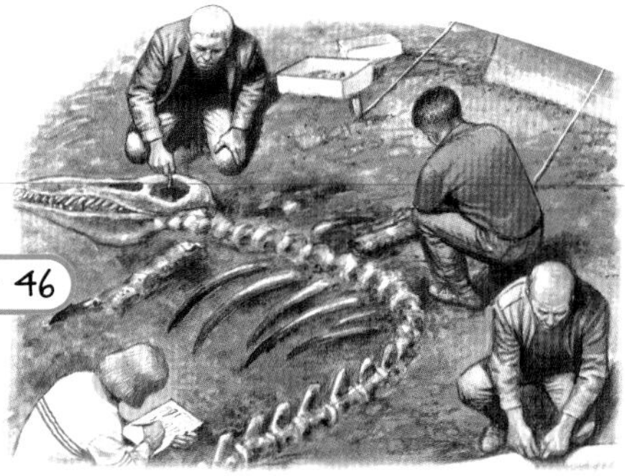

page 46

5. What is a range?

page 49

6. Can earthquakes start fires?

page 51

7. Can ice be fun?

page 53

page 59

11. What is a stalactite?

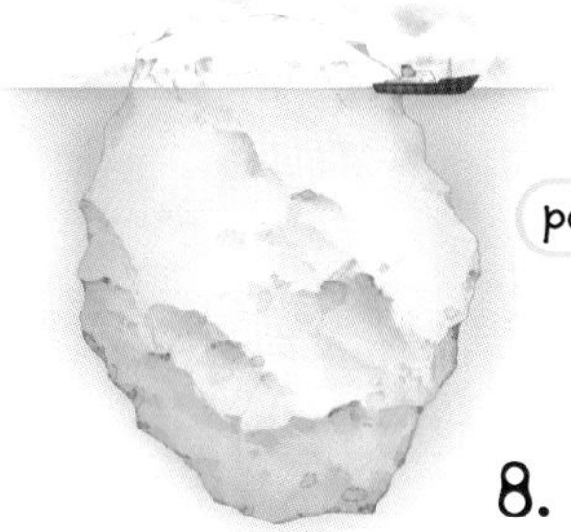

page 53

8. What is an iceberg?

page 61

12. What is a rainforest?

page 54

9. Why are there waterfalls?

page 63

13. Do storms have eyes?

page 59

10. Can lava make caves?

Answers

1. Because there are craters on its surface
2. Because the Earth is always spinning
3. Lots of different layers of rocks
4. A living thing that has turned to stone
5. A group of mountains
6. Yes, they can
7. Yes, people skate on ice for fun
8. A big chunk of ice that has broken off a glacier
9. Because water flows over cliffs
10. Yes it can
11. A rocky spike that hangs from the ceiling of a cave
12. A large, thick, green forest that grows in a hot place
13. Yes, the centre of a hurricane is called the eye

Questions about...

Oceans

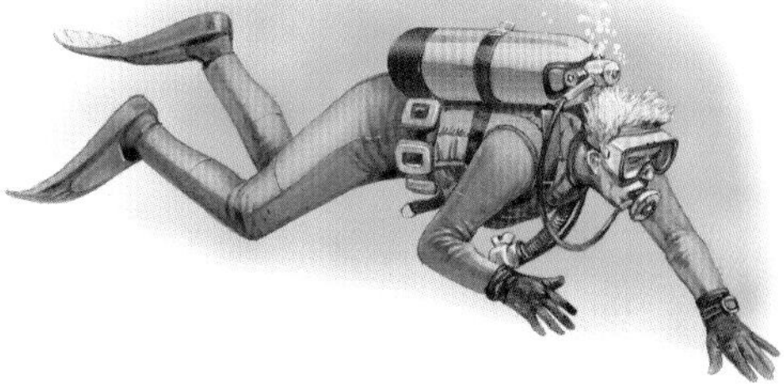

Is there only one big ocean?

It seems that way. All the oceans flow into each other, but we know them as four different oceans – the Pacific, Atlantic, Indian and Arctic. The land we live on, the continents, rises out of the oceans. More than two-thirds of the Earth's rocky surface is covered by oceans.

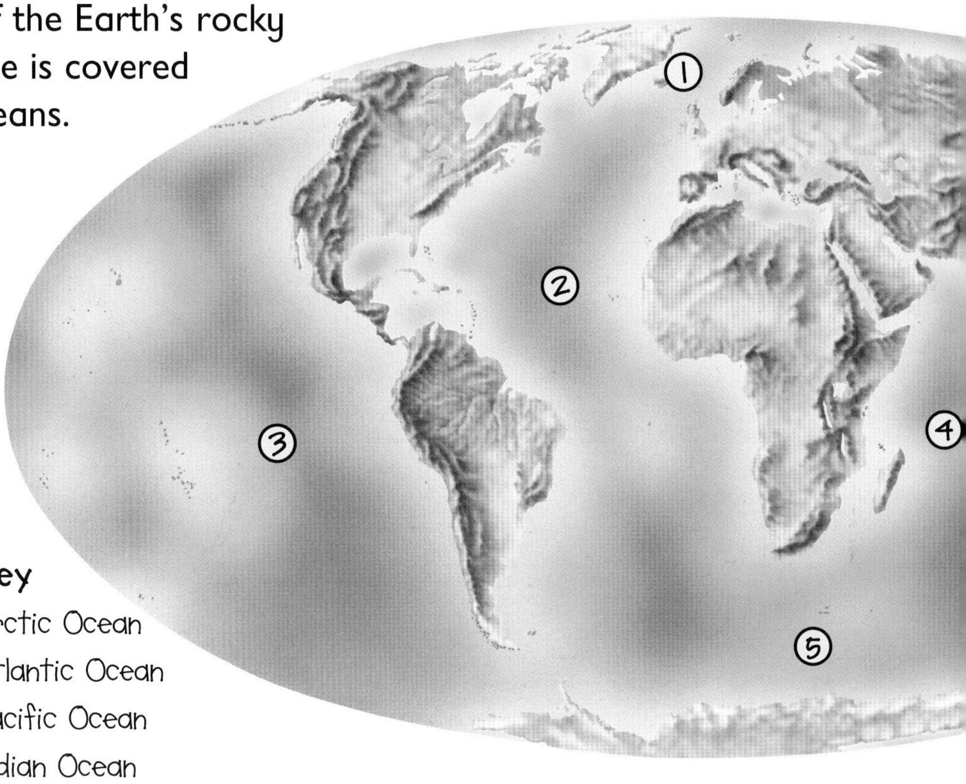

Key

1. Arctic Ocean
2. Atlantic Ocean
3. Pacific Ocean
4. Indian Ocean
5. Southern Ocean

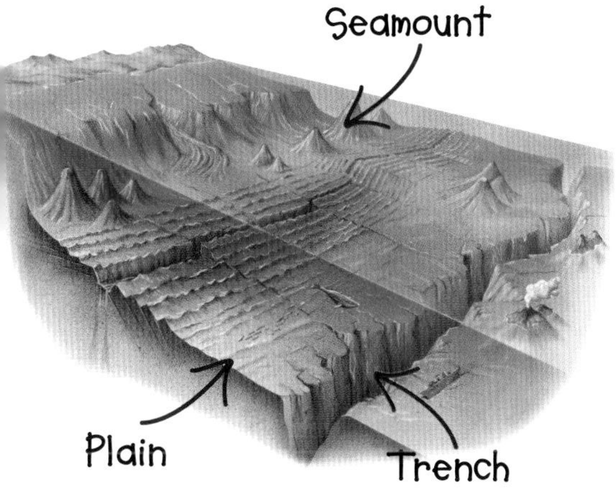

Are there mountains under the sea?

Yes there are. The land beneath the sea is covered by mountains, flat areas called plains and deep valleys called trenches. There are also huge underwater volcanoes called seamounts.

Salty or fresh!

Almost all of the world's water is in the oceans. Only a tiny amount is in freshwater lakes and rivers.

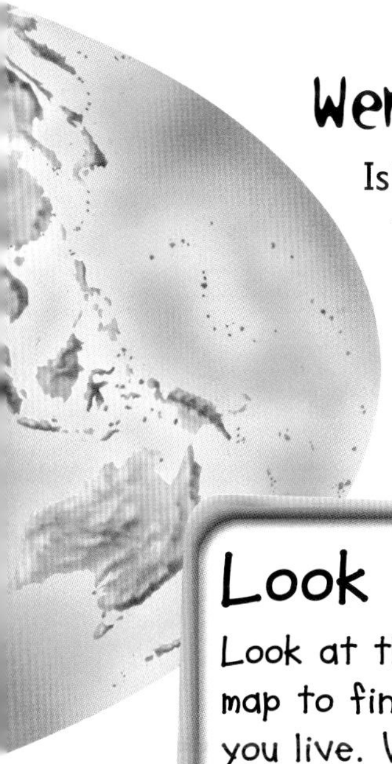

Were do islands come from?

Islands are 'born' beneath the sea. If an underwater volcano erupts, it throws out hot, sticky lava. This cools and hardens in the water. Layers of lava build up and up, until a new island peeps above the waves.

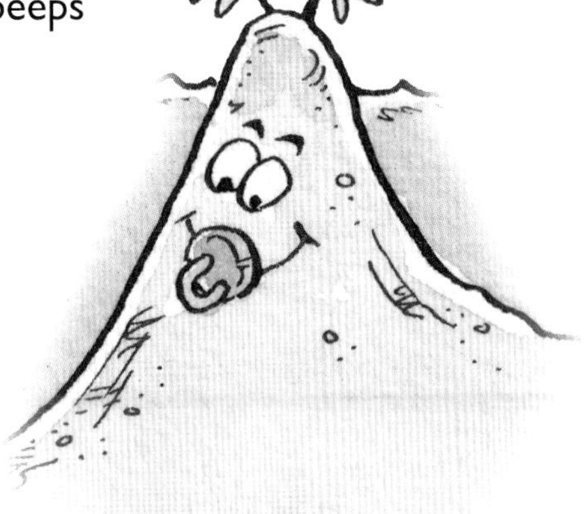

Look

Look at the world map to find where you live. Which ocean is nearest to you?

Do seashells have feet?

Tiny animals called limpets live inside some seashells. They stick to rocks at the shoreline where they eat slimy, green plants called algae. When the tide is out, limpets stick to the rocks like glue, with a strong muscular foot. They only move when the tide crashes in.

Can starfish grow arms?

Yes they can. Starfish may have as many as 40 arms, called rays. If a hungry crab grabs hold of one, the starfish abandons its arm, and uses the others to make its getaway. It then begins to grow a new arm.

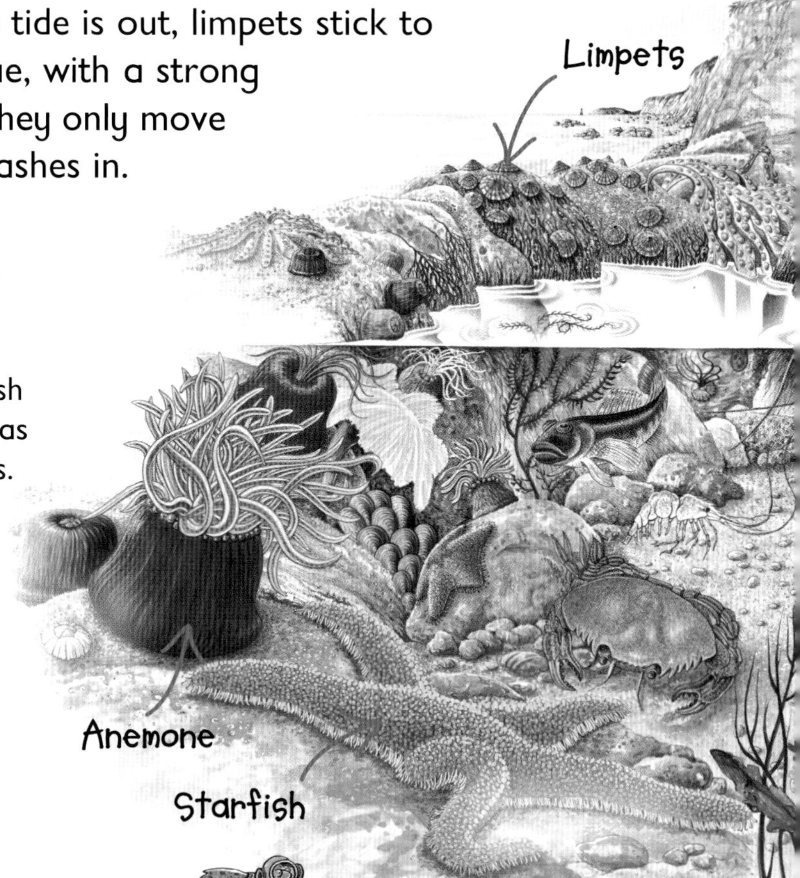

Fighting fit!

Anemones are a kind of sea-living plant. Some anemones fight over their feeding grounds. Beadlet anemones shoot sharp, tiny hooks at each other until the weakest one gives in.

When is a sponge like an animal?

Sponges are animals! They are very simple creatures that filter food from sea water. The natural sponge that you use in the bath is a long-dead dried-out sponge!

Find

When you next visit a beach, try to find a rockpool. Write a list of what you see.

Are there schools in the sea?

Some fish live in big groups called schools. This may protect them from hungry hunters. There are thousands of different types of fish in the sea. Most are covered in shiny scales and use fins and tails to swim. Fish have gills that take in oxygen from the water so that they can breathe.

Read

What is a big group of fish called? Read this page to find out.

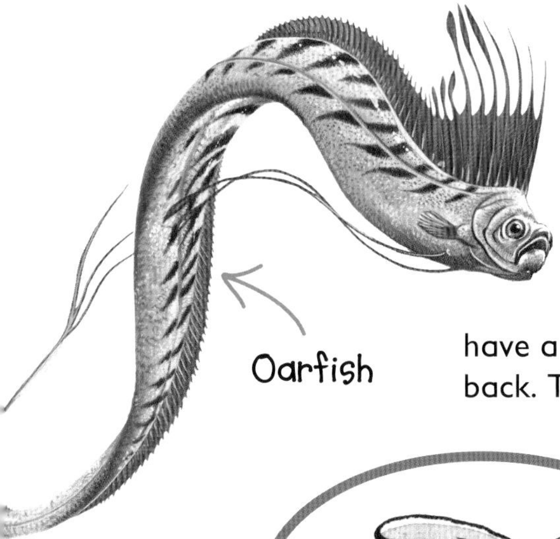

Oarfish

Which fish looks like an oar?

The oarfish does – and it can grow to be as long as four canoes! It is the longest bony fish and is found in all the world's oceans. Oarfish have a bright red fin along the length of their back. They swim upright through the water.

Flying high!

Flying fish cannot really fly. Fish can't survive out of water, but flying fish sometimes leap above the waves when they are swimming at high speed. They use their long fins to glide through the air for as long as 30 seconds.

School of fish

Do fish like to sunbathe?

Sunfish like sunbathing. Ocean sunfish are huge fish that can weigh as much as one tonne – as heavy as a small car! They like to swim at the surface of the water, as if they're sunbathing.

What is the scariest shark?

Great whites are the scariest sharks. These huge fish speed through the water at 30 kilometres an hour. Unlike most fish, the great white shark has warm blood. This allows its muscles to work well but it also means that it needs to eat lots of meat. Great white sharks are fierce hunters. They will attack and eat almost anything, but prefer to feed on seals.

Great white shark

Draw

Using felt-tip pens, draw your own underwater picture. Include a great white shark.

Do some sharks use hammers?

Not really! Hammerhead sharks have hammer-shaped heads to search for food. With a nostril and an eye on each end of the 'hammer', they swing their heads from side to side, looking for a meal.

Hammerhead shark

Yum yum!

Most sharks are meat eaters. Herring are a favourite food for sand tiger and thresher sharks, while a hungry tiger shark will gobble up just about anything!

When is a shark like a pup?

When it's a baby. Young sharks are called pups. Some grow inside their mother's body. Others hatch from eggs straight into the sea.

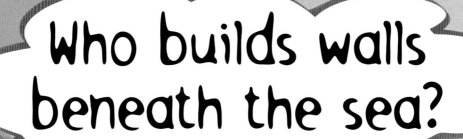

Who builds walls beneath the sea?

Tiny animals build underwater walls. These walls are made of coral, the leftover skeletons of tiny sea animals called polyps. Over millions of years, enough skeletons pile up to form walls. These make a coral reef. All kinds of creatures live around a reef.

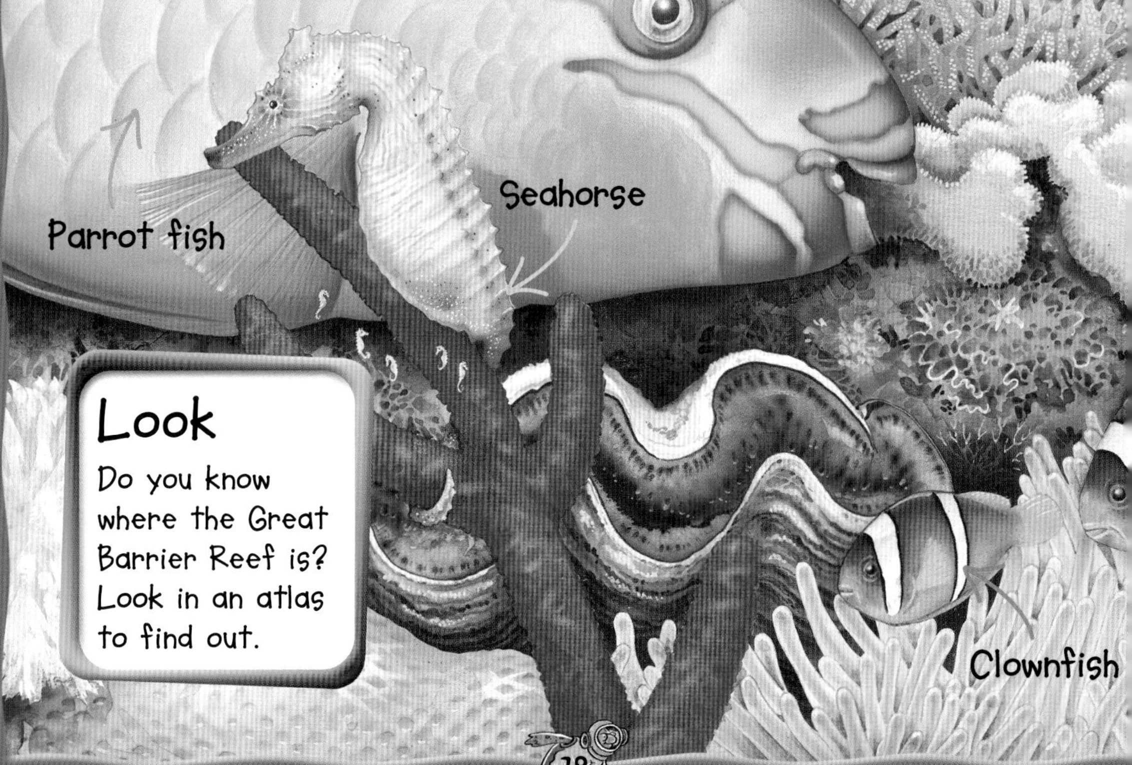

Look

Do you know where the Great Barrier Reef is? Look in an atlas to find out.

How do fish keep clean?

Cleaner wrasse are little fish that help other fish to keep clean! Larger fish, such as groupers and moray eels, visit the cleaner wrasse, which nibbles all the bugs and bits of dirt off the bigger fishes' bodies – what a feast!

Super reef

You can see the Great Barrier Reef from space! At over 2000 kilometres long, it is the largest thing ever built by living creatures.

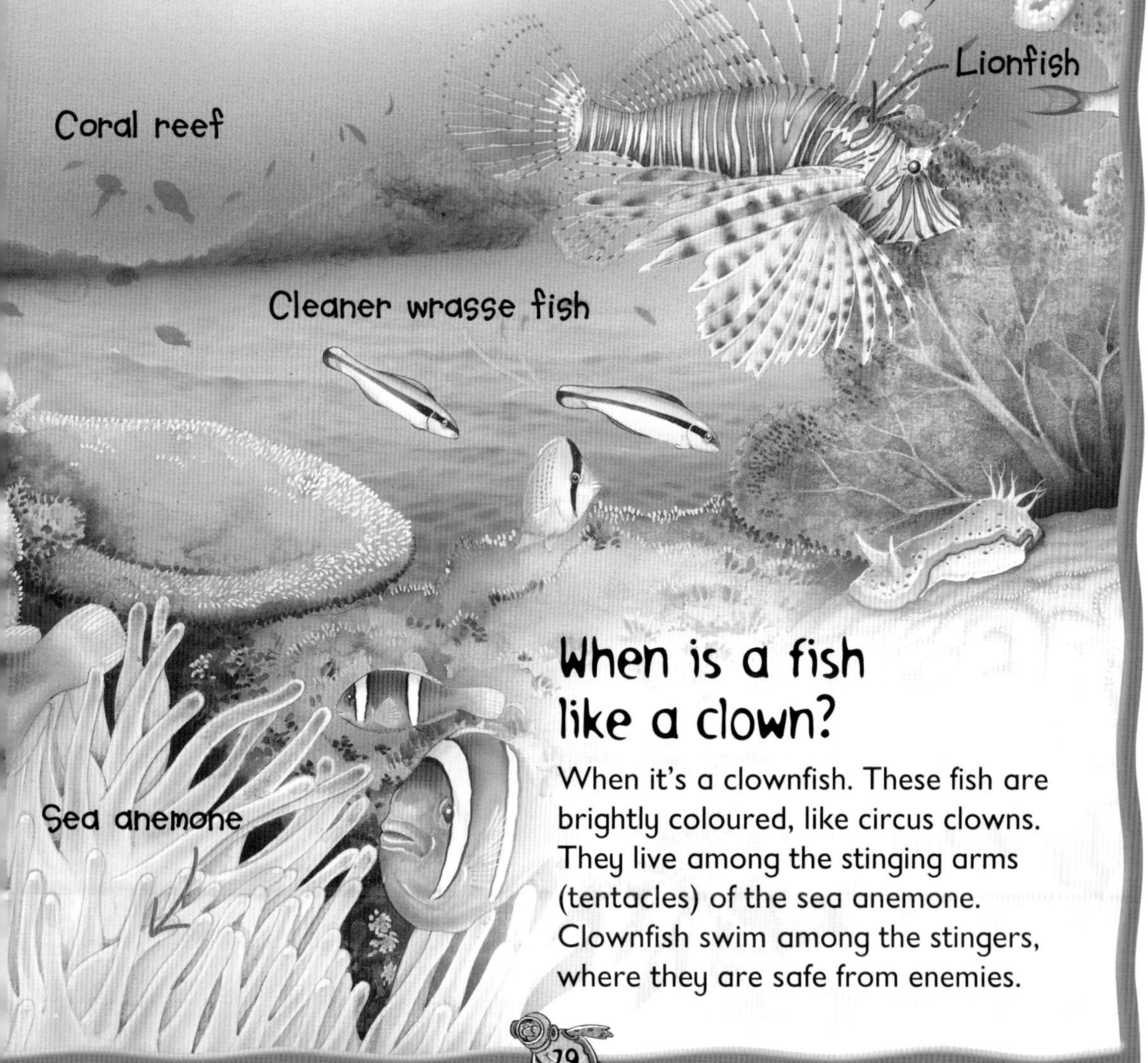

When is a fish like a clown?

When it's a clownfish. These fish are brightly coloured, like circus clowns. They live among the stinging arms (tentacles) of the sea anemone. Clownfish swim among the stingers, where they are safe from enemies.

What is the biggest sea animal?

The blue whale is the biggest animal in the ocean – and the whole planet. It is about 30 metres long and can weigh up to 150 tonnes. It feeds on tiny, shrimp-like creatures called krill – and eats about four tonnes every day! Like other great whales, the blue whale has special, sieve-like parts in its mouth that are called baleen plates.

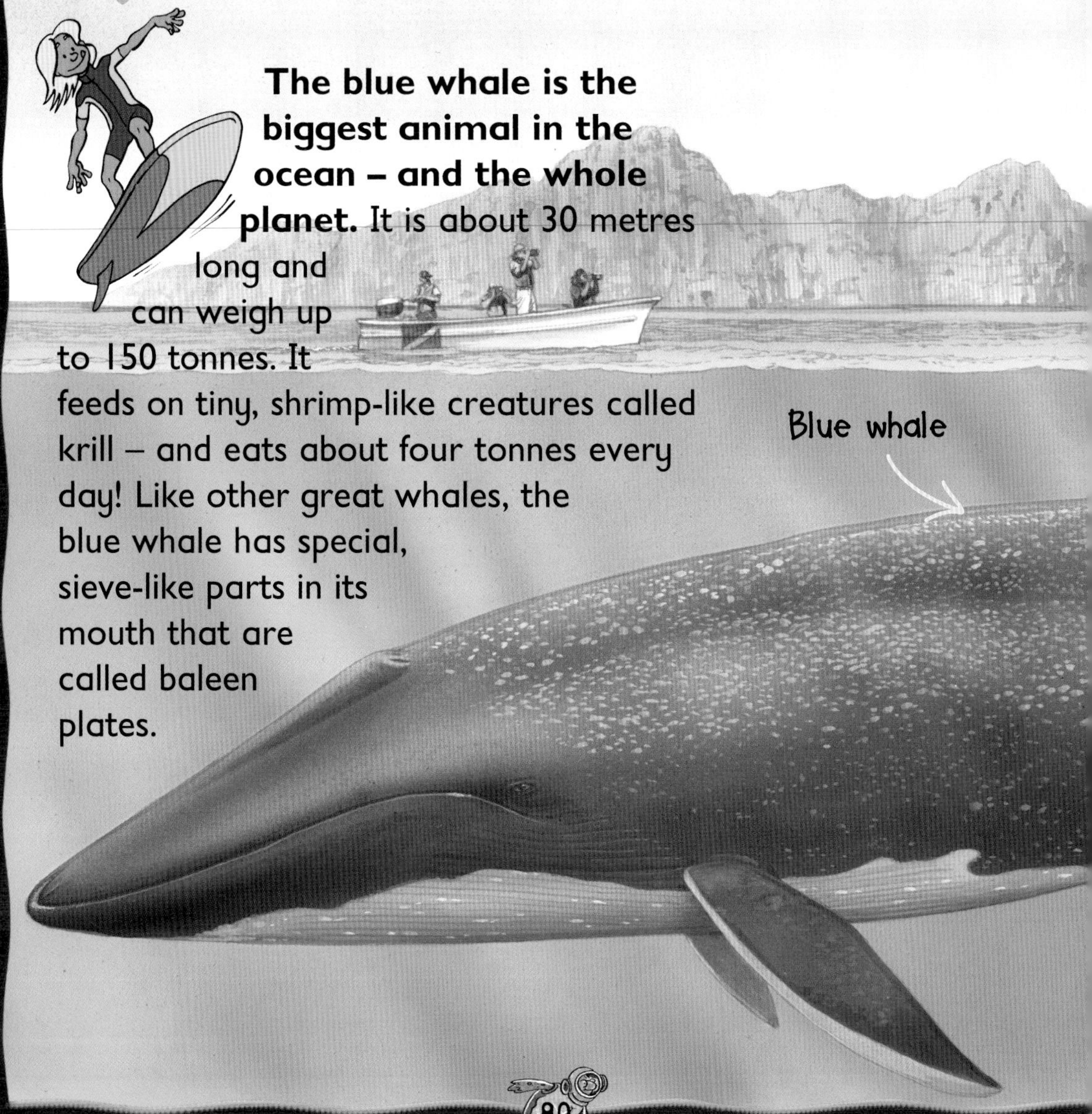

Can whales sing songs?

All whales make sounds, such as squeaks and moans. The humpback whale really does seem to sing. The males probably do this to attract a mate. He may repeat his song for up to 20 hours!

Humpback whale

Stick around!

Barnacles are shellfish. They attach themselves to ships, or the bodies of grey whales and other large sea animals.

Do whales grow tusks?

The narwhal has a tusk like a unicorn's. This tusk is a long, twirly tooth that comes out of the whale's head. The males use their tusks as weapons when they fight over females. The tusk can grow to 3 metres in length.

Measure

The blue whale is 30 metres long. Can you measure how long you are?

Do lions live in the sea?

There are lions in the sea, but not the furry, roaring kind. Sea lions, seals and walruses are all warm-blooded animals that have adapted to ocean life. They have flippers instead of legs – far more useful for swimming. A thick layer of fat under the skin keeps them warm in cold water.

Think

What do you think whales, dolphins and seals have in common with humans?

Sea lion

Who sleeps in seaweed?

Sea otters do! They live in forests of giant seaweed, called kelp. When they sleep, they wrap strands of kelp around their bodies to stop themselves being washed out to sea.

Sea otter

Singing seal!

Leopard seals sing in their sleep! These seals, found in the Antarctic, chirp and whistle while they snooze.

:an a walrus change colour?

Valruses seem to change colour. n cold water, a walrus can look pale rown or even white. This is because lood drains from the skin to stop the ody losing heat. On land, blood returns o the skin and the walrus looks pink!

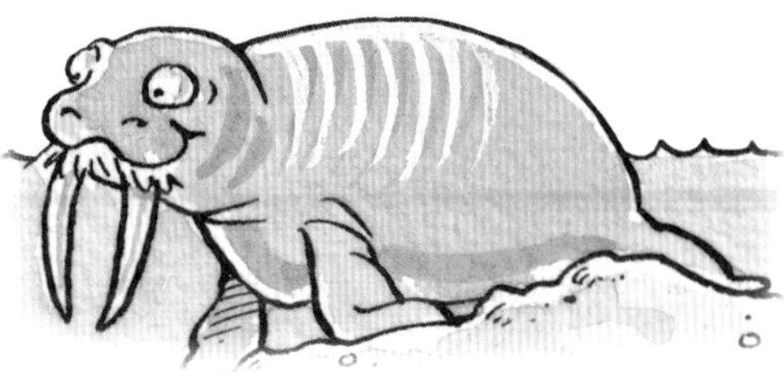

Are there crocodiles in the sea?

Most crocodiles live in rivers and swamps. The saltwater crocodile also swims out to sea – it doesn't seem to mind the salty water. These crocodiles are huge, and can grow to be 7 metres long and one tonne in weight.

Saltwater crocodile

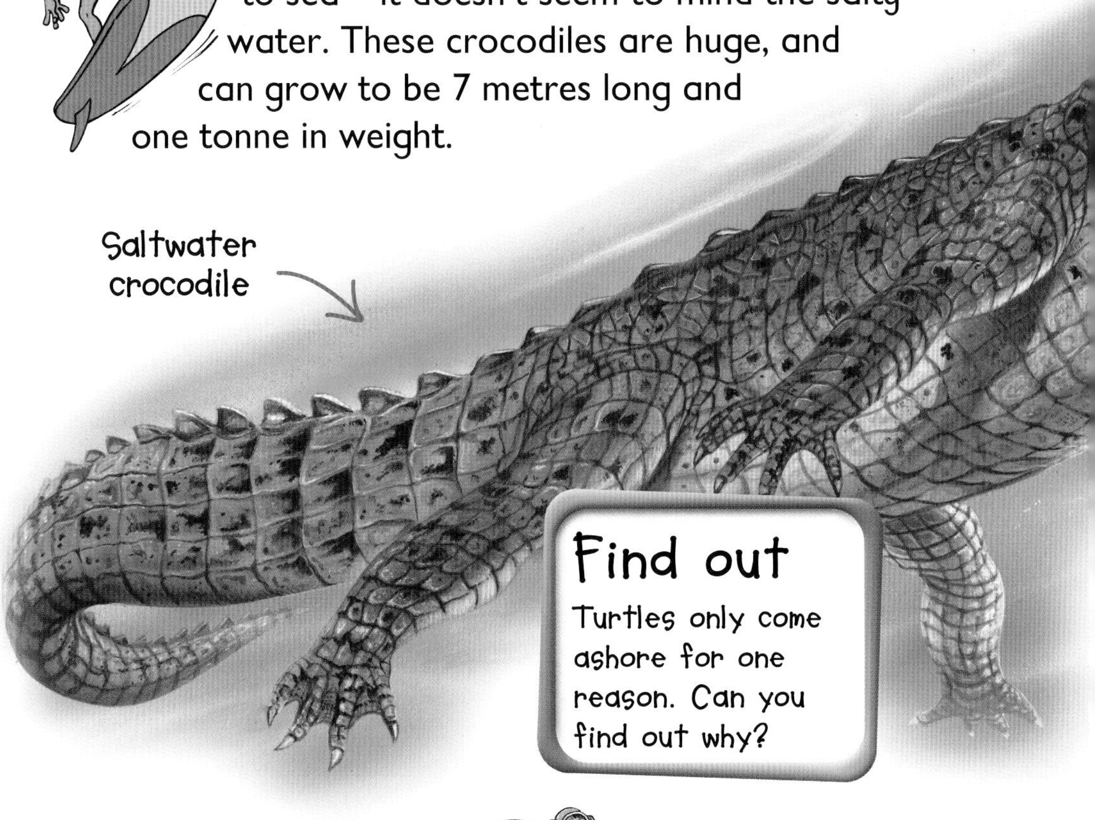

Find out

Turtles only come ashore for one reason. Can you find out why?

Which lizard loves to swim?

Most lizards live on land, where it is easier to warm up their cold-blooded bodies. Marine iguanas depend on the sea for food. They dive underwater to eat seaweed growing on rocks. When they are not diving, they sit on rocks and soak up the sunshine.

How deep can a turtle dive?

Leatherback turtles can dive up to 1200 metres for their dinner. They are the biggest sea turtles and they make the deepest dives. Leatherbacks feed mostly on jellyfish but also eat crabs, lobsters and starfish.

Leatherback turtle

Slithery snakes!

There are poisonous snakes in the sea. The banded sea snake and the yellow-bellied sea snake both use poison to kill their prey. Their poison is far stronger than that of land snakes.

Can seabirds sleep as they fly?

Wandering albatrosses are the biggest seabirds and spend months at sea. They are such good gliders that they even sleep as they fly. To feed, they sit on the surface of the water, where they catch creatures such as squid. An albatross has a wingspan of around 3 metres – about the length of a family car!

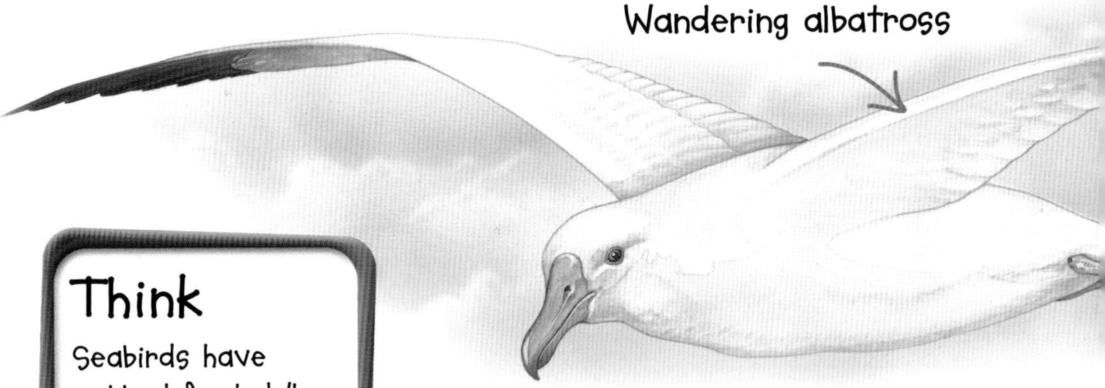

Think

Seabirds have webbed feet. Why do you think this is? Do you have webbed feet?

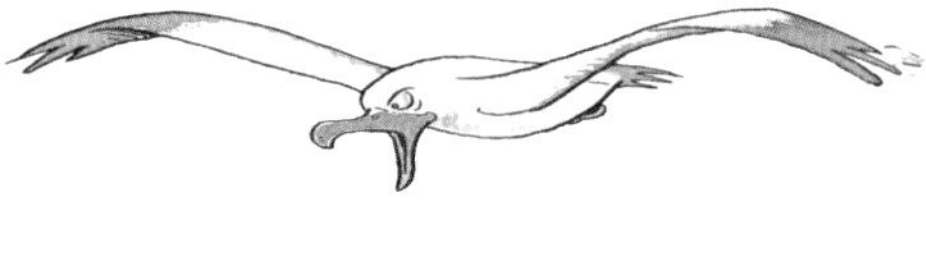

Do seabirds dig burrows?

Most seabirds make nests on cliffs. The puffin digs a burrow on the clifftop, like a rabbit. Sometimes, a puffin even takes over an empty rabbit hole. Here it lays its egg. Both parents look after the chick when it hatches.

Puffins

Dancing birds!

Boobies are a type of seabird that live in large groups. The males have bright red or blue feet. When they are looking for a mate, they dance in front of the female, trying to attract her with their colourful feet!

Which bird dives for its dinner?

The gannet dives headfirst into the ocean to catch fish in its beak. It dives at high-speed and hits the water hard. Luckily, the gannet is protected by cushions of air inside its head that absorb most of the shock.

How do polar bears learn to swim?

Polar bears are good swimmers and they live around the freezing Arctic Ocean. They learn to swim when they are cubs, by following their mother into the water. With their big front paws, the bears paddle through the water. They can swim for many hours.

Polar bears

Imagine

Pretend to be a penguin. Imagine what life is like at the South Pole.

Are penguins fast swimmers?

Penguins are birds – but they cannot fly. All penguins are fast swimmers. The fastest swimmer is the gentoo penguin. It can reach speeds of 27 kilometres an hour underwater.

Gentoo penguin

Small and tall!

The smallest penguin is the fairy penguin at just 40 centimetres tall. The biggest is the emperor penguin at 1.3 metres in height – as tall as a seven-year-old child!

Which penguin dad likes to babysit?

Emperor penguin dads look after the baby chicks. The female lays an egg and leaves her mate to keep it warm. The penguin dad balances the egg on his feet to keep it off the freezing ice. He goes without food until the chick hatches. When it does, the mother returns and both parents look after it.

Is seaweed good to eat?

Seaweed can be very good to eat. In shallow, warm seawater, people can grow their own seaweed. It is then dried in the sun, which helps to keep it fresh. Seaweed is even used to make ice cream!

Growing seaweed

List

Make a list of the things you can eat that come from the ocean. Which of these things have you eaten before?

How do we get salt from the sea?

Sea water is salty. Salt is an important substance. In hot, low-lying areas, people build walls to hold shallow pools of sea water. The water dries up in the sun, leaving behind crystals of salt.

How are lobsters caught?

Lobsters are large shellfish that are good to eat. Fishermen catch them in wooden cages called pots. The lobsters are attracted to dead fish placed in the pots. They push the door of the pot open to get to the fish, but once inside, the lobster can't get out again.

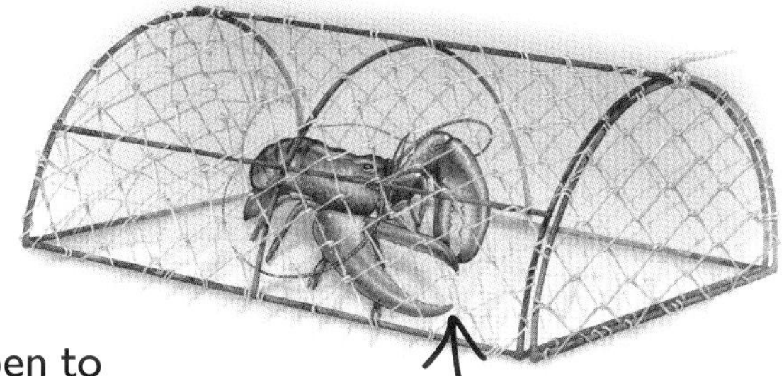

Do pearls grow at sea?

Yes they do. Pearls grow inside oysters, a kind of shellfish. If a grain of sand gets stuck in an oyster's shell, it irritates its soft body. The oyster coats the grain with a substance that it uses to line the inside of its shell. In time, more coats are added and a pearl begins to form.

Are there chimneys under the sea?

Rocky chimneys on the ocean floor give off clouds of hot water. These chimneys lie deep beneath the ocean. The hot water feeds strange creatures such as tube worms and sea spiders.

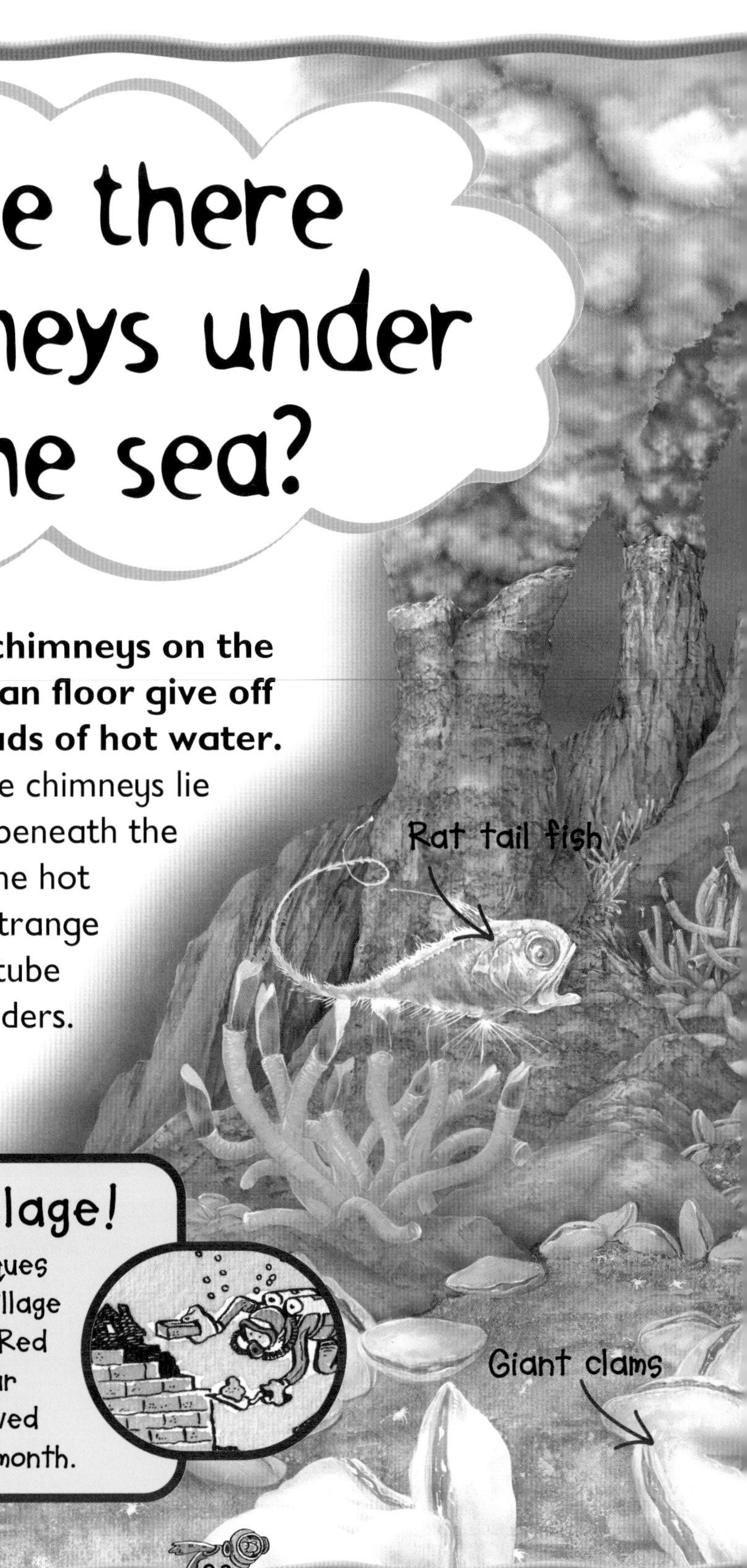

Watery village!

In 1963, diver Jacques Cousteau built a village on the bed of the Red Sea. Along with four other divers, he lived there for a whole month.

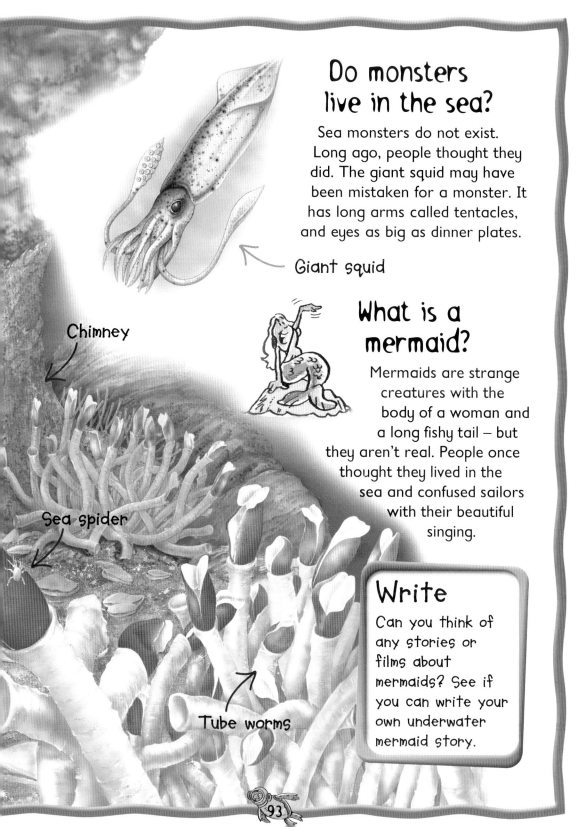

Do monsters live in the sea?

Sea monsters do not exist. Long ago, people thought they did. The giant squid may have been mistaken for a monster. It has long arms called tentacles, and eyes as big as dinner plates.

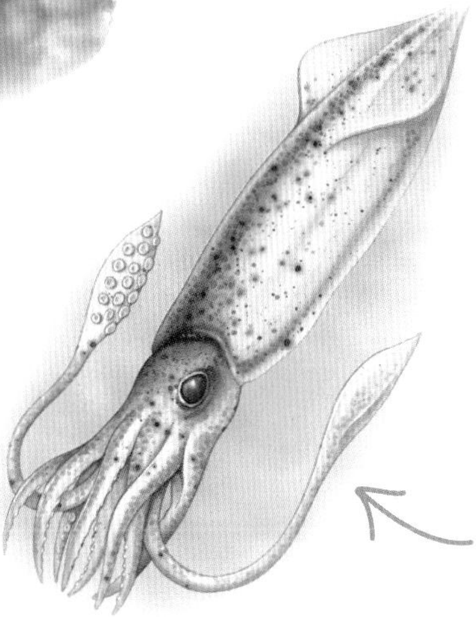

What is a mermaid?

Mermaids are strange creatures with the body of a woman and a long fishy tail – but they aren't real. People once thought they lived in the sea and confused sailors with their beautiful singing.

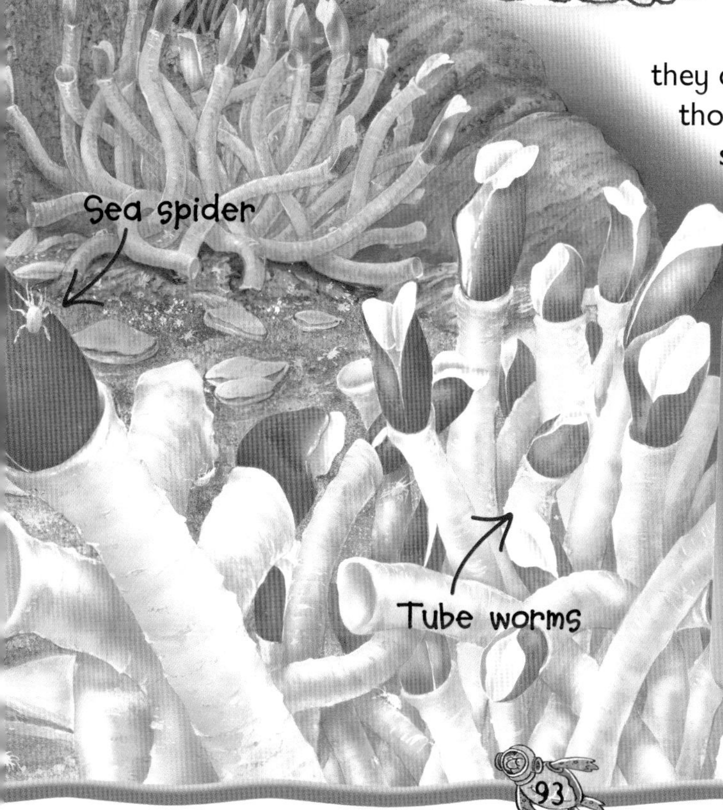

Write

Can you think of any stories or films about mermaids? See if you can write your own underwater mermaid story.

How do divers breathe underwater?

Divers have a spare pair of lungs. Scuba divers carry a special piece of breathing equipment called an 'aqua lung'. These are tanks filled with oxygen (air) that sit on the divers' backs. A long tube supplies the diver with air.

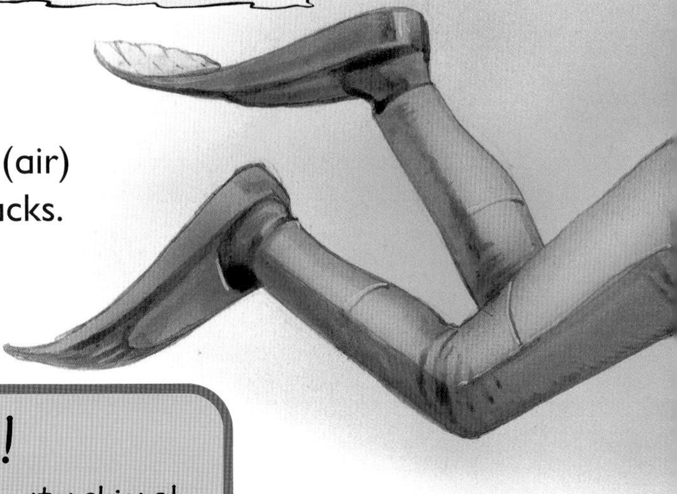

Water record!

A single boat towed 100 waterskiers! This record was made off the coast of Australia in 1986 and no one has beaten it yet. The drag boat was a cruiser called 'Reef Cat'.

Can people ride the waves?

Yes they can, on surfboards. Surfing became popular in the 1950s. Modern surfboards are made of super-light material. People stand up on their boards and ride the waves. The best places to surf are off the coasts of Mexico and Hawaii.

Surfer

Wear

Try wearing some goggles in the bath. What can you see?

What is a jetski?

A jetski is like a motorbike without wheels that travels on water. It pushes out a jet of water behind it, which pushes it forward. Some jetskiers can reach speeds of 100 kilometres an hour.

Quiz time

Do you remember what you have read about oceans? Here are some questions to test your memory. The pictures will help you. If you get stuck, read the pages again.

1. Are there mountains under the sea?

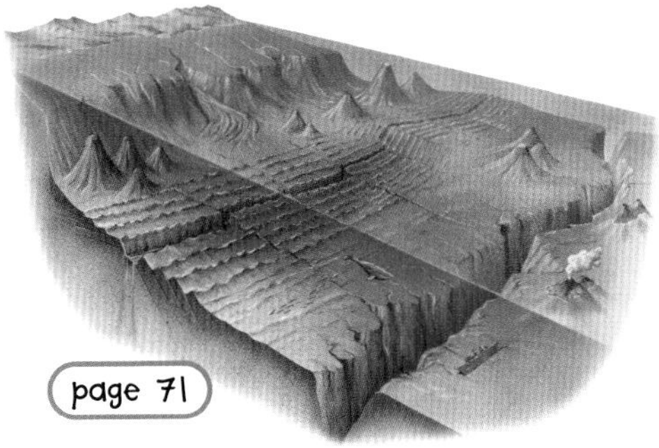

page 71

2. When is a sponge like an animal?

page 73

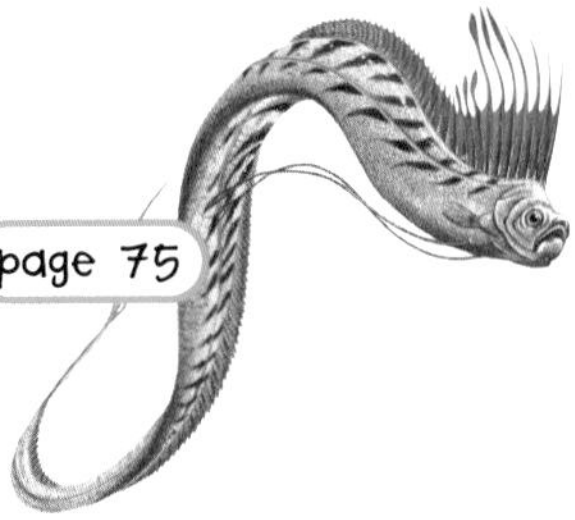

page 75

3. Which fish looks like an oar?

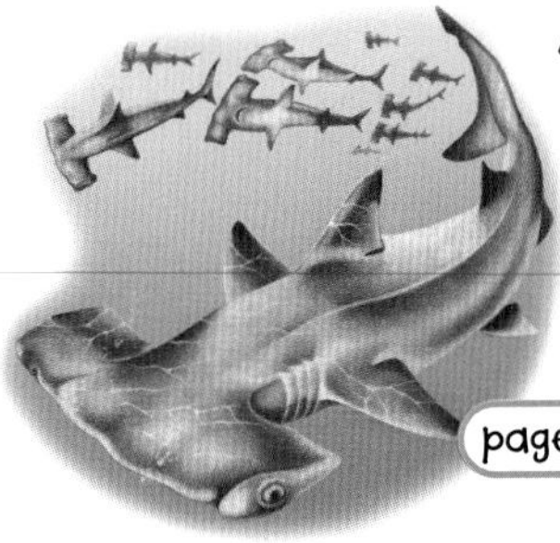

4. Do some sharks use hammers?

page 77

page 77

5. When is a shark like a pup?

page 83

6. Who sleeps in seaweed?

7. Are there crocodiles in the sea?

page 84

8. Can seabirds sleep as they fly?

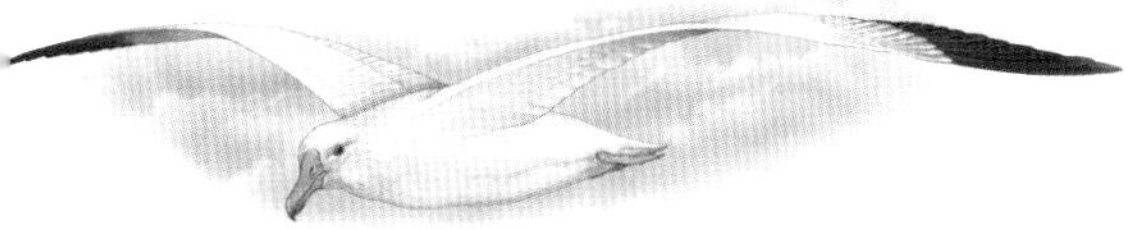

page 86

9. How do polar bears learn to swim?

page 88

10. Which penguin dad likes to babysit?

page 89

11. Is seaweed good to eat?

page 90

12. What is a mermaid?

page 93

page 94

13. How do divers breathe underwater?

Answers

1. Yes, there are
2. A sponge is an animal
3. The oarfish
4. No, but the hammerhead shark has a hammershaped head
5. When it's a baby – young sharks are called pups
6. The sea otter
7. The saltwater crocodile swims in the sea
8. Yes, the wandering albatross can
9. By following their mother into the water
10. The emperor penguin
11. Yes, it can be
12. A creature that is half–woman, half–fish
13. By using an aqua lung

Questions about...

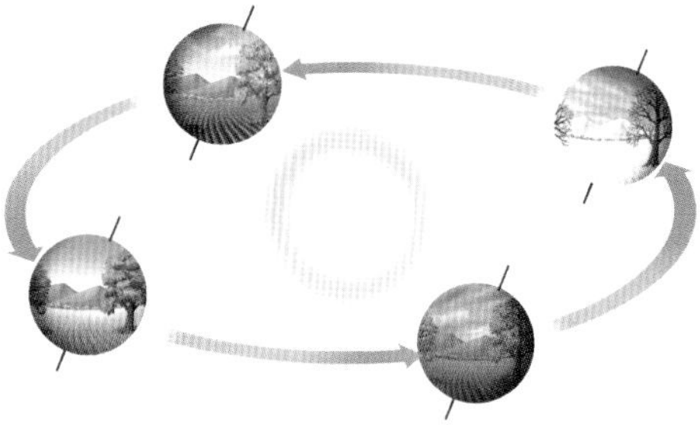

Weather

Why is summer warm and sunny?

The Earth is tipped to one side as it moves round the Sun. Some of the year, the north half of the Earth faces the Sun. Then the Sun is higher in the sky, making the weather warm. This is summer. When the southern half of the Earth faces the Sun, it is winter in the north.

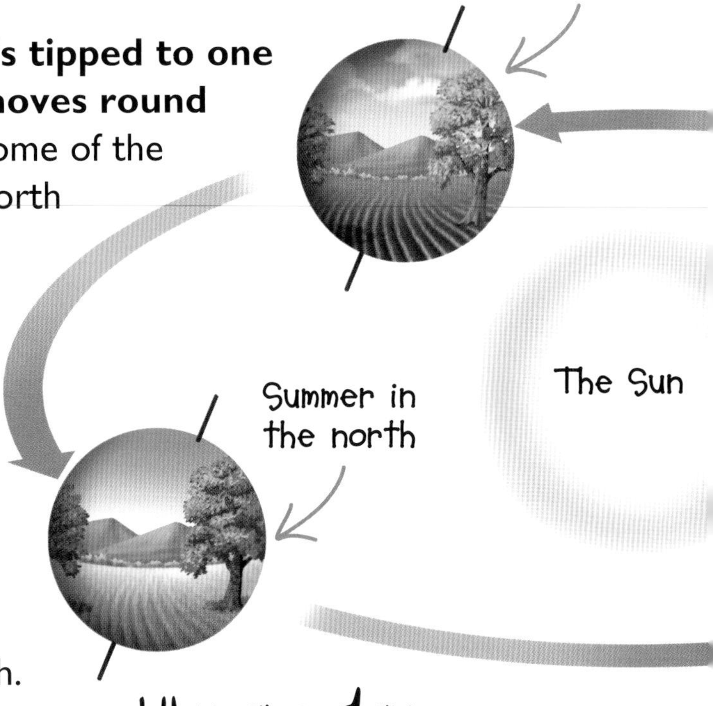

Why are days longer in summer?

Summer days are longer because the Earth is tilted and spins round. In summer, the Sun rises earlier and sets later. This makes daytime last longer than night. In the middle of summer in Sweden it is light for 21 hours!

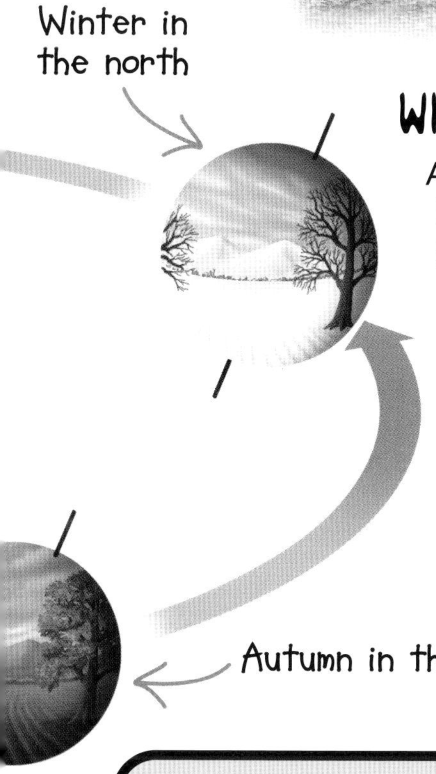

Why do leaves fall in autumn?

Autumn comes between summer and winter. Many trees lose their leaves in autumn because it is hard for them to grow in the dark winter months. The leaves turn from green to red, orange or brown. Then they fall to the ground.

Find

Can you find photographs of red, orange and brown leaves in autumn?

Sunshine at midnight!

At the North and South Poles, the Sun never sets in summer. It is light all day. In winter, the Sun never rises. Then it is dark all day long!

What is the sunniest place?

The Sahara Desert in North Africa is the sunniest place on Earth. It is sunny for nearly 12 hours every day! It hardly rains, which makes it hard for plants and animals to live here. People dress in loose clothes to stop being sunburnt.

Sea makes fire!

Water flowing around the sea can change the weather. El Niño is a warm water current in the Pacific Ocean. Scientists think that this could cause droughts.

When is a lake not a lake?

When it's a mirage! A mirage often happens on a hot day. Hot air near the ground makes light from the bright sky bend upwards. This makes it seem as if there is a lake on the ground in the distance. Really the ground is dry!

People living in the desert

Remember

Can you remember why desert people wear loose clothes, even when it is very hot?

Drought

What happens when it doesn't rain?

Sometimes it is dry for a long time in places where it normally rains a lot. This is called a drought. There was a drought in the United States in the 1930s. Crops didn't grow and fields turned to dust. Many people had to leave their farms.

Does Earth have a blanket?

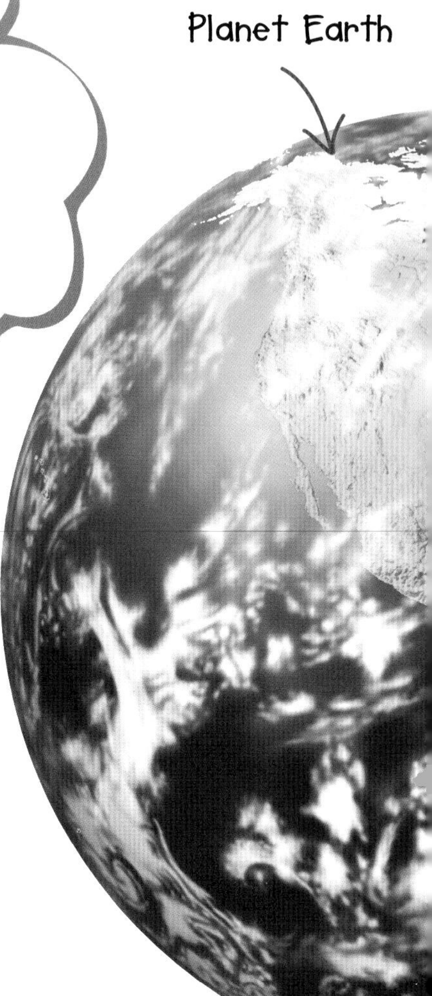

Yes, it does. The Earth is wrapped in a thick blanket of air. It is called the atmosphere. This is where all the weather happens. The atmosphere also helps to keep the Earth's surface warm at night. In the day it protects us from harmful rays coming from the Sun.

Where does it rain every day?

In a tropical rainforest the weather is always very hot and very wet. The Sun shines every day, and there are downpours of heavy rain, too. Rainforest plants grow very quickly in this steamy weather.

Monsoon downpour!

In some countries it pours with rain for a few weeks every year. This is called a monsoon. In India, enough rain falls in one year to cover the ground with water 26 metres deep!

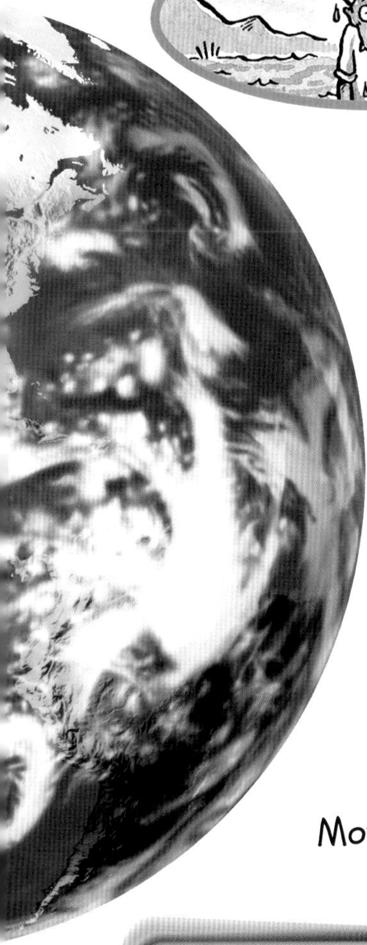

How deep is the atmosphere?

The atmosphere stretches hundreds of kilometres above our heads. If you go up through the atmosphere, the air gets thinner and thinner. High up in mountains, mountaineers find it difficult to breathe so they take breathing equipment with them.

Look

Look at the picture of the Earth above. What do you think the white swirly patterns are?

Where does rain come from?

Most rain comes from the sea! Some seawater turns to gas in the air. If the air rises, the gas becomes water drops. These make clouds. If the drops get big enough, they fall as rain. The water flows back to the sea.

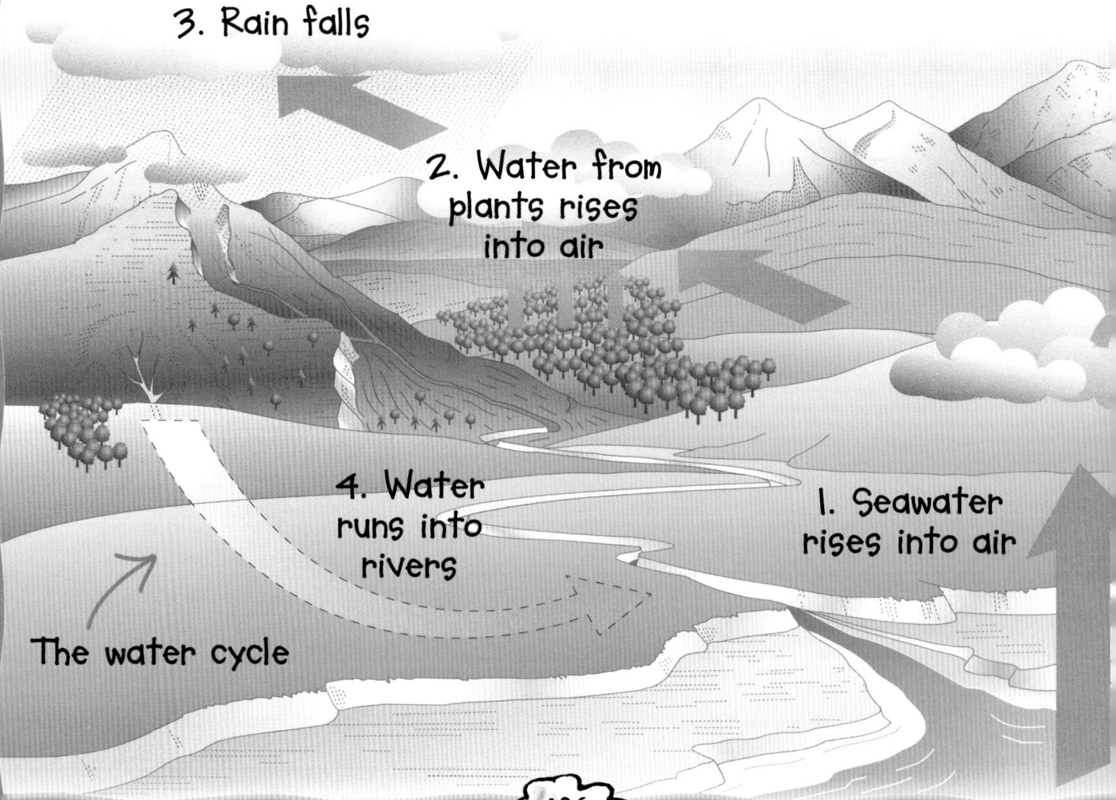
3. Rain falls
2. Water from plants rises into air
4. Water runs into rivers
1. Seawater rises into air
The water cycle

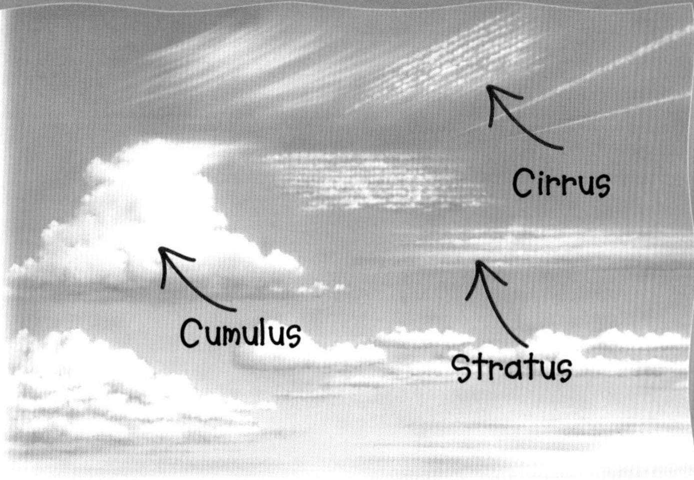

Head in the clouds!

The tops of tall mountains are often in the clouds. At the top it looks misty. Mountaineers sometimes get lost in these clouds!

Are all clouds small and fluffy?

Clouds come in lots of different shapes and sizes. Weather experts give the different clouds names. Fluffy clouds are called cumulus clouds. Some are small and some are giant. Flat clouds are called stratus clouds. Wispy clouds high in the sky are called cirrus clouds.

What rain never lands?

Sometimes rain that falls from a cloud never reaches the ground. If the drops of rain fall into very dry air, the water in them turns into gas. This means that the drops disappear and never reach the ground.

Look

Look at the clouds outside today. Are they fluffy or flat? The picture above will help you.

What happens in a flood?

Sometimes a lot of rain falls in a few hours. So much water flows into rivers that they fill up and burst their banks. The rivers flood the land on each side. Sometimes houses disappear under the flood water.

Floods of tears!

The river Nile in Egypt floods every year. Thousands of years ago, the Egyptians made up a story about the flood. It said that a goddess called Isis cried so much that the river filled up with her tears.

Did Noah build an ark?

The Bible tells the story of a man called Noah. He built a great boat called an ark to escape a flood. We don't know if Noah's ark existed. Scientists have found out that there probably was a huge flood thousands of years ago.

Noah's ark

Flooded house

Find

Can you find the country of Egypt and the river Nile in an atlas?

Can there be a flood in a desert?

Yes there can. Most of the time there is no rain in a desert. The hot Sun bakes the ground hard. Once in a while, it rains heavily. The water flows off the ground instead of soaking in. This can cause a flood.

What is snow made of?

Snow is made of ice, which is water that has frozen. When it is very cold in a cloud, tiny bits of ice (crystals) begin to form, instead of water drops. The pieces clump together to make snowflakes that fall to the ground. The weather must be very cold for snow to fall. If it is too warm, the snowflakes melt and turn to rain.

Shiver!

Antarctica is the coldest place on Earth. The lowest temperature ever recorded there is –89°C. That's much, much colder than inside a freezer!

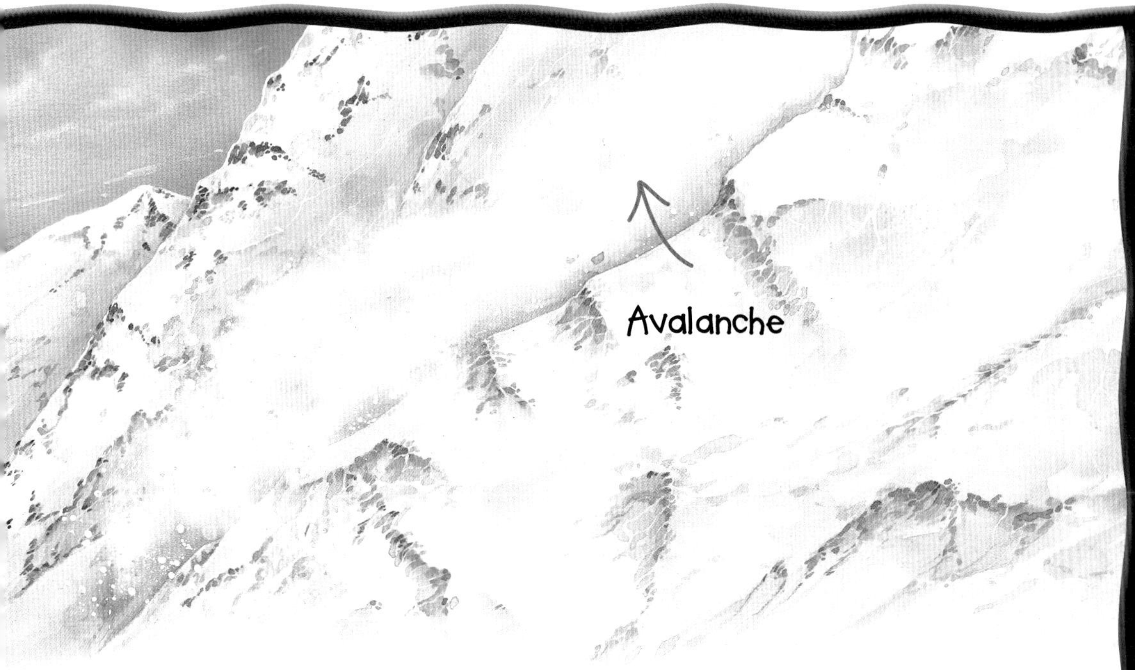

When is snow dangerous?

When lots of snow falls on mountains, deep layers build up on the slopes. The snow may suddenly slide down the mountain. This is an avalanche. A big avalanche can bury a town. A loud noise or even a person walking on the snow can start an avalanche.

Are all snowflakes the same?

It's hard to believe, but all snowflakes are different – even though there are millions and millions of them. This is because every ice crystal in a snowflake has its own shape. No two crystals are the same. Most ice crystals in snowflakes looks like stars with six points.

Think

Can you think why it could be dangerous to ski across a steep hillside covered with snow?

Where are the fastest winds?

Inside a tornado. A tornado is like a spinning funnel made of air. They reach down from giant thunderstorms. The winds can blow at 480 kilometres an hour. That's twice as fast as an express train! Tornadoes can rip trees from the ground and destroy houses.

Which storm has an eye?

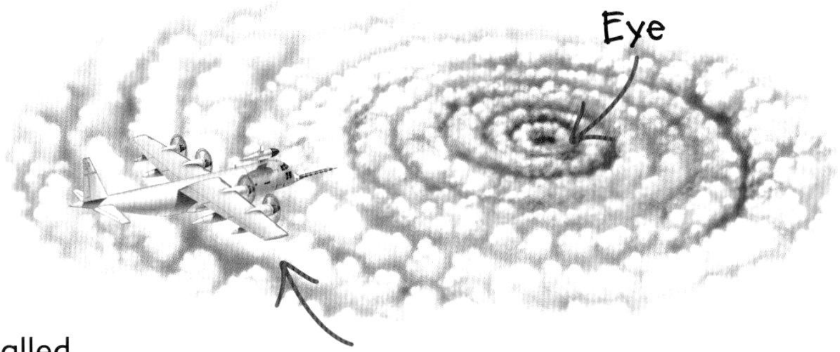

A hurricane is a giant spinning storm made up of super-strong winds. The centre is a hole called the eye. Here it is calm and sunny. If a hurricane reaches land, the winds can damage buildings and heavy rain causes floods. Hurricane hunters are planes that fly into hurricanes to measure the wind speed.

Draw

Look at the pictures on this page. Can you draw a picture of a tornado and a hurricane?

Stormy names!

A tropical storm that starts in the Atlantic Ocean is called a hurricane. In the Pacific Ocean, a tropical storm is called a typhoon. In the Indian Ocean it is called a cyclone.

How do we measure wind?

We measure the wind on a scale called the Beaufort Scale. The slowest wind is Force 1 on the scale. This is called a light breeze. The strongest wind is Force 12. This is called a hurricane. Force zero means there is no wind at all.

What makes the sky clap?

A thunderstorm! Inside a big thundercloud, water drops and bits of ice move up and down, bumping into each other. This makes electricity build up. When the electricity jumps around, we see a spark of lightning and hear a loud clap of thunder.

Huge hail!

Hail is made up of lumps of ice called hailstones. Hail can fall from thunderclouds. The biggest hailstone ever fell in Bangladesh in 1986. It was the size of a grapefruit!

When is lightning like a fork?

When lightning jumps from a thundercloud to the ground, it looks like huge forks in the sky. If lightning jumps from one cloud to another, the clouds light up. This is called sheet lightning. Lightning can be red, blue, yellow or white.

Lightning

Does lightning hit buildings?

Lightning often hits tall buildings. The buildings have a metal spike on top called a lightning conductor. When lightning hits a building, the lightning conductor carries the electricity to the ground. If there was no lightning conductor, the building could be damaged by the lightning.

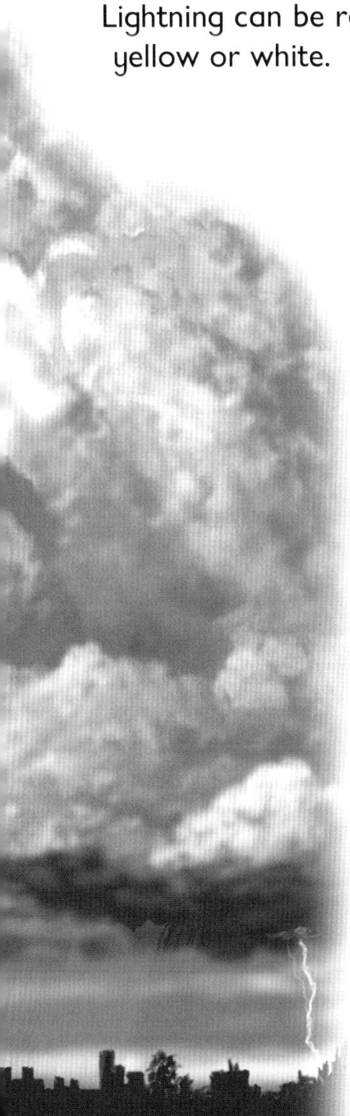

Thundercloud

Count

Count the seconds between a flash of lightning and a clap of thunder. The bigger the number, the further away the thunderstorm.

What is a rainbow made of?

A rainbow is made of sunlight. The light bounces through raindrops. This splits the light into different colours. The colours of a rainbow are always the same. They are red, orange, yellow, green, blue, indigo and violet.

Northern lights

Remember

Can you remember all seven colours of a rainbow?

When does the sky have curtains?

In the far north and the far south of the world, amazing patterns of light sometimes appear in the sky. They look like colourful curtains. The patterns are called auroras (or-roar-rers). They happen when tiny light particles from the Sun smash into the air.

Rainbow with no colour!

A fogbow is a rainbow that is white. You might see a fogbow when the Sun shines through fog. It is white because the water drops in fog are too small to split up the light into rainbow colours.

When can you see three suns?

If there are thin clouds high in the sky, you might see three suns. The clouds are made of bits of ice. These bend light from the Sun. This makes it look as if there are two extra suns in the sky. We call these mock suns, or sun dogs.

What is a rain dance?

In many hot places, such as Africa, it only rains once or twice a year. People may dance traditional rain dances if the rain does not fall. In the past, people believed that rain dances really could bring clouds and rain.

Who first recorded the weather?

Over 3000 years ago in China, people made notes about the weather. They studied how windy it was, or if it rained or snowed. They carved the information onto pieces of tortoiseshell.

Are weather sayings true?

There are many sayings about the weather. Most of them are true. One saying is 'Clear Moon, frost soon'. If there are no clouds in the sky you can see the Moon clearly. It also means it will get cold quickly at night. So the saying is true.

Rain dance

Full Moon

Weather cows!

Some people think that cows lie down when it is going to rain. But this weather saying is not true. Cows lie down on sunny days, too!

Discover

Can you find some more sayings about the weather? You could ask your teacher, or try looking in a book.

Which bird spins in the wind?

A metal cockerel on a weather vane. The cockerel spins so it can point in any direction. When the wind blows, the cockerel spins and points to where the wind is coming from. If the wind is blowing from the north, it is called a north wind. The wind blows from the north, south, east and west.

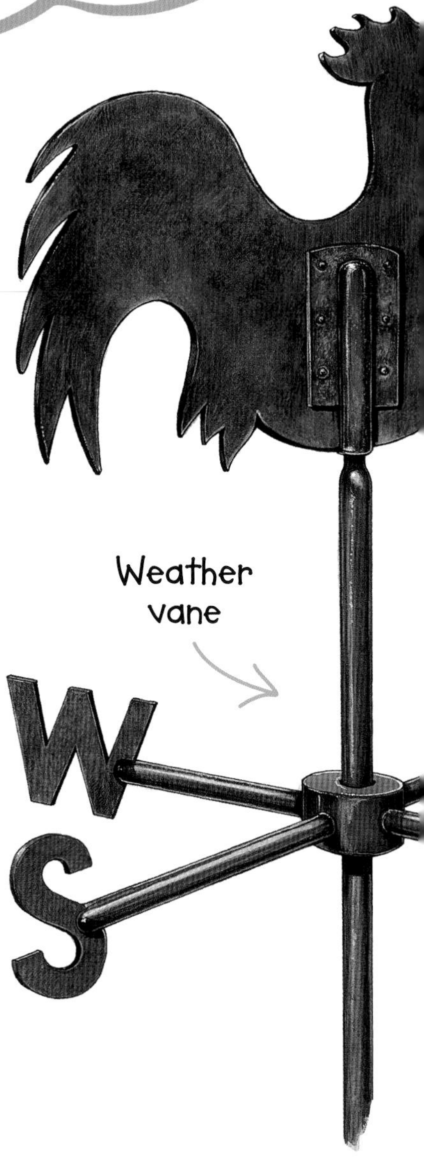

Groundhog Day!

In the USA, 2 February is called Groundhog Day. If people see an animal called a groundhog, they think that it will stay cold for another six weeks!

What is a weather house?

A weather house is a model that can tell how much moisture is in the air. If it is going to be dry, a lady in summer clothes comes out. If it is going to be rainy, a man with an umbrella comes out.

Weather house

How do we know how hot it is?

By reading a thermometer. A thermometer shows the temperature, which is how hot the air around us is. The first thermometer was made in 1714 by Gabriel Daniel Fahrenheit.

Think

From which direction does a southerly wind blow? North or south?

Can planes tell the weather?

Weather planes don't carry any passengers. Instead they fly through the air recording the weather. They measure the temperature of the air, the speed of the wind and how much water is in the air. This information helps weather forecasters tell us what the weather is going to be like.

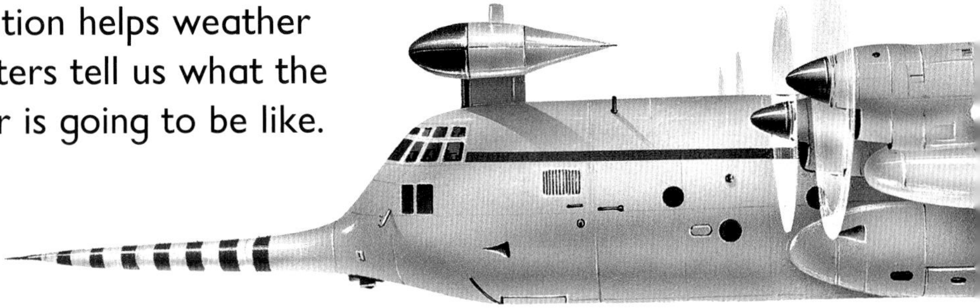

Weather plane

Astronaut snaps!

Astronauts who travel on the space shuttle and live on space stations take cameras with them. They often take amazing photographs of clouds and thunderstorms from space.

Why do scientists fly balloons?

Scientists fly balloons to find out about the weather. The balloons are filled with a gas called helium. They float up through the air and carry instruments that measure the weather. The information is sent back to the ground by radio.

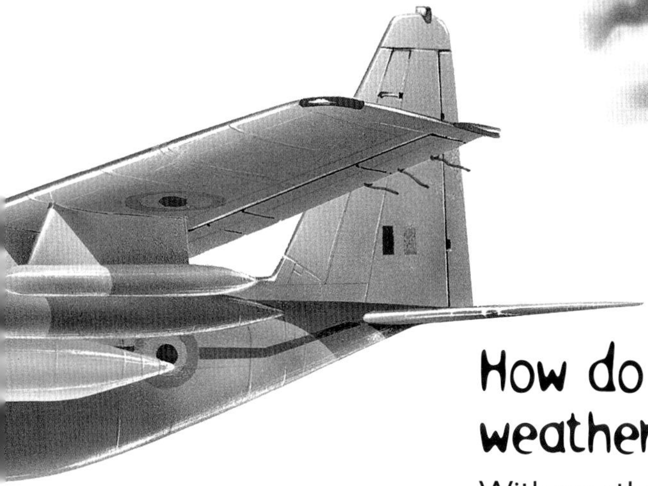

How do we watch weather from space?

With weather satellites. A satellite moves around the Earth in space. It takes photographs of the clouds below and sends them back to Earth. Satellite photographs show which way hurricanes are moving. They help forecasters to warn people if a hurricane is heading their way.

Remember

Can you remember how information gets from a weather balloon down to the ground?

Did weather kill the dinosaurs?

Dinosaurs lived millions of years ago. Scientists think that they may have died because the weather all over the world got colder. They think this happened when a giant rock (meteorite) from space hit the Earth. This threw lots of dust into the air, which blocked out the Sun.

Can trees affect the weather?

Yes, they can. Many rainforests are being cut down for farming. When trees are burned, the fires release a gas called carbon dioxide. This gas acts as a blanket over the Earth and does not let heat escape. High levels of carbon dioxide can raise the temperature too much causing damage to the Earth.

Rainforest

Windy tower!

The Tower of Winds is a tower in Athens, Greece. It was built 2000 years ago. It had a giant wind vane on top to measure the direction of the wind.

Find

Can you find Greenland on a map of the world?

Is our weather changing?

Weather experts think the weather is getting warmer. If the average world temperature rises by as little 1.5°C it will mean more storms, including hurricanes and tornadoes, and more droughts too.

Quiz time

Do you remember what you have read about weather? These questions will test your memory. The pictures will help you. If you get stuck, read the pages again.

1. Why do leaves fall in autumn?

page 101

2. When is a lake not a lake?

page 103

3. Where does it rain every day?

page 104

4. How deep is the atmosphere?

page 105

5. Are all clouds small and fluffy?

page 107

6. What rain never lands?

page 107

7. What happens in a flood?

page 108

8. Did Noah build an ark?

page 109

9. When is snow dangerous?

page 111

10. Which storm has an eye?

page 113

11. What makes the sky clap?

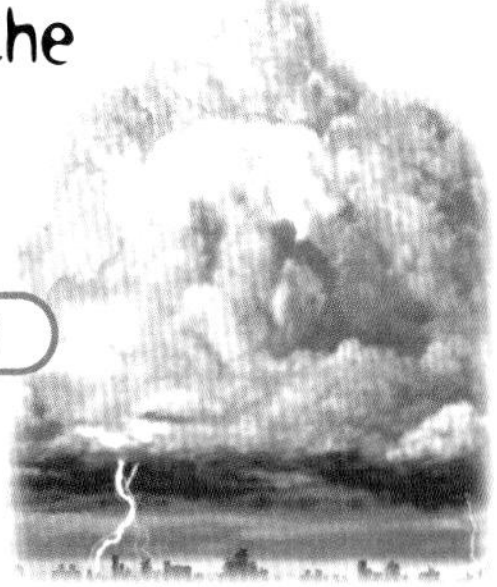

page 114

12. Who first recorded the weather?

page 118

13. What is a rain dance?

page 118

Answers

1. Because it is hard for them to grow in the dark winter months
2. When it's a mirage
3. In a tropical rainforest
4. Hundreds of kilometres
5. No, they come in different shapes and sizes
6. Drops that fall into very dry air
7. A lot of rain falls and floods the land
8. We don't know if Noah's ark existed
9. In an avalanche
10. A hurricane
11. A thunderstorm
12. The Chinese
13. A traditional dance to bring on clouds and rain

Questions about...

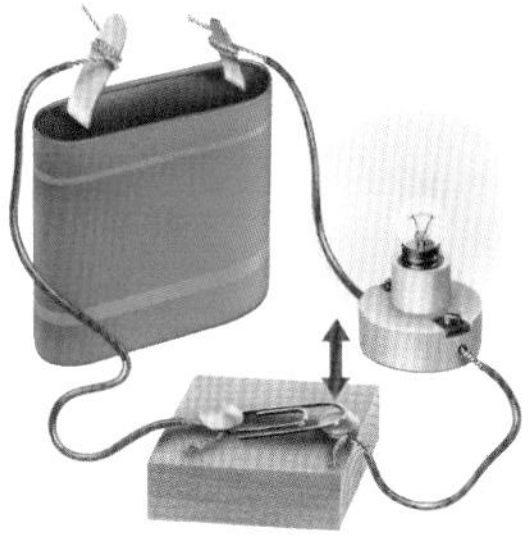

Science

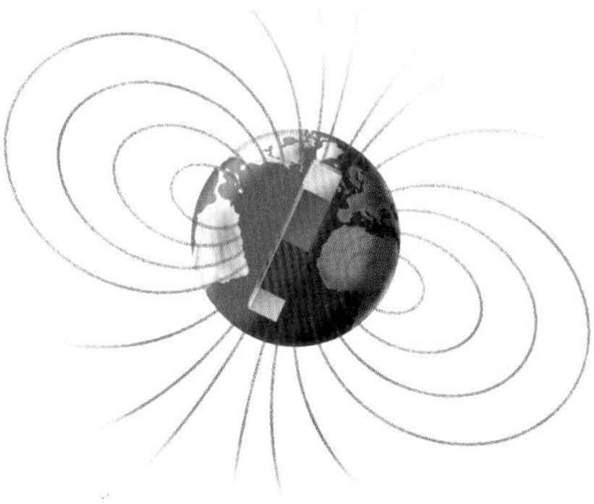

Is science in the playground?

Yes, it is! Lots of science happens in a playground. The playground rides could not work without science. A see-saw is a simple machine called a lever. It has a long arm and a point in the middle called a pivot. As you ride on the see-saw, the lever tips up and down on the pivot.

Sloping machine!

A ramp is the simplest machine of all. It is easier to walk up a ramp to the top of a hill than it is to climb a steep hillside.

What is a wheel?

A wheel is a very simple machine that can spin around. Wheels let other machines, such as skateboards, bicycles, cars and trains, roll along smoothly. They also make it easy to move heavy weights in carts and wheelbarrows.

Feel

Press the palm of your hand onto a table. A force called friction stops you sliding your hand along.

What makes things stop and start?

Pushes and pulls make things stop and start. Scientists use the word 'force' for pushes and pulls. Forces are all around us. The force of gravity pulls things downwards. It makes a rollercoaster car hurtle downhill. It also slows the car on the uphill parts of the track.

Why do fireworks flash and bang?

Fireworks flash and bang because they are full of chemicals that burn. The chemicals have lots of energy stored in them. When they burn, the energy changes to light, heat and sound. We use chemicals that burn in other places too, such as cookers, heaters and car engines.

Fireworks

How do candles burn?

Candles are made of wax and a wick (string). When the wick is lit, the wax around it melts. The wick then soaks up the liquid wax and the heat of the flame turns the wax into a gas (vapour), which burns away. As the wax becomes vapour it cools the wick, allowing the candle to burn slowly.

Hot! Hot! Hot!

The hottest-ever temperature recorded was in a science laboratory. It was four hundred million degrees Celsius (400,000,000°C).

What is a thermometer?

A thermometer tells us how hot something is. This is called temperature. The numbers written on a thermometer are normally degrees Celsius (°C). If you put a thermometer in cold water, it shows 0°C. If you put it in boiling water it shows 100°C. A thermometer can also measure your body temperature.

Remember

Which piece of equipment is used to measure how hot or cold something is?

What is in an electric motor?

Magnets and wires. Electricity from a battery passes through the wires. This turns the wires into a magnet. Two more magnets on each side of the motor push and pull against the wires. This makes a thin metal rod (spindle) spin around.

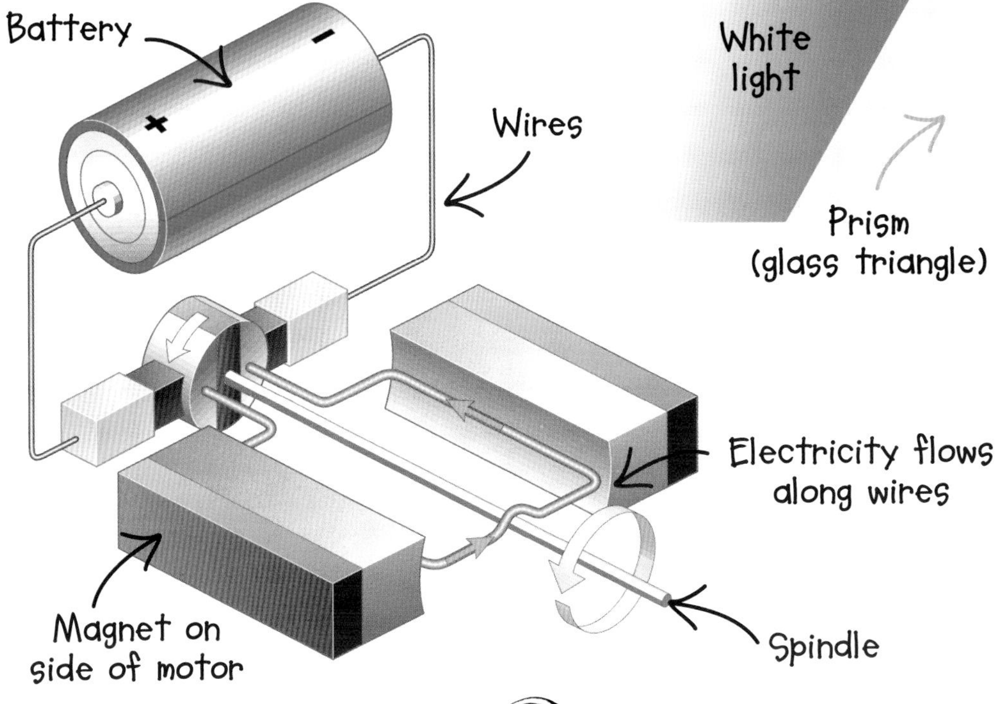

Why does light bend?

Light rays travel in straight lines. When light shines through a prism, the rays bend because light travels more slowly through glass than air. Sunlight is called white light, but it is made up of a mixture of colours. When white light passes through a prism it splits into many colours, like a rainbow.

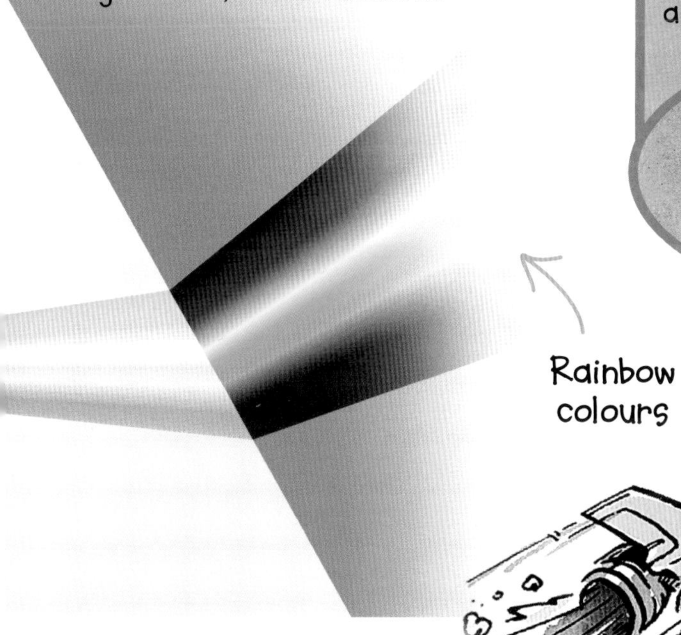

Fast as light!

Light is the fastest thing in the Universe. It travels 300,000 kilometres every second. That means it could travel around the Earth seven times in less than a second!

Make

On a sunny day, stand with your back to the Sun. Spray water into the air and you should see a rainbow!

What is the loudest sound?

The roar of a jet engine is the loudest sound we normally hear. It is thousands of times louder than someone shouting. Sounds this loud can damage our ears if we are too close to them. The quietest sounds we can hear are things like rustling leaves.

Where is science in a city?

Everywhere! In a big city, almost every machine, building and vehicle is based on science. Cars, buses and trains help us move around the city. Scientists and engineers have also worked out how to build tall skyscrapers where people live and work.

Look

Look at the city picture. How many different forms of transport can you see?

Who works railway signals?

Nobody does! The signals work by themselves. Electronic parts on the track work out if a train is passing. Then a computer changes the signals to red, to stop another train moving onto the same piece of track.

How do skyscrapers stay up?

Skyscrapers stay up because they have a strong frame on the inside. The frame is made from steel and concrete. These are very strong materials. Normally you can't see the frame. It is hidden by the skyscraper's walls. The walls hang on the frame.

Plane spotters!

There's science at an airport, too. A radar machine uses radio waves to find aircraft in the sky. This helps people at the airport to guide the aircraft onto the runway.

How do you make magnets?

By using another magnet! Magnets are made from lumps of iron or steel. You can turn a piece of iron into a magnet by stroking it with another magnet. A magnet can also be made by sending electricity through a coil of wire. This is called an electromagnet. Some electromagnets are so strong, they can pick up cars.

Electromagnet picking up scrap cars

Count

Find a magnet at home (you can use a fridge magnet). How many paper clips can your magnet pick up?

Does a magnet have a field?

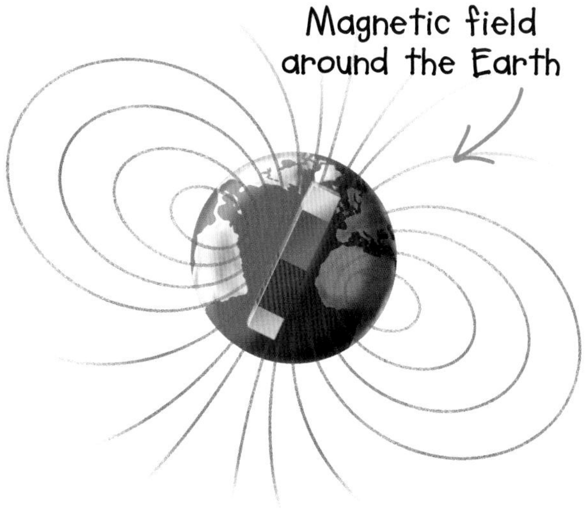

Yes – but it's not a field of grass! The area around a magnet is called a magnetic field. A magnetic field is shown by drawing lines around a magnet. The Earth has a magnetic field, too. It is as though there is a giant magnet inside the Earth.

What are poles?

Every magnet has two poles. These are where the pull of a magnet is strongest. They are called the north pole and the south pole. A north pole and a south pole always pull towards each other. Two north poles always push each other away. So do two south poles.

Handy rock!

Some rocks act like magnets. Years ago, people used magnetic rocks to find their way. If they let the rock spin round, it always pointed in the same direction.

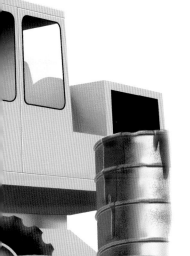

Where does electricity come from?

Electricity comes to your home along cables from power stations. The cables are held off the ground by pylons. Around your home are holes in the wall called sockets. When a machine is plugged into a socket, electricity flows out to work the machine.

Electric!

Our homes are full of machines that work using electricity. If there was no electricity we wouldn't have televisions, lights, washing machines or computers!

Remember

Mains electricity is very dangerous. It could kill you. Never play with mains sockets in your home.

Light bulb
Switch

What is a circuit?

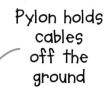

A circuit is a loop that electricity moves around. This circuit is made up of a battery, a light bulb and a switch. If the switch is turned off, the loop would be broken. Then the electricity would stop moving and the light would go out.

When is electricity in the sky?

When there's a thunderstorm! During a storm, a kind of electricity called static electricity builds up. This can make a big flash, that lights up the sky. This is lightning. The hot lightning heats up the air around it and this makes a loud clap. This is thunder.

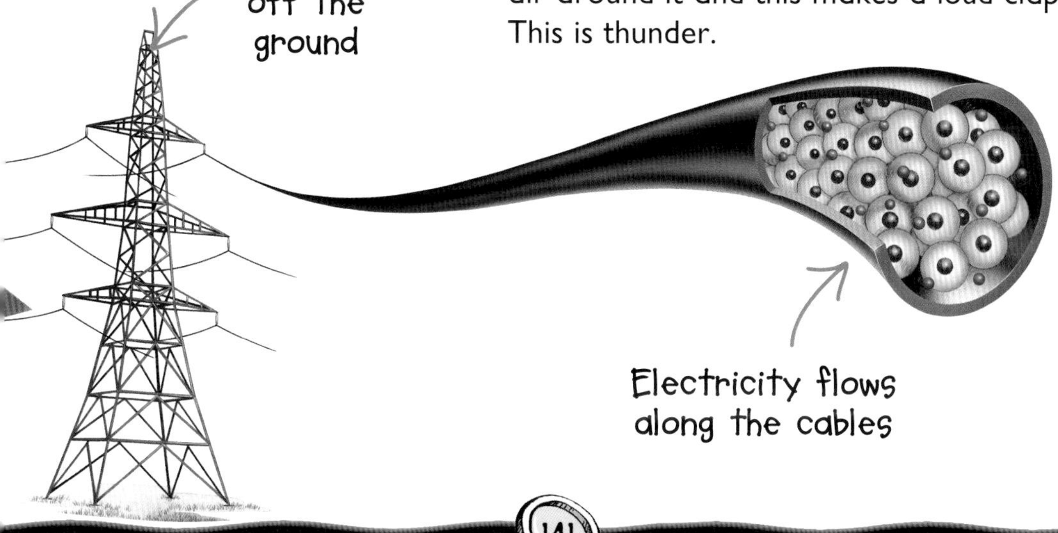
Pylon holds cables off the ground
Electricity flows along the cables

What waves are invisible?

Radio waves are all around us, but we can't see them. We use radio waves to send sounds and pictures to radios and televisions. Some radio waves come from satellites in space. A radio set receives radio waves through a metal rod called an aerial. A dish-shaped aerial picks up radio waves for television programmes.

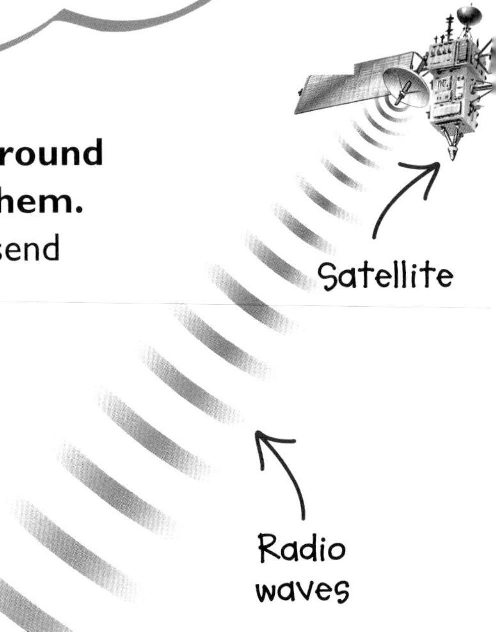

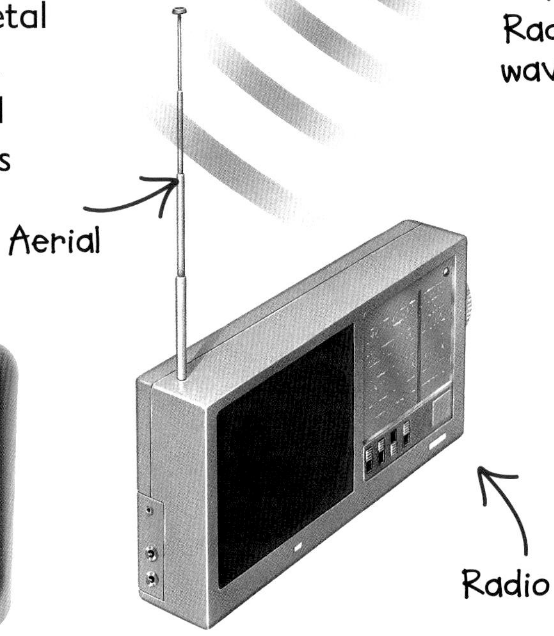

Remember

Which part of your body would stop an X-ray? Skin or bone?

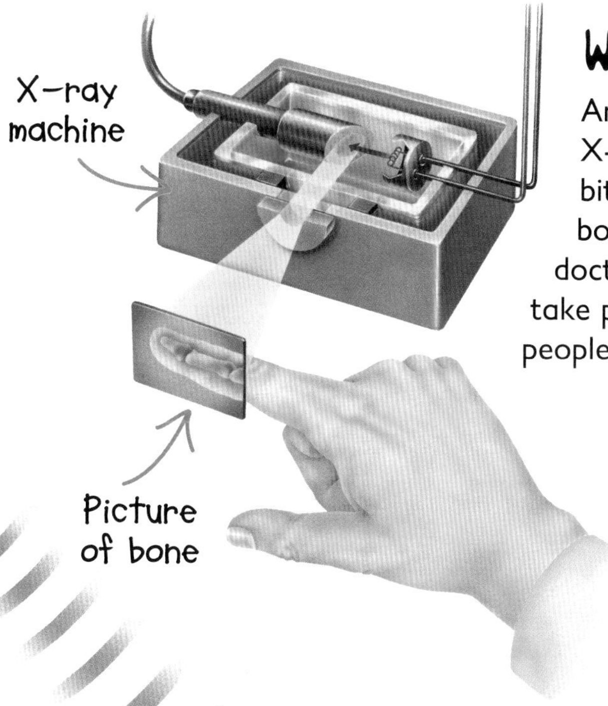

What is an X-ray?

An X-ray is like a radio wave. X-rays can go through the soft bits of your body. However, hard bones stop them. That's why doctors use X-ray machines to take pictures of the inside of people's bodies.

Space radio!

Radio waves can travel through space. But they can't travel through water. So you can listen to a radio in a space station, but not in a submarine!

What waves can cook food?

Microwaves can. These are a kind of radio wave. They have lots of energy in them. A microwave uses this energy to cook food. Microwaves are fired into the oven. They make the particles in the food jiggle about. This makes the food hot.

Are computers clever?

Not really! Computers are amazing machines, but they can only do what they are told. They carry out computer programs written down by people. These are full of instructions that the computer follows. You can also tell a computer what to do by using its keyboard and mouse.

Remember

Can you remember the name for a computer's electronic brain? Read these pages again to help you.

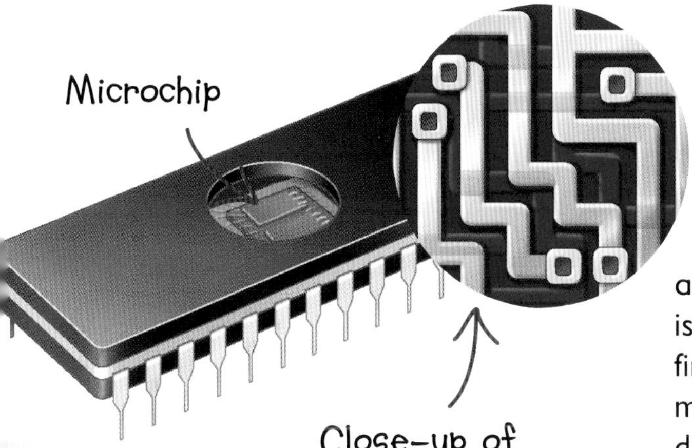

Does a computer have a brain?

A computer doesn't have a brain like yours. It has an electronic brain called a central processing unit. This is a microchip the size of your fingernail. This amazing mini machine can do millions of difficult sums in a split second.

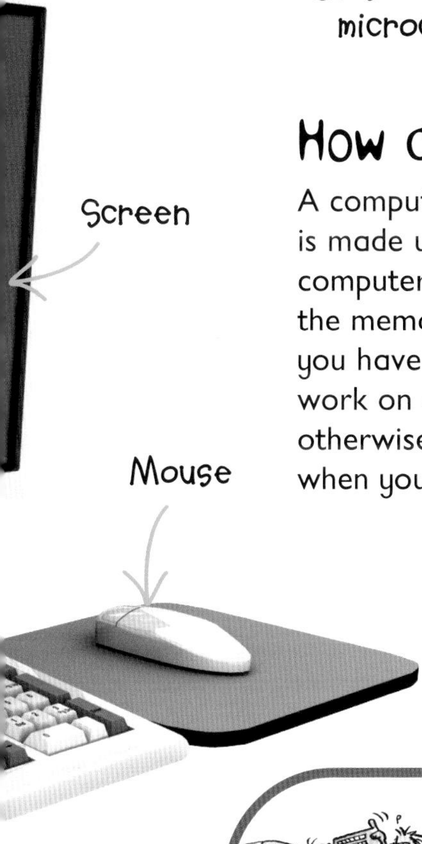

How does a computer remember?

A computer remembers with its electronic memory. This is made up of lots of tiny microchips. When you turn the computer off, everything in the memory is lost. So you have to save your work on a disc, otherwise you lose it when you switch off.

Computer room!

The first computer was made 60 years ago. It was so big that it filled a whole room. A modern calculator can do sums much more quickly!

Is the Internet like a web?

The Internet is made up of millions of computers around the world. They are connected like a giant spider's web! A computer connects to a machine called a modem. This sends signals to a server. The server lets you connect to the Internet. People can send emails and open web pages.

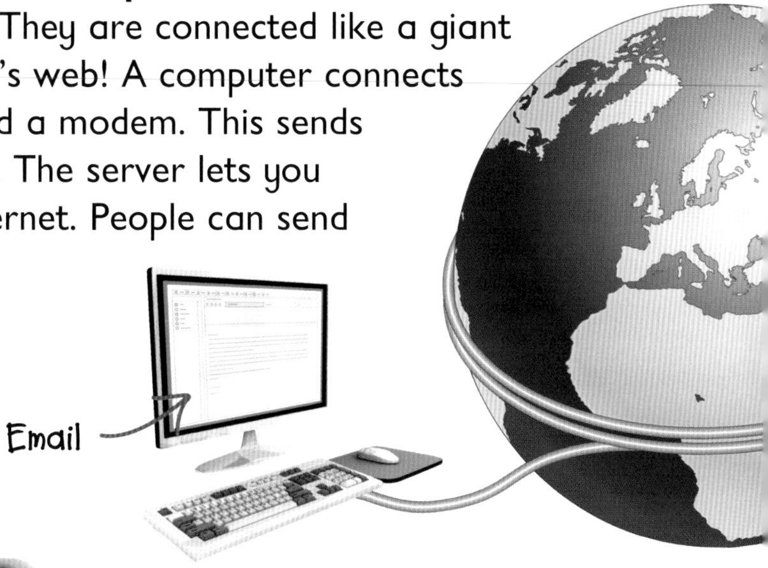

Find out

Look at the main picture on these pages. See if you can find out what the word 'email' is short for.

What does www stand for?

The letters www are short for World Wide Web. The World Wide Web is like a giant library of information, stored on computers all over the world. There are also thousands of shops on the World Wide Web, where you can buy almost anything.

Can I use the Internet without a computer?

Yes. Other machines can link to the Internet, too. You can see simple information from the Internet on a mobile phone. You can send and get emails, too. A mobile phone connects to the Internet by radio.

Mobile phone

Web page

Millions of pages!

The World Wide Web has more than 8000 million pages of information. That's two pages for every person on the planet!

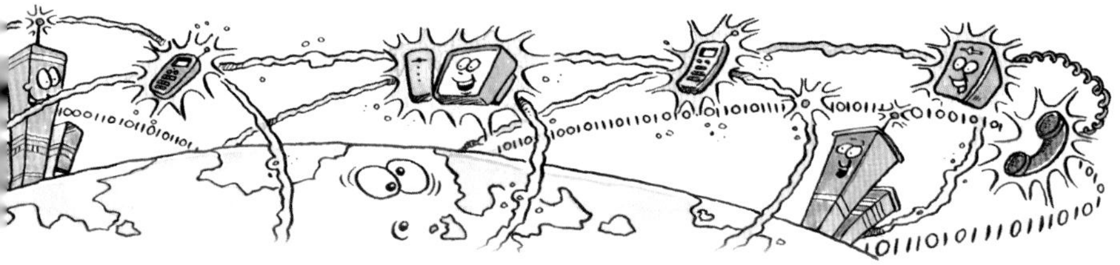

Can a car be made from card?

Yes, it can – but it would break if you sat inside it! It is always important to use the right material to make something. Cars are made from tough, long-lasting materials. Metal, plastic and rubber are all materials used to make cars.

A racing car is made up of hundreds of parts and different materials

Think

Think of three more materials from which things are made. If you get stuck, ask an adult.

Cotton plants make clothes

What materials grow?

Many of the materials we use every day come from plants. Wood comes from the trunks and branches of trees. Cotton is made from the seeds of cotton plants to make clothes such as T-shirts. Some rubber is made from a liquid (sap) from rubber trees.

Rubber tree makes tyres

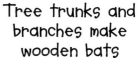

Tree trunks and branches make wooden bats

Bullet proof!

Some glass is extra-strong. Toughened glass is so hard that even a bullet from a gun bounces off it!

Does glass grow?

Glass doesn't grow! It is made from sand and two other materials called limestone and soda. These materials are mixed together and melted to make a gooey liquid. When the mixture cools down, it forms the hard glass that we use to makes windows, drinking glasses and other objects.

What do scientists do at work?

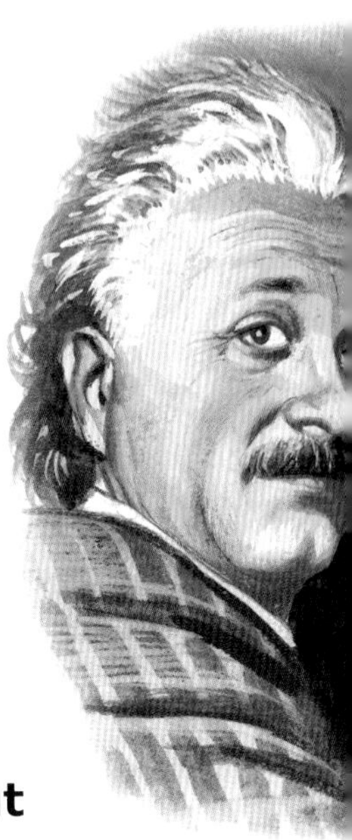

Some scientists try to find out about the world around us. Others find out about space, planets and stars. Some scientists discover useful materials that we can use. Scientists carry out experiments in laboratories to test their ideas.

Scientist in a laboratory

Who is the most famous scientist?

The most famous scientist is called Albert Einstein (1879–1955). He made many discoveries about time, space, the force of gravity and nuclear energy. The ideas that Einstein wrote down were so amazing that they made him famous across the world.

Albert Einstein

Atom pie!

One hundred years ago, scientists thought that the pieces in an atom were all spread out, like the raisins in a pudding. Now we know they are all bunched together.

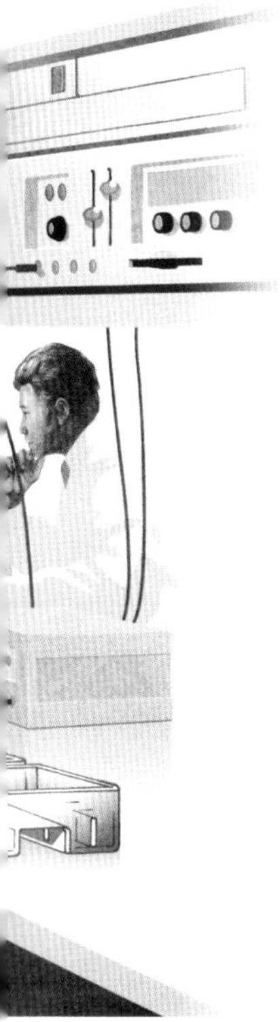

Do scientists help doctors?

Yes, they do. Many scientists make medicines that the doctor gives you when you are ill. They also help to make the complicated machines that doctors use in hospitals. Scientists also try to find out what makes us ill, and how we can stay healthy.

Find

Find out the name of the country where Albert Einstein was born. An encyclopedia will help you.

Are animals part of science?

Yes, they are! Scientists who study animals and plants work everywhere in the world. They study in hot rainforests, dusty deserts, high mountains, at the freezing poles and in rivers and seas.

Many scientists study animals and plants

Look

Study the picture. Can you see something that might harm the animals and plants?

Which way?

Some animals travel great distances around the world. They use the Earth's magnetic field to guide them.

What is an ecologist?

An ecologist is a scientist. Ecologists study where plants and animals live. They also look at how plants and animals live alongside each other, and the things that animals eat. Ecologists study the harm that we do to plants and animals.

How do ecologists follow animals?

With complicated radio equipment. First they catch the animal and put a collar on its neck, wing or leg. The collar has a tiny radio aerial that sends out radio waves. The ecologist finds the animal by listening with a machine that picks up the radio waves.

Are we harming the Earth?

Many of the things we do are harming the world around us. Machines such as cars put dangerous gases into the air. These gases can harm plants and make people ill. They are also making the weather change.

Scientists are always looking for new ways to reduce damage to the Earth.

Dirty cars!

Cars and other vehicles can produce so much pollution that in some cities it has become difficult for people to breathe.

What is recycling?

Recycling is using materials again, instead of throwing them away. This helps to make less waste. Ask your parents to take empty glass bottles to a bottle bank. The glass in the bottles is made into new bottles. Paper, metal and plastic are also recycled.

1. Bottle bank
2. Bottles are crushed
3. Glass is melted
4. Liquid glass is put in moulds
5. New bottles are ready

Glass recycling

Save

Ask your family to save electricity. Get them to switch off the lights when nobody is in the room.

Does electricity harm the Earth?

Yes, it does. Lots of coal, oil and gas are burned to make electricity. These make harmful gases that go into the air. You can help by turning things off to save electricity. Scientists are inventing new ways of making electricity from the wind, the Sun and water.

Quiz time

Do you remember what you have read about science?

These questions will test your memory. The pictures will help you. If you get stuck, read the pages again.

1. Is science in the playground?

page 130

2. How do candles burn?

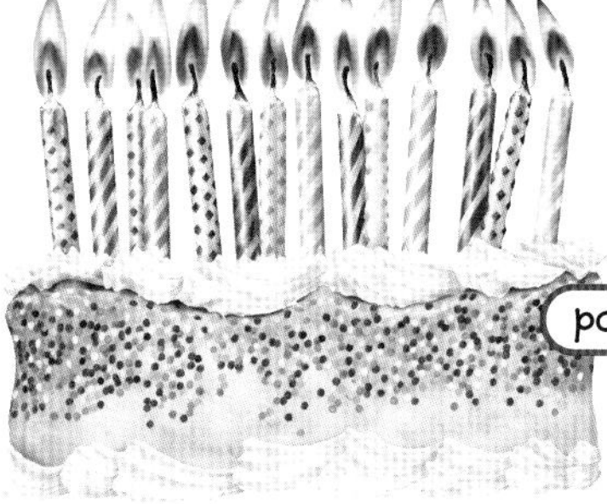

page 133

3. What is a thermometer?

page 133

4. What is in an electric motor?

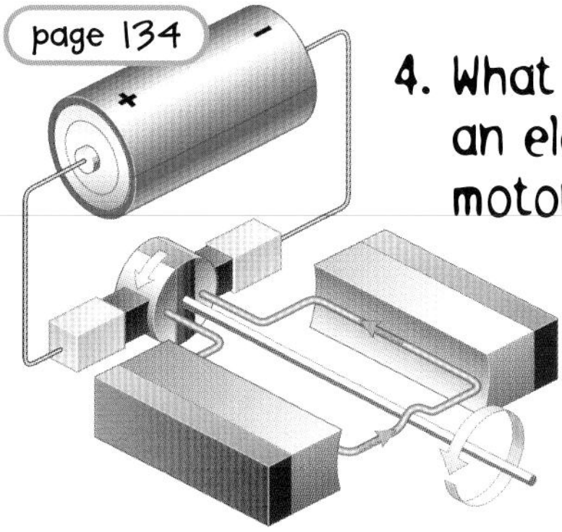

page 134

5. How do skyscrapers stay up?

page 137

6. Does a magnet have a field?

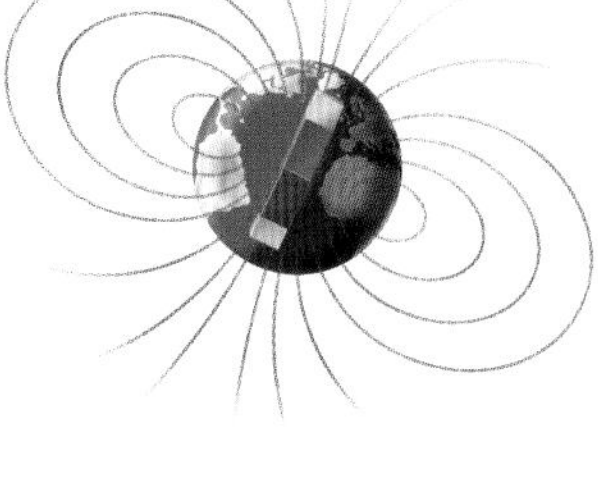

page 139

7. What is a circuit?

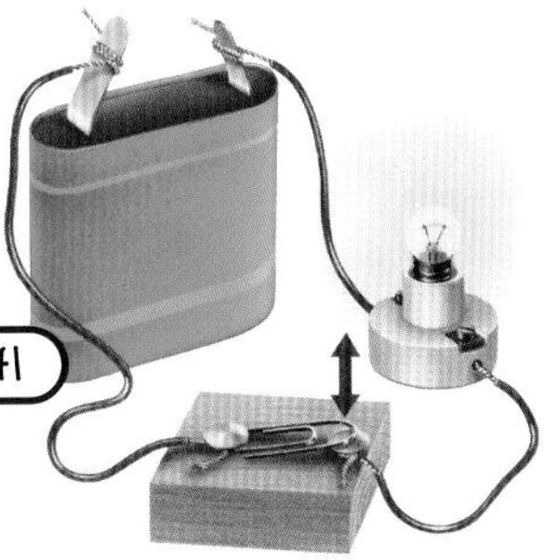

page 141

8. What is an X-ray?

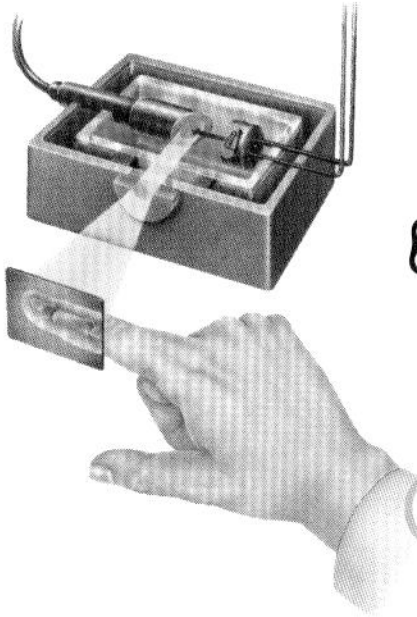

page 143

9. What waves can cook food?

page 143

page 144

10. Are computers clever?

page 146

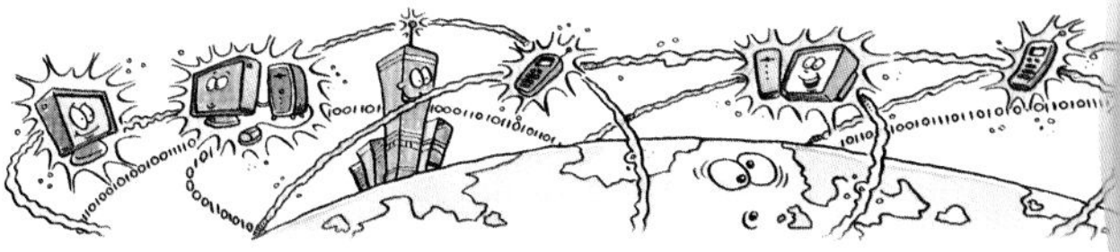

11. What does www stand for?

12. Who is the most famous scientist?

page 151

13. Does electricity harm the Earth?

page 155

Answers

1. Yes it is, in rides such as see-saws
2. By melting wax, which becomes a vapour that burns.
3. A machine that measures heat
4. Magnets and wires
5. They have a strong frame that supports them
6. Yes, a magnetic field
7. When the candle is lit, the wax melts and disappears into the air
8. It is a radio wave
9. Microwaves
10. No, but they can follow instructions
11. World Wide Web
12. Albert Einstein
13. Yes, it can

Questions about...

Inventions

What were the first inventions?

The first inventions were stone tools, which early people began to make about two million years ago. During the Stone Age, about 30,000 years ago, people discovered how to sew animal skins together to make clothes. They also learnt how to keep warm and dry by building shelters.

Stone Age people using tools

How did early people see in the dark?

Prehistoric people used lamps to light up caves. The lamps were made of clay or stone saucers, which were filled with animal fat. The animal fat was then burnt using a wick made of moss.

Fire-makers!

Early people discovered how to make fire more than 250,000 years ago! Thousands of years later, flint stones were used to make sparks, which lit dried grass and wood.

Who invented the wheel?

The Sumerian people invented wheels 5500 years ago. They were heavy and made with carved wood that was fastened together. Later, the ancient Egyptians made spoked wheels, which were lighter.

Spoked wheels

Count

In this book, how many inventions can you find that use the wheel?

Who invented the first car?

Karl Benz invented the first car in 1896. It had a petrol-powered engine but could not travel very fast. The first popular car was the Model T, built in 1908 by the Ford company in the United States. Over 15 million of them were sold worldwide.

Model T Ford

Why do tractors have such big tyres?

Tractors were invented in 1892 and are used to pull farm machinery, such as ploughs. Tractors have huge tyres to stop them getting stuck in mud. Big weights at the front stop tractors tipping over when pulling heavy machinery.

Tractor

Wooden lines!

Railway tracks were once made of wood! Wheels move more easily along rails, so horses pulled wagons on wooden rails more than 400 years ago. Metal rails were invented in 1789.

What was a boneshaker?

A boneshaker was one of the first bicycles. It had solid tyres and was so uncomfortable to ride that it made people's bones shake. In 1888, John Dunlop invented air-filled rubber tyres that made cycling more comfortable.

Try

If you have a bike, try riding it in the garden. Is it a smooth or bumpy ride?

Who used the first sails?

Sails were invented by the Egyptians more than 5000 years ago. About 2000 years ago, the best sailors were the Phoenician people. They sailed in boats made of cedar wood and reeds. These ships had sails and oars and were used to make long journeys.

Draw

Using coloured pens or pencils, draw your own super sail boat. Try adding your own amazing inventions.

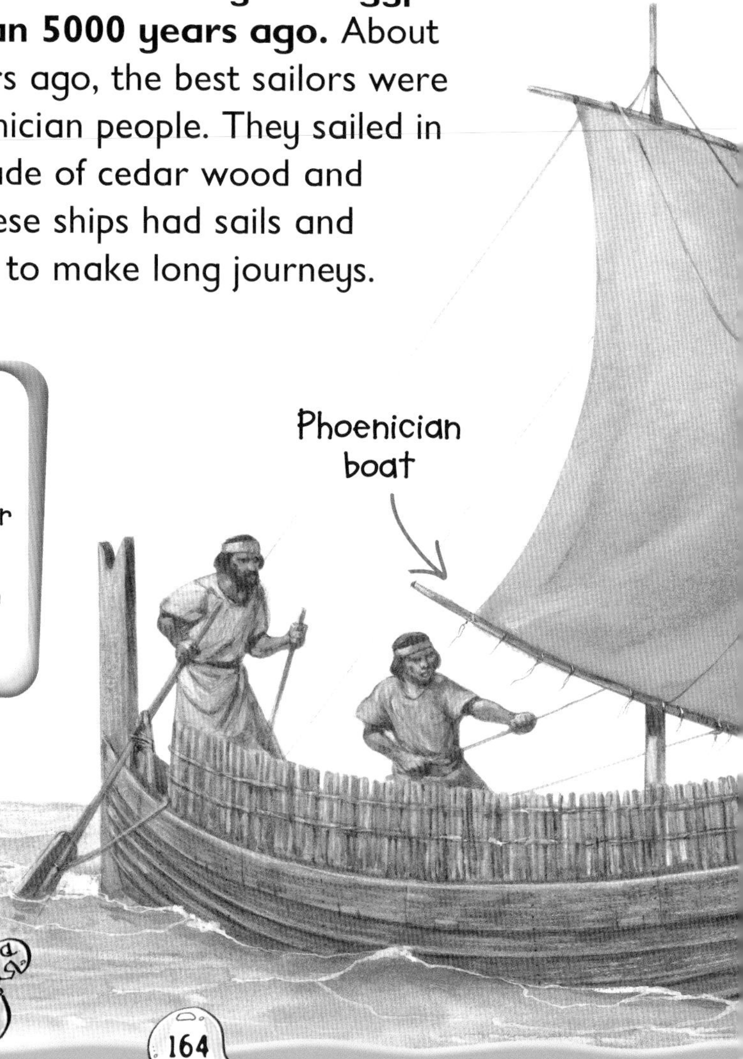

Super sailing!

Modern boats use inventions such as machines that roll up the sails and special gears that let the boat steer itself.

Why did coal miners need steam power?

Before steam power, miners had to pull coal carts out of mines by hand. This was very hard work. Then in 1814, a coal miner named George Stephenson invented an engine that pulled the carts out of the mines using steam power.

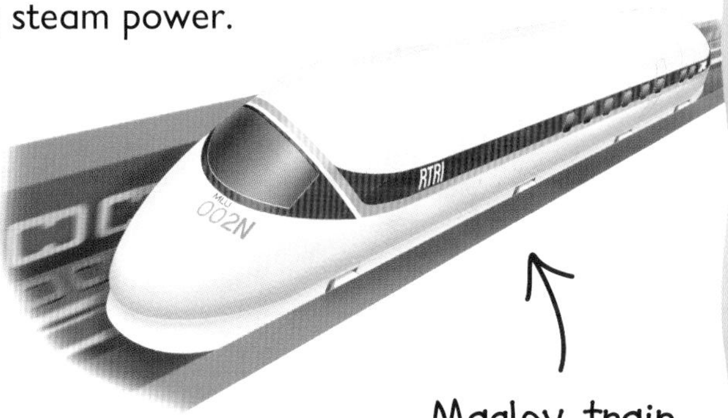

Maglev train

Can trains float?

Yes they can, in a way. In 1909 Robert Goddard discovered a way to make trains travel using magnets. These trains are called Maglevs. They run on a magnetic rail that pushes the train up so it seems to be floating. Maglevs can reach very high speeds.

What is a combine harvester?

A combine harvester is a big farm machine that cuts crops and separates grain. The first combine harvester was invented in 1836 and was pulled by horses. Today, farmers all over the world use these machines so they can harvest their crops quickly.

Plant power!

Scientists are changing the way plants grow. They have invented ways of creating crops with built-in protection from pests and diseases.

Airship

Can ships fly?

Airships can! They are filled with a special gas called helium. This gas is lighter than air, and makes the airship float in the sky. Today, airships are used to display adverts in the sky and are not used for people to travel in.

Did people pull ploughs?

Ploughs were invented in Egypt around 2000 BC and were first pulled by people. They helped farmers break up the ground and turn the soil over. Later, people began to use horses and oxen to pull ploughs.

Think

Can you think of any other machines or animals that you would find on a farm?

Who invented jumbo jets?

A jumbo jet is a plane. In 1970, the first jumbo jet flight took place between New York and London. The planes are powered by jet engines that were invented by Dr Hans von Ohain of Germany, and Sir Frank Whittle of England. Their inventions developed to become modern jet engines.

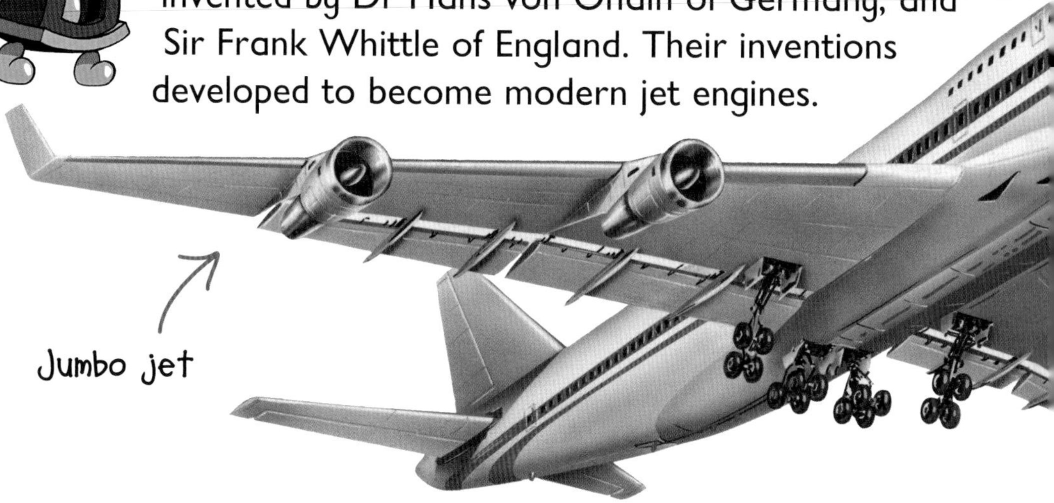

Bird brains!

Many inventors have tried to fly by flapping birdlike wings. All have failed. One of the first bird-men crashed to his death at a Roman festival in the 1st century AD.

Can balloons carry people?

Hot-air balloons were invented in 1783. They can carry people high up into the sky. The first ever passengers to fly in a hot air balloon were not humans but a cockeral, a duck and a sheep!

Do planes perform tricks?

Yes, they do. The Red Arrows are a team of highly skilled pilots that can make their planes perform tricks. Their red aircrafts can fly upside down and on their sides and are very fast. The Red Arrows perform in front of large crowds at airshows and other special occasions.

Make

With some paper, make a plane and colour it in. How far can you get it to fly?

How can we see into space?

People can look at the stars and planets by using a telescope. The first telescope was invented by a Dutchman called Hans Lippershey in 1608. In 1609, the Italian scientist Galileo built his own telescope. He was the first person to see the craters on the Moon.

Who invented spectacles?

The Italians did. In the 14th century in Italy people made their own glass lenses to look through. These small lenses were put into frames and were used to help people to read.

Write

Imagine you have found a pair of magic spectacles. Write a story about what you see when you put them on.

Microscope

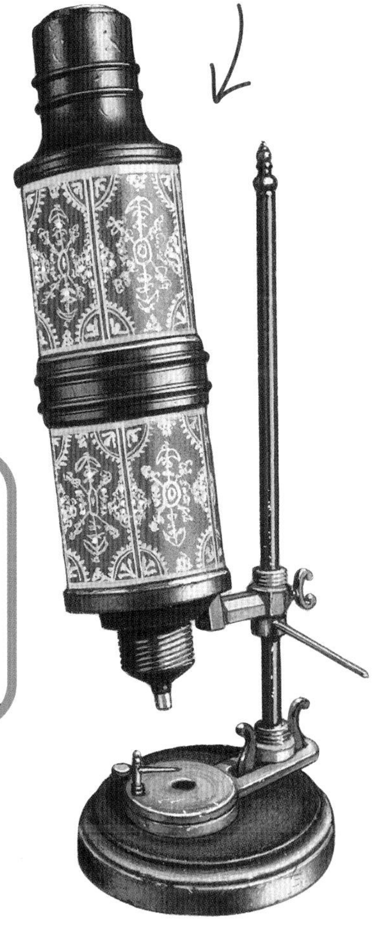

How can we make small things bigger?

By using a microscope. A microscope uses pieces of glass called lenses. These make small things look bigger than they really are. The first microscope was invented in the 1600s and had one lens. Later microscopes had two lenses to make them more powerful.

Marvellous maths!

Around AD 300, the Chinese invented a counting machine called an abacus. It was a wooden frame with beads strung on wires and it helped people do complicated sums.

Who made the streets light up?

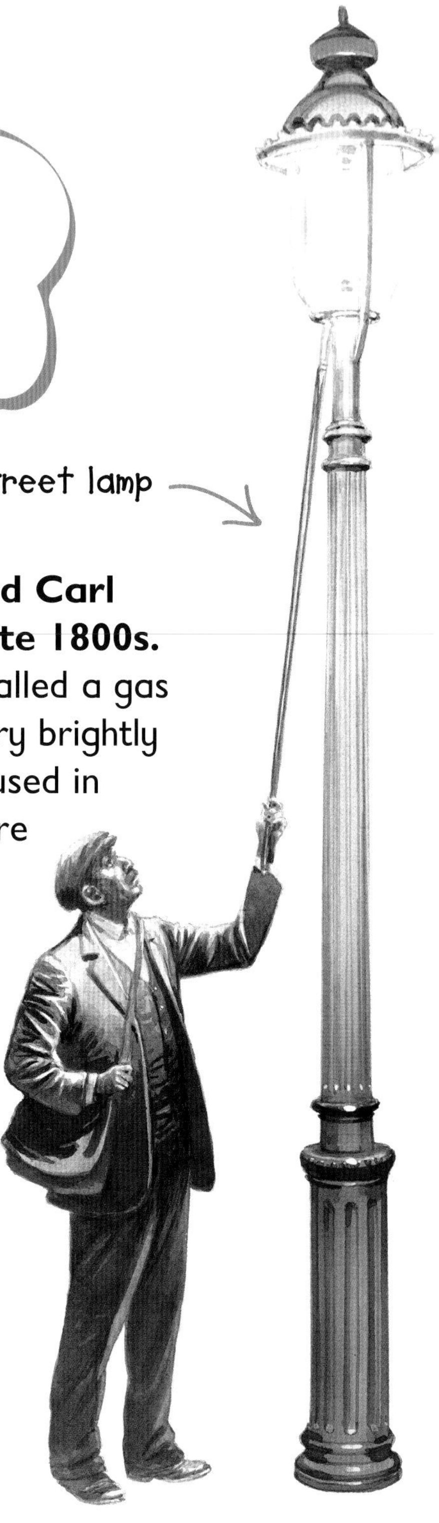

An Austrian named Carl Auer did, in the late 1800s. He invented a lamp called a gas mantle that glowed very brightly when heated up. The gas mantle was used in the first street lamps. Long torches were needed to light the lamps.

Wind power!

The first windmills were invented thousands of years ago. They helped to grind grain into flour. Today, windmills are used to pump water, make electricity and power machinery.

How big was the first computer?

The first computer was so big that it took up a whole room. In 1975, the first home computers were made but they were expensive and not very powerful. Computers today are small, cheap and powerful.

Who made electricity from the wind?

In 1888, Charles F Brush invented a modern-day windmill called a wind turbine. Wind turbines have blades that turn in the wind. These power a motor inside the turbine, which makes electricity. Wind turbines can power entire towns.

Remember

In ancient times, what was the name of the counting machine that was invented by the Chinese?

Why do clocks have hands?

Clocks have hands so that people can tell the time. The hands point to different numbers on the clock face and these tell us what time it is. Clocks work by using a series of springs and wheels that move the hands of the clock around. The first mechanical alarm clock was invented in 1787.

Make

Use a paper plate to make a clock. Write the numbers on the face and use plastic straws for the hands.

Alarm clock

How does the Sun tell the time?

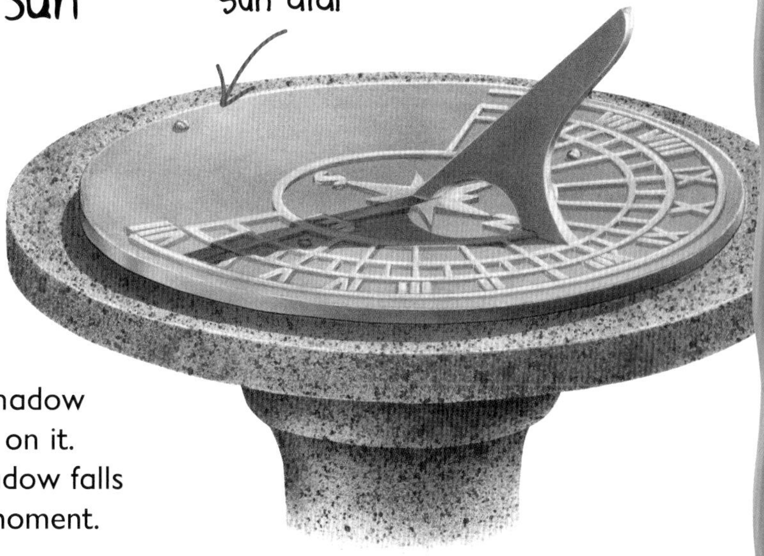

The Sun was used to help people tell the time before clocks were invented. Sundials have a stone face marked with the hours, and a pointer that makes a shadow when the Sun is shining on it. Whatever hour the shadow falls on is the time at that moment.

Watch it!

The wrist watch was invented in the 1600s by a French mathematician. He attached a piece of string to his pocket watch and tied it around his wrist.

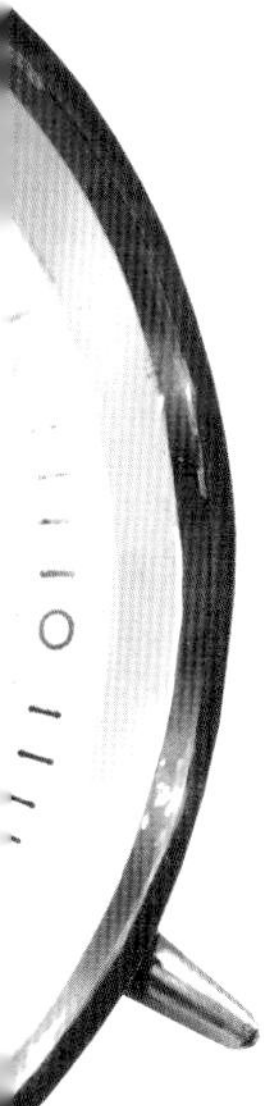

Can candles tell the time?

Candles were once used as clocks to tell the time. They were marked with rings so that when the wax burnt down, people could tell how much time has passed by.

When was cooking invented?

Cooking was invented in prehistoric times by some of our earliest relatives. When people discovered fire, they realized that if food was placed in the fire, it tasted better. Cooking also made food safer because it killed germs that might cause sickness.

The first cooks

Write

Using pictures instead of words, write a secret message. Can your friends work out what it says?

Who wrote the first words?

The Sumerian people wrote the first words more than 5500 years ago. They scratched words onto clay tablets. The first writing was made up of pictures. Ancient picture-writing used hundreds of different signs. Today, modern alphabets have far fewer letters.

Smoky signals!

Before inventions such as the telephone, sending long-distance messages had to be simple. Native Americans used smoke signals to send messages to each other.

Who made the first phone call?

Alexander Graham Bell made the first telephone call in 1876. The telephone worked by turning vibrations in the human voice into electrical signals. These signals travelled down a wire to another phone, where they were turned back into sound.

What was a gramophone?

In 1887, Emile Berlin invented a machine that could play music. The machine was called a gramophone. To make it work, a handle was turned, which turned a disc under a steel needle. The needle allowed the music to play.

Find out

Today we use CDs to play music. Can you find out what the letters CD are short for?

Marvellous movies!

Only one person at a time could watch the very first films. The viewer went into a special room and looked through a hole in a box.

Who invented television?

John Logie Baird invented the first television in 1926. The pictures were black and white and very blurry. Modern televisions show clear, sharp pictures in colour.

Flat screen television

Who took the first photo?

Joseph Nicephore took the first-ever photograph in 1826. The picture was of rooftops and took eight hours to take. The first cameras were very big, and instead of paper, the photos were printed on glass plates.

Why were fridges dangerous?

The first electric refrigerators were invented in 1805, but they were dangerous to use. This was because they used a poisonous gas to keep them cold. In 1929, a safer gas called freon was used. However freon causes damage to the planet, so scientists want to change this, too.

Stone cold!

Stone Age people invented the first refrigerators! They buried any spare food in pits dug in ground that was always frozen.

Early fridge

Microwave oven

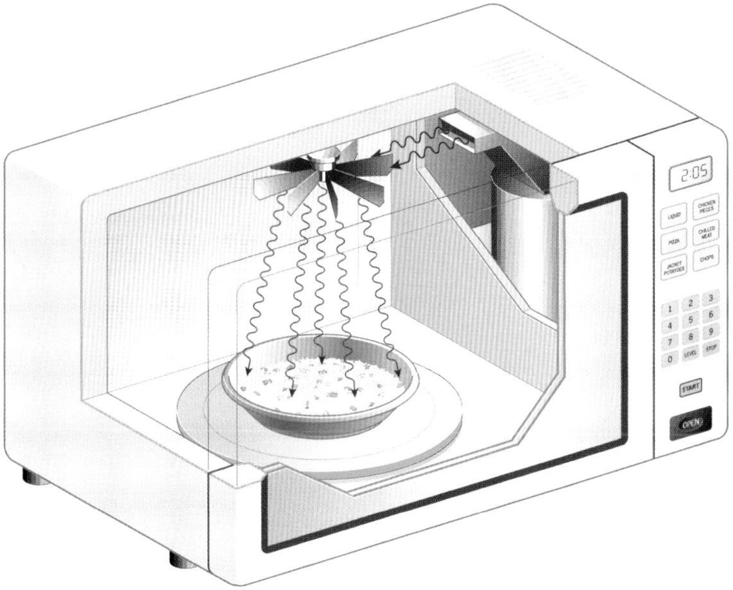

How do microwaves cook food?

A microwave oven produces waves that make food heat itself up. In 1945, Percy L. Spencer invented the microwave oven after noticing that a microwave machine at his workplace had melted a chocolate bar in his pocket.

Look

Take a look around your house. How many inventions help you and your family every day?

Have toilets always flushed?

4000 years ago in Greece, royal palaces had flushing toilets that used rainwater. Thomas Twyford invented the first ceramic flushing toilet in 1885. His design is still used today.

What is special about the shuttle?

The space shuttle is a very special spacecraft. This is because it is reusable. Most spacecraft can only go into space once, but the shuttle is like a space plane. It can return into space up to ten times. The first space shuttle was launched in 1981.

Write

Imagine you are living on board a space station. Write a letter to tell people about your adventure.

Who invented fireworks?

The Chinese invented fireworks thousands of years ago. The loud sound that they made was supposed to frighten off evil spirits. Today, fireworks are used to celebrate special occasions.

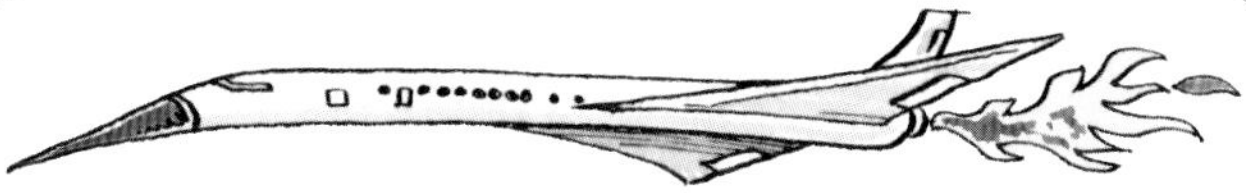

Fast flyer!

Concorde was a superfast plane that flew people across the Atlantic in record time. Trips from London to New York only took three hours.

Space station

Can people live in space?

Yes, they can. A space station is a home in space for astronauts. It has a kitchen for making meals, and cabins with sleeping bags. The first space station was launched in 1971.

Do zips have teeth?

Yes, zips do have teeth! A zip has two rows of teeth that can be opened and shut by a slider. The first zip was invented in 1891. It was called the Talon Slide Fastener and was used on a boot called the zipper. This is where the zip got its name from.

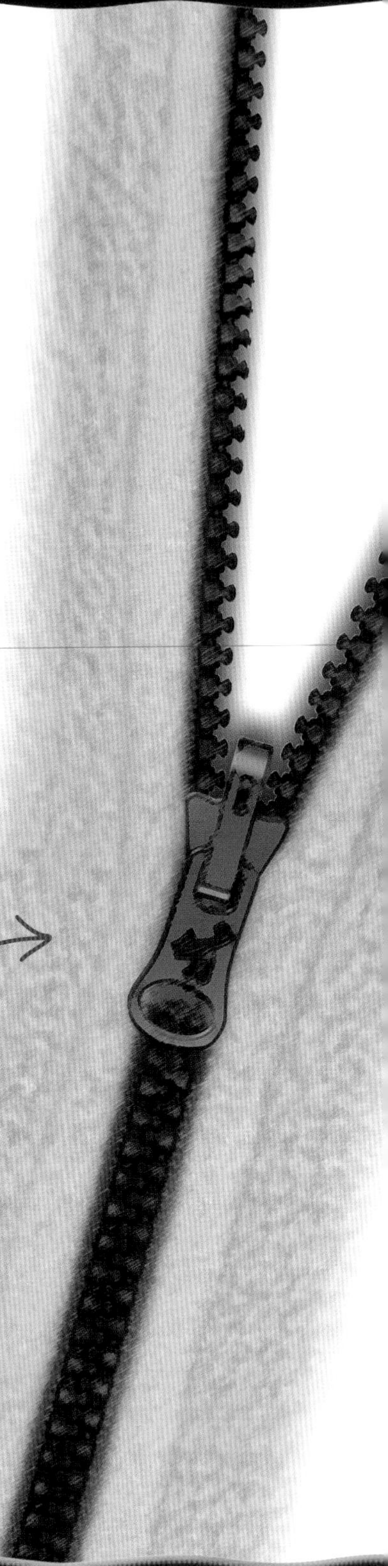

Bone brush!

The first toothbrush was made out of animal bone. The bone had small holes drilled into it where bristles were placed.

How did teddy bears get their name?

The teddy bear was named after US President Theodore Roosevelt in 1903. The president's nickname was Teddy. One day he spared the life of a bear cub when out hunting. The teddy bear became the most popular soft toy ever.

Which horse can rock?

The rocking horse was invented in 1780. It was a toy horse that children could ride on without hurting themselves. Early rocking horses were usually dapple-grey in colour and rocked on wooden bow rockers.

Draw

Design your own perfect toy. Draw a picture of it and colour it in.

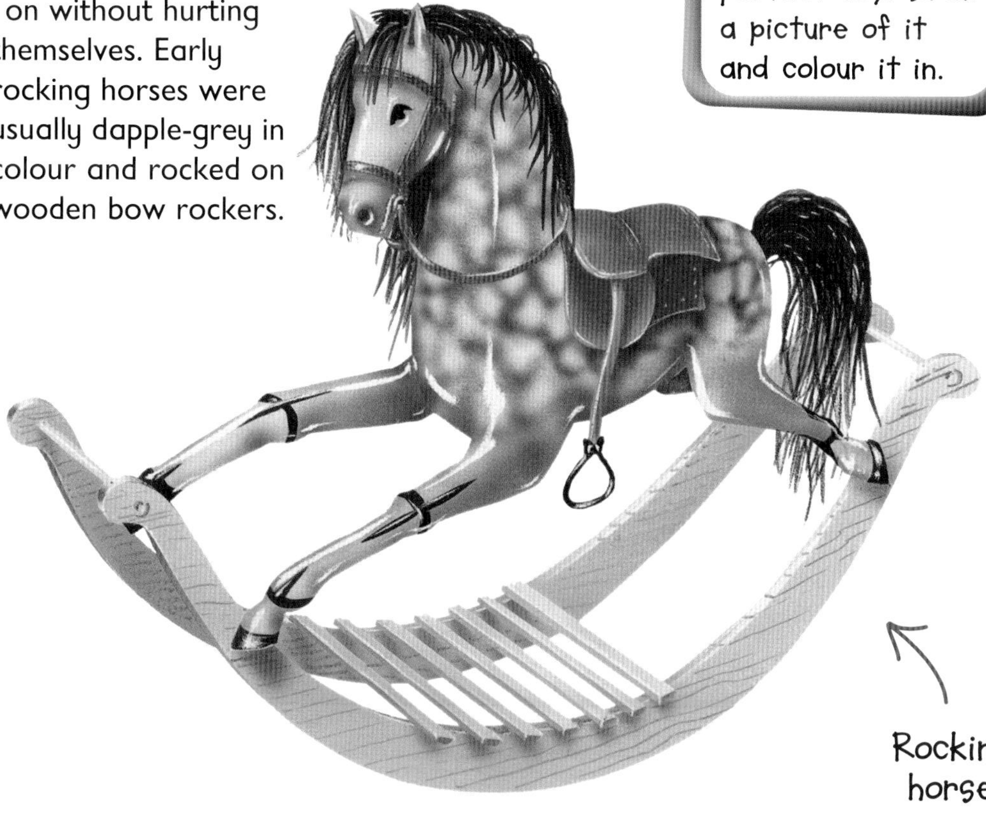

Rocking horse

Quiz time

Do you remember what you have read about inventions? These questions will test your memory. The pictures will help you. If you get stuck, read the pages again.

page 160

1. How did early people see in the dark?

page 161

2. Who invented the wheel?

3. What was a boneshaker?

page 163

4. Can trains float?

page 165

5. Did people pull ploughs?

page 167

6. Can ships fly?

page 167

7. Who invented jumbo jets?

page 168

page 179

8. Who invented spectacles?

page 171

11. Who took the first photo?

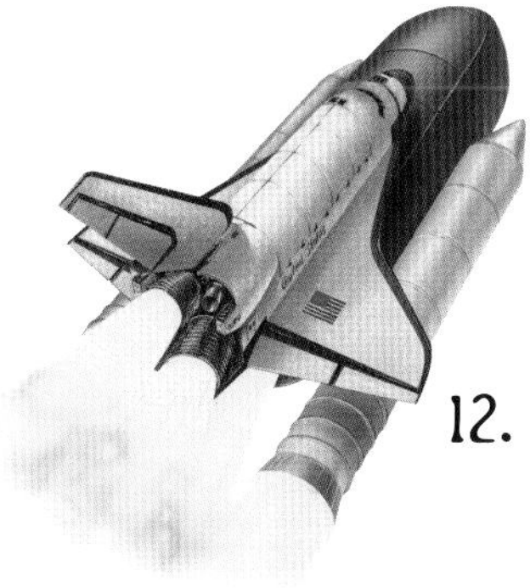

page 182

12. What is special about the shuttle?

9. How does the Sun tell the time?

page 175

page 183

13. Who invented fireworks?

10. Who wrote the first words?

page 177

Answers

1. They used lamps made of clay and animal fat
2. The Sumerian people
3. One of the very first bicycles
4. Yes, the Maglev train can
5. Yes, the first ploughs were pulled by people
6. Airships can fly
7. Dr Hans von Ohain
8. The Italians
9. With a sundial
10. The Sumerian people
11. Joseph Nicephore
12. It can be reused
13. The Chinese

Questions about...

Your Body

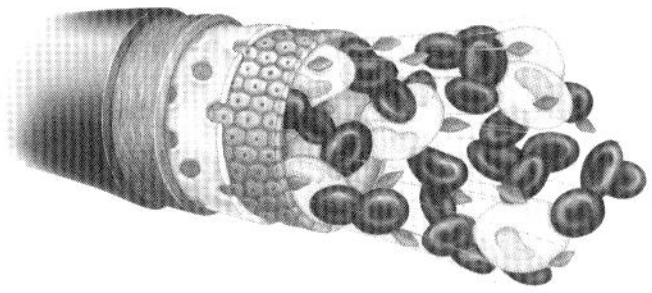

Why do babies grip so tightly?

Tiny babies can do simple things. If something touches a baby's cheek, it turns its head and tries to suck. If something touches the baby's hand, it grips tightly. These actions are called reflexes. They help the baby survive.

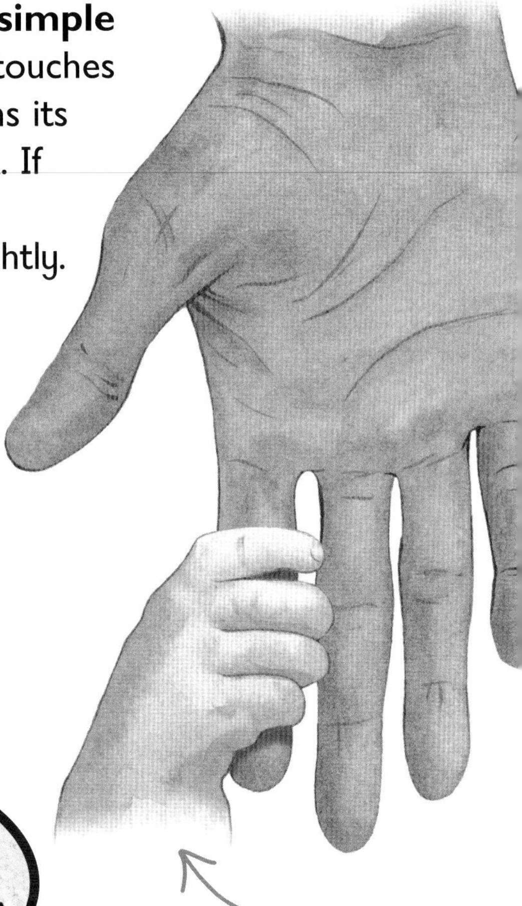

Baby gripping

Giant baby!

A baby grows quickly before it is born. If it grew this fast for 50 years, it would be taller than Mount Everest!

When do babies start to walk?

When they are about one year old. Babies can roll over at three months. At six months, they can sit up. At nine months they start to crawl. Then babies learn to stand and take their first steps.

Children playing

Am I always learning?

Yes, you are! Most children start school when they are five years old. They learn to count, read, write and draw. Children learn outside of the classroom, too. Playing and having fun with friends is a great way to learn new things!

Find out

Find out three reasons why a newborn baby cries? Ask a grown-up if you need any help.

What does my skin do?

Skin protects you from bumps and scratches. It stops your body from drying out, and prevents germs from getting in. When you play on bikes or skateboards, you should wear gloves and knee pads to protect your skin.

Knee pads protect from cuts
Gloves protect from scrapes

Ouch! Ouch! Ouch!

There are millions of tiny touch sensors in your skin. They tell your brain when something touches your skin. Some sensors feel hot and cold. Others feel pain. Ouch!

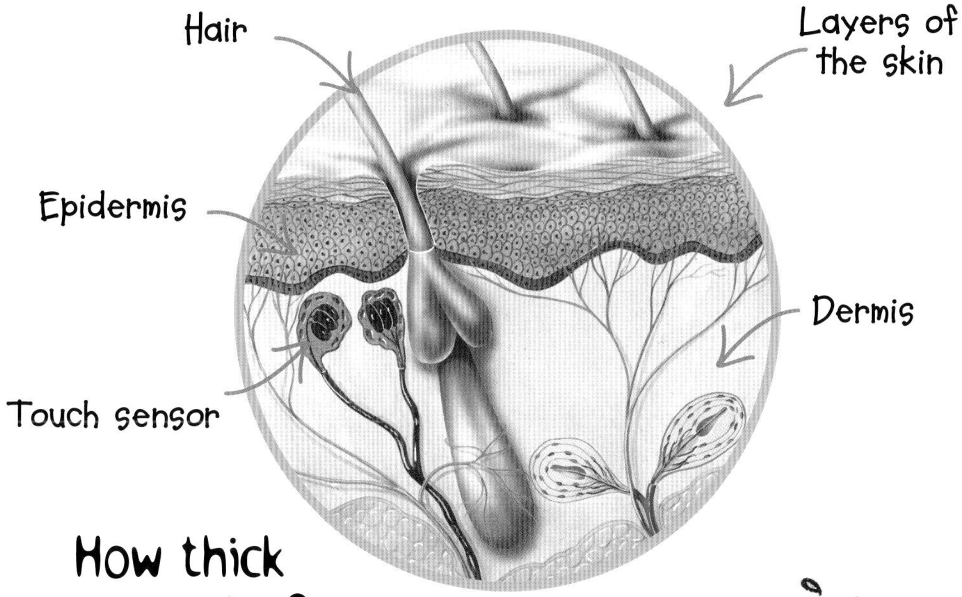

How thick is my skin?

Your skin is very thin. It is only 2 millimetres thick. On top is a layer of tough, dead cells called the epidermis. These cells gradually rub off. New cells grow underneath to replace them. Underneath is another layer of skin called the dermis. This contains areas that give you your sense of touch.

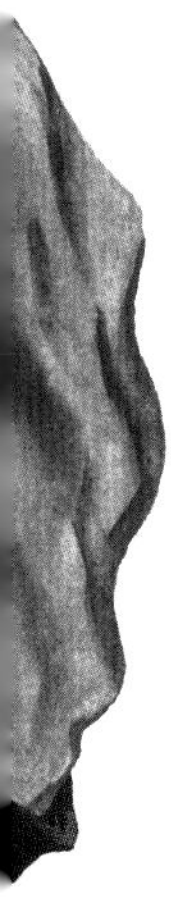

Why do I sweat when I'm warm?

To cool down again. Your body warms up on a hot day or when you run about. You sweat to get rid of the heat. Your body lets sweat out through your skin. As the sweat dries, it takes away heat. This cools you down.

Think

If you are riding a bike or playing on a skateboard, what should you wear on your head, and why?

How much hair do I have?

Your whole body is covered in about five million hairs! You have about 100,000 hairs on your head. Hair grows out of tiny pits in your skin, called follicles. Hair grows in different colours and it can be wavy, curly or straight.

For the chop!

The hair on your head grows about 2 millimetres a week. If a hair is never cut, it reaches about one metre in length before it falls out. It is replaced by a new hair.

What are nails made from?

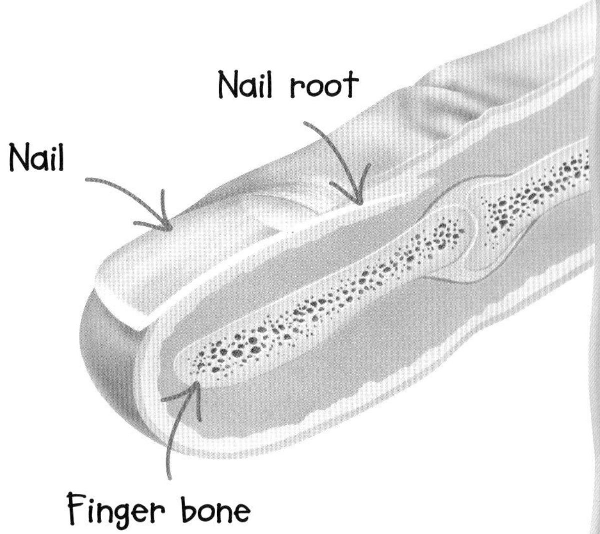

Fingernails and toenails are made from a hard material called keratin. It is the same material that hair is made from. Nails grow out of the nail root. In a week, a nail grows by about half a millimetre. They grow faster at night than in the day!

Look

Have a look in the mirror. Is your hair straight, wavy or curly? Use the pictures on page 194 to help you.

Why do we have fingernails?

Fingernails protect your fingertips. The nail stops your fingertip bending back when you touch something. This helps your fingers to feel things. Nails are useful for picking up tiny objects.

How many bones do I have?

Most people have 206 bones. Half of them are in your hands and feet. All your bones together make up your skeleton. The skeleton is like a frame. It holds up the other parts of your body. It also protects the squashy bits inside.

Find

Can you find your collarbone? It starts at your shoulder and runs to the top of your rib cage.

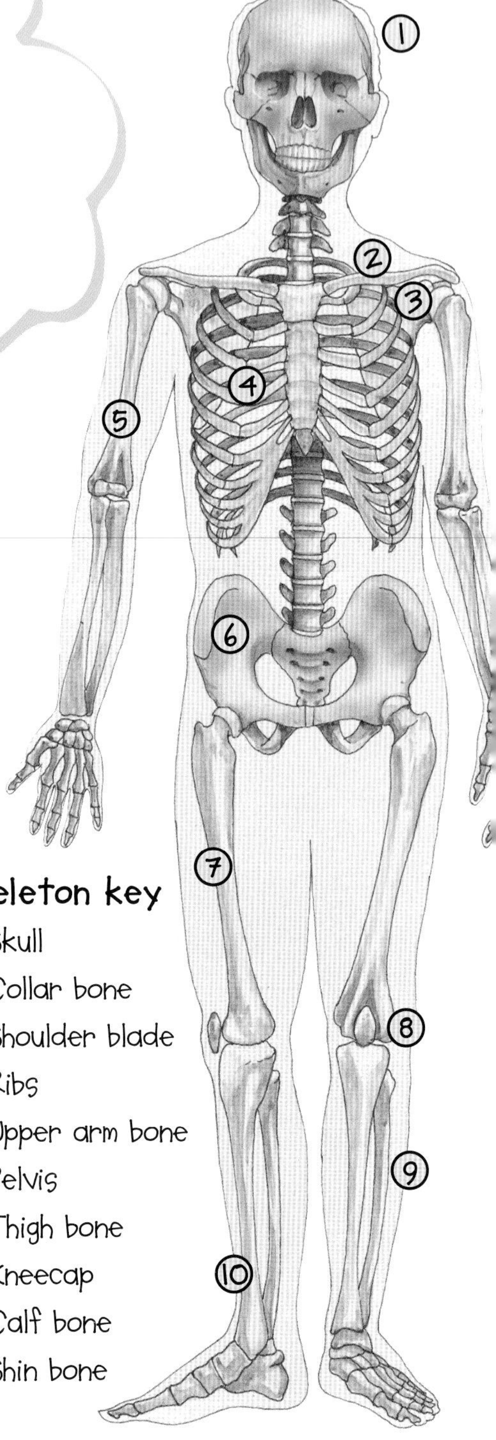

Skeleton key

1. Skull
2. Collar bone
3. Shoulder blade
4. Ribs
5. Upper arm bone
6. Pelvis
7. Thigh bone
8. Kneecap
9. Calf bone
10. Shin bone

What are bones made from?

Bones are made from different materials mixed together. Some of the materials are very hard and some are tough and bendy. Together they make bones very strong. There is a kind of jelly called marrow inside some bones. This makes tiny parts for your blood, called red and white cells.

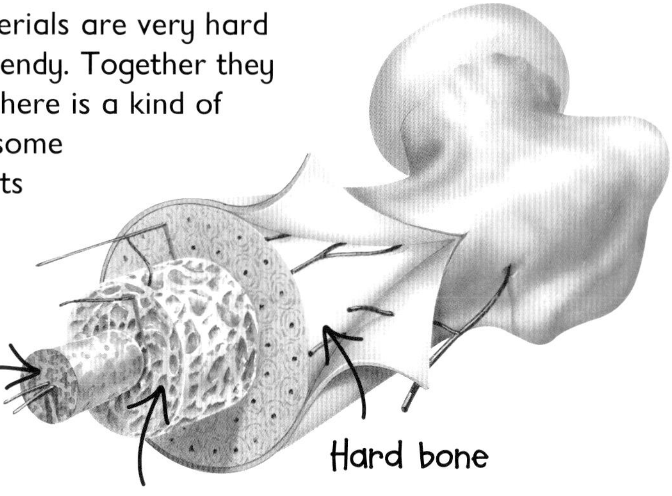

Strong bones!

Your bone is lightweight but super-strong. It is stronger than concrete or steel, which are used for making buildings and bridges! But bones can still break if they are bent too much.

How are bones joined together?

Your bones are connected by joints. They let your back, arms, legs, fingers and toes move. You have about 100 joints. The largest joints are in your hips and knees. The smallest joints are inside your ear.

How do muscles work?

Muscles are made from fibres that look like bits of string. The fibres get shorter to make the muscle pull. Many muscles make your bones move. They help you to run, jump, hold and lift things. Some muscles move your eyes, your heart and other body parts.

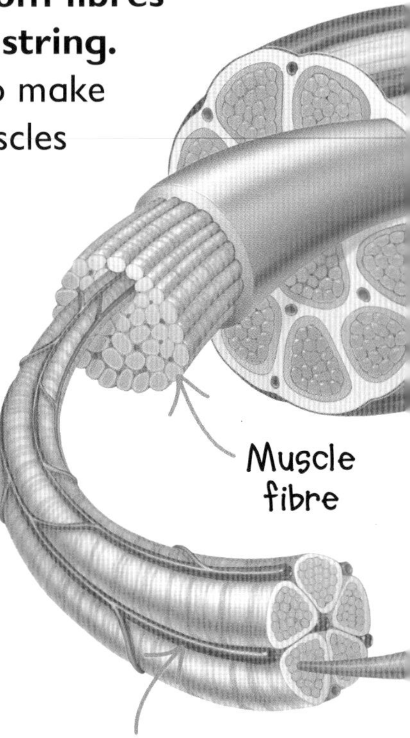

What is my biggest muscle?

The biggest muscles in your body are the ones that you sit on – your bottom! You use them when you walk and run. The strongest muscle in your body is in your jaw. It scrunches your teeth together.

Cheeky muscles!

Your face is full of muscles. You use them to smile, to wrinkle your nose, or to cry. You use more muscles to frown than to smile!

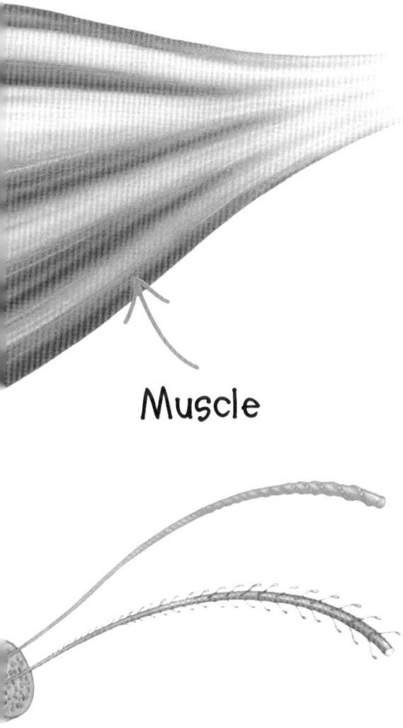

Muscle

What makes my muscles move?

Your brain does. It sends messages along nerves to your muscles. Lots of muscles are needed, even for small movements, like writing with a pen. Your brain controls other muscles without you thinking about it. For example, the muscles in your heart keep working even when you are asleep.

Feel

Bend and unbend your arm. Can you feel your arm muscles getting shorter and longer?

Why do I need to breathe?

You breathe to take air into your body. There is a gas in the air called oxygen that your body needs to work. The air goes up your nose or into your mouth. Then it goes down a tube called the windpipe and into your lungs.

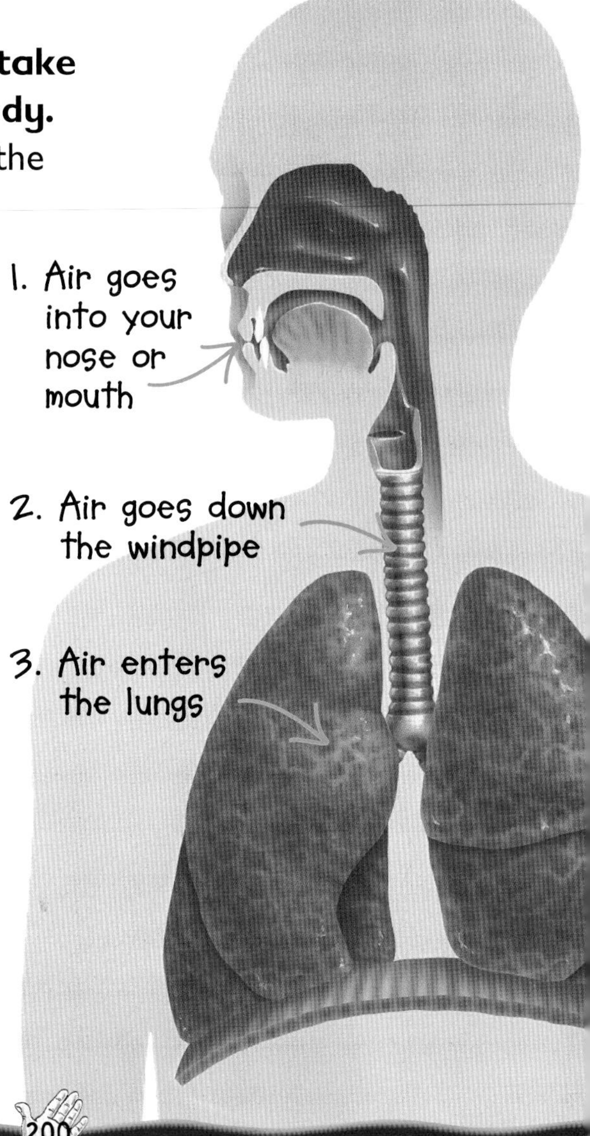
1. Air goes into your nose or mouth
2. Air goes down the windpipe
3. Air enters the lungs

Count

How many times do you breathe in and out in one minute?

Is my voice kept in a box?

Not quite! The real name for your voicebox is the larynx. It's at the top of the windpipe, and makes a bulge at the front of your neck. Air passing through the voicebox makes it shake, or vibrate. This is the sound of your voice. Your voice can make lots of sounds, and helps you to sing!

Singing

What makes air go into my lungs?

There is a big muscle under your lungs that moves down. More muscles make your ribs move out. This makes your lungs bigger. Air rushes into your lungs to fill the space. When your muscles relax, the air is pushed out again.

Fill 'em up!

When you are resting, you take in enough air to fill a can of fizzy drink in every breath. When you are running, you breathe in ten times as much air.

What food is good for me?

Lots of food is good for you! Different foods give your body the goodness it needs. Fruit and vegetables are very good for you. Bread and pasta give you energy. Small amounts of fat, such as cheese, keep your nerves healthy. Chicken and fish keep your muscles strong.

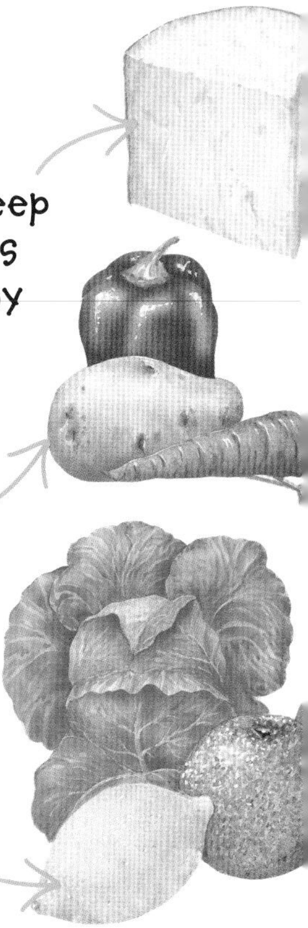

Fats keep nerves healthy

Vegetables help digestion

Fruit is full of goodness

Eating elephants!

You eat about one kilogram of food every day. During your life, you will eat about 30 tonnes of food. That's the same weight as six elephants!

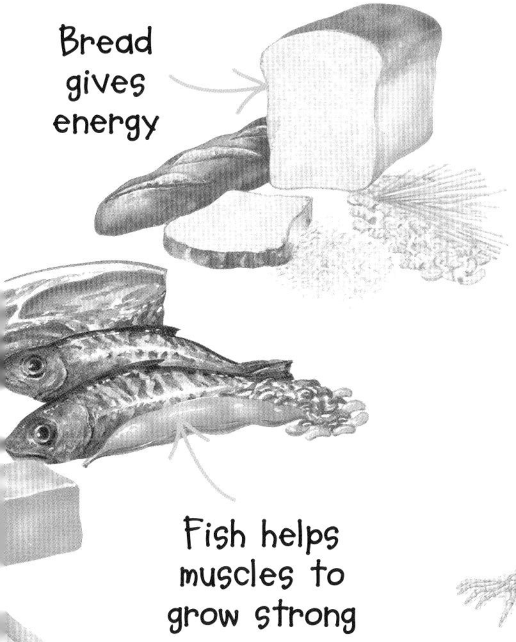
Bread gives energy
Fish helps muscles to grow strong

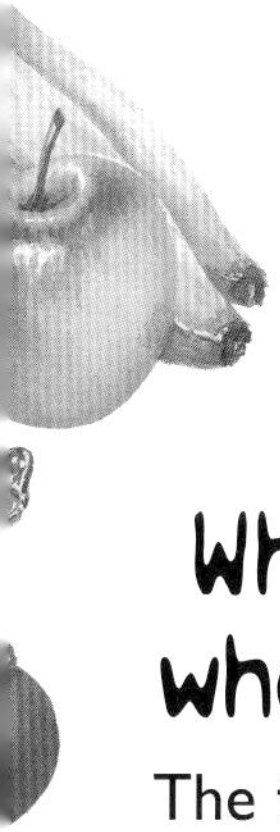

Why do I need to eat food?

Food keeps your body working. It is like fuel for your body. It keeps your body going through the day and night, and works your muscles. Food also contains things your body needs to grow, repair itself and fight illness.

Your whole body needs food

What happens when I swallow?

The first thing you do with food is chew it. Then you swallow lumps of the chewed food. When you swallow, the food goes down a tube called the gullet. Muscles in the gullet push the food down into your stomach.

Draw

Look at some of the pictures on these pages. Can you draw a healthy meal that you would like to eat?

What are teeth made of?

Teeth are covered in a material called enamel. This is harder than most kinds of rock! Teeth are fixed into your jaw bones by roots. Sharp front teeth (incisors) bite food into small pieces. Tall, pointy teeth (canines) tear and pull food. Flat back teeth (molars) chew food to a mush.

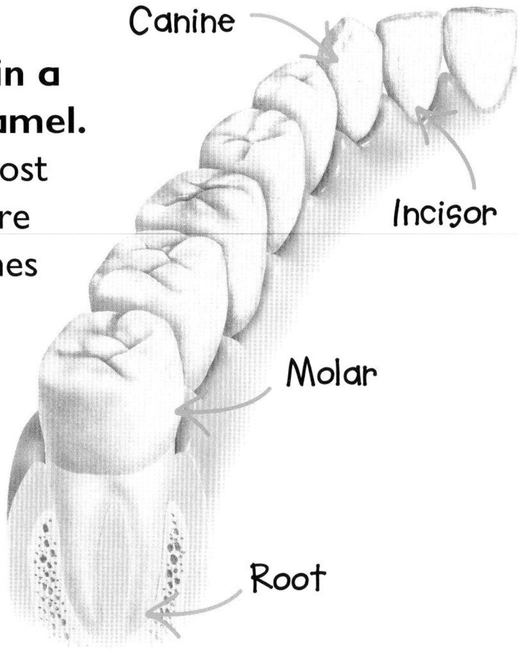

How many sets of teeth do I have?

You have two sets. A baby is born without teeth. The first set of teeth appears when a child is six months old. This set has 20 teeth. These teeth fall out at about seven years old. They are replaced by 32 adult teeth.

Discover

Do you still have your first set of teeth, or have your baby teeth begun to fall out?

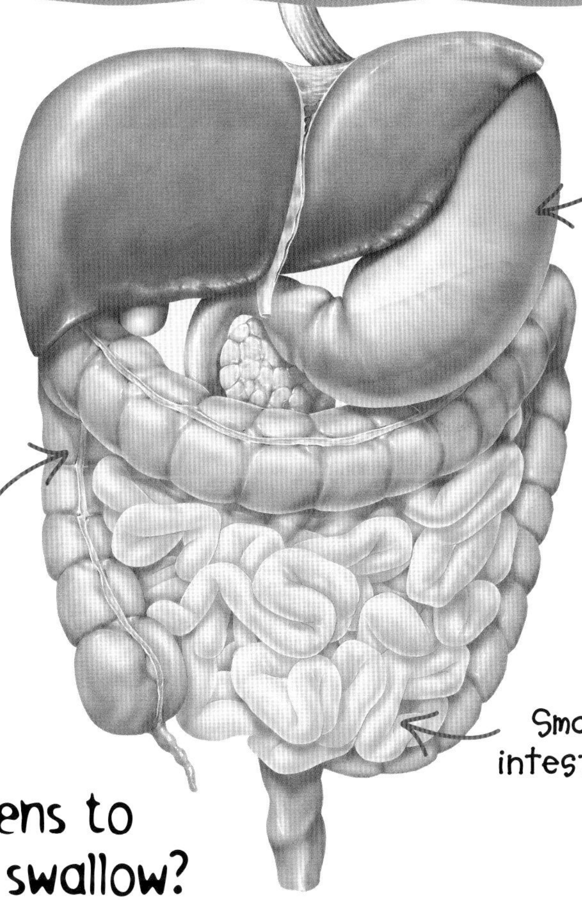

What happens to the food I swallow?

The food you swallow goes into your stomach. Here, special juices and strong muscles break the food up into a thick mush. The mushy food then goes into a long tube called the intestines. Here, all the goodness from the food is taken out, to be used by our body.

All gone!

When you go to the toilet, you get rid of waste. This is leftover food. It is stored in your large intestine until you go to the toilet.

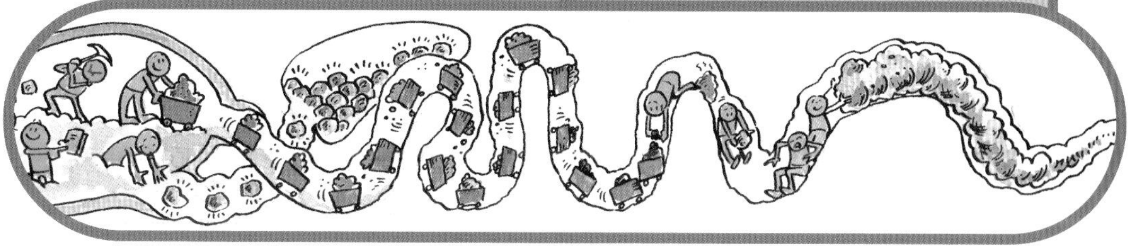

Why does my heart beat?

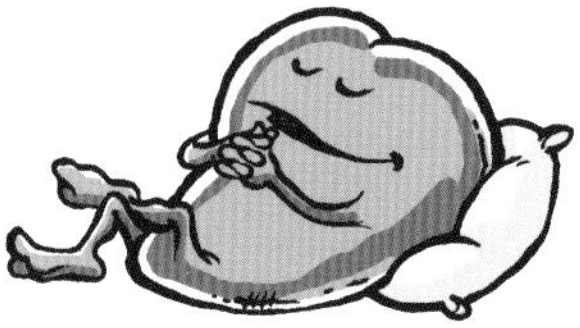

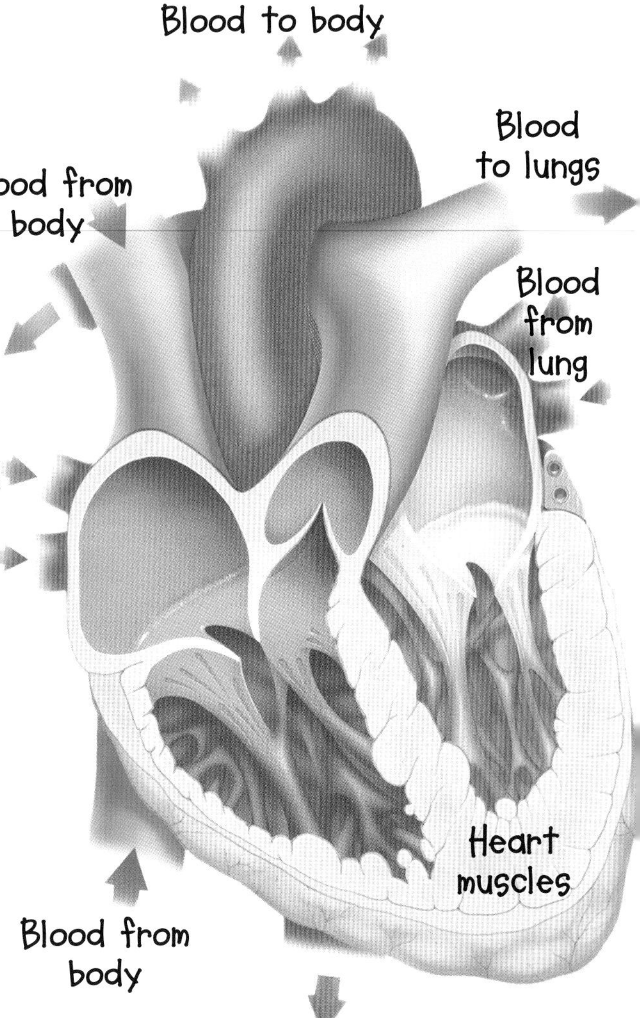

To pump blood and oxygen around your body. Your heart is about the size of your fist and is made of muscle. When it beats, your heart squeezes blood into tubes. These carry blood and oxygen around your body. The blood then comes back to the heart from the lungs, with more oxygen.

Beat of life!

Your heart beats once a second for the whole of your life. That is 86,000 beats a day, and 31 million beats a year. In total, this is 2000 million beats in your life.

What does blood do?

Your whole body needs oxygen to work. Blood carries oxygen to every part of your body in its red cells. Blood also contains white cells that fight germs. Tubes called arteries and veins carry blood around your body.

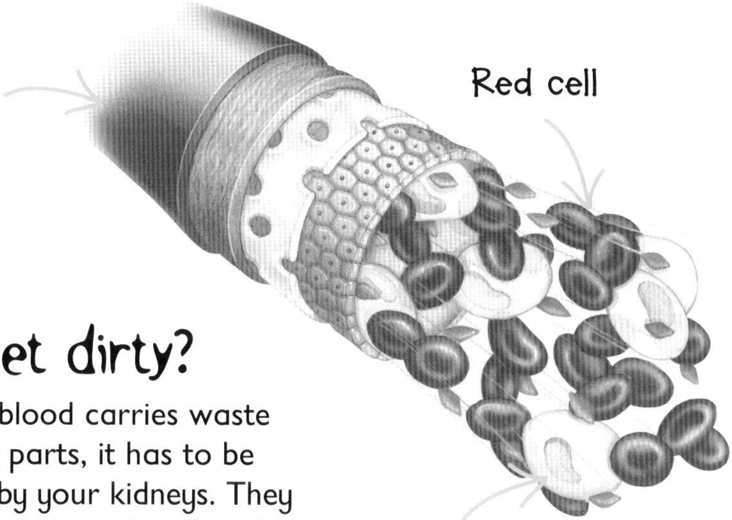

Does blood get dirty?

Yes, it does. Because blood carries waste away from your body parts, it has to be cleaned. This is done by your kidneys. They take the waste out of the blood and make a liquid called urine. This liquid leaves your body when you go to the toilet.

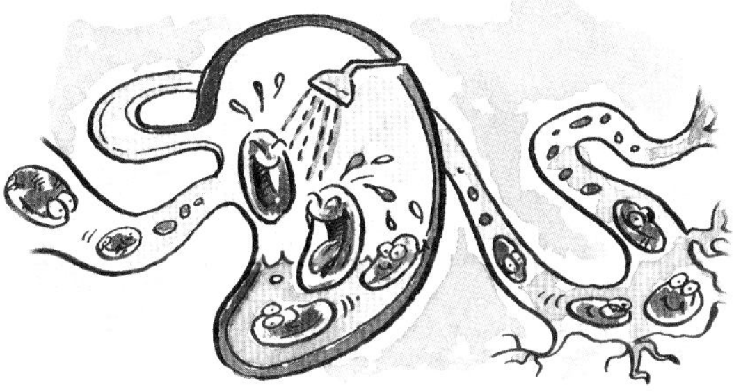

Feel

Touch your neck under your chin. Can you feel the blood flowing through an artery to your brain?

Are my eyes like a camera?

Your eyes work like a tiny camera. They collect light that bounces off the things you are looking at. This makes tiny pictures at the back of the eyes. Here, millions of sensors pick up the light. They send a picture to your brain along a nerve.

In a spin!

Inside your ear are loops full of liquid. They can tell when you move your head. This helps you to balance. If you spin around, the fluid keeps moving. This makes you feel dizzy!

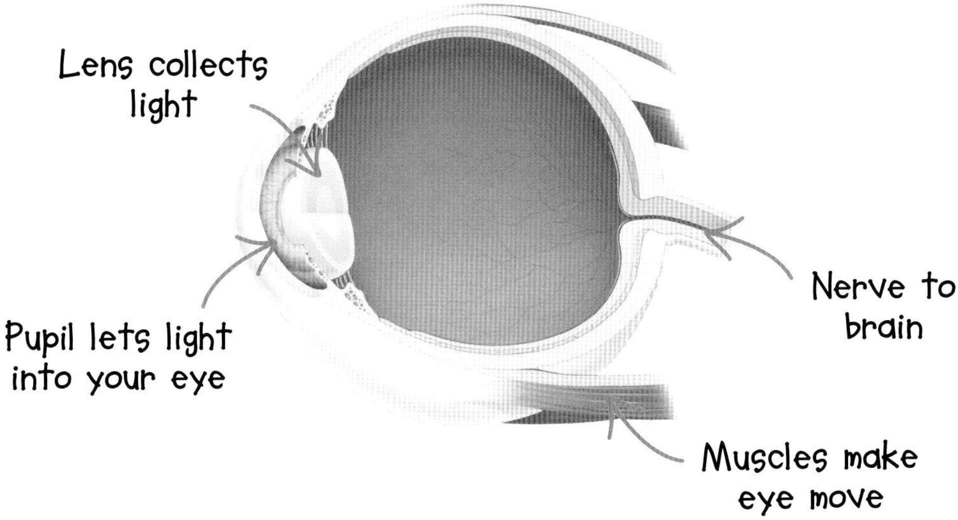
Lens collects light
Pupil lets light into your eye
Nerve to brain
Muscles make eye move

What is inside my ears?

The flap on your head is only part of your ear. The hole in your ear goes to a tiny piece of tight skin, called an eardrum. Sounds enter your ear and make the eardrum move in and out. Tiny bones pass these movements to the cochlea, which is shaped like a snail. This is filled with liquid.

Look

Look in the mirror at your eye. Can you see the dark pupil where light goes in?

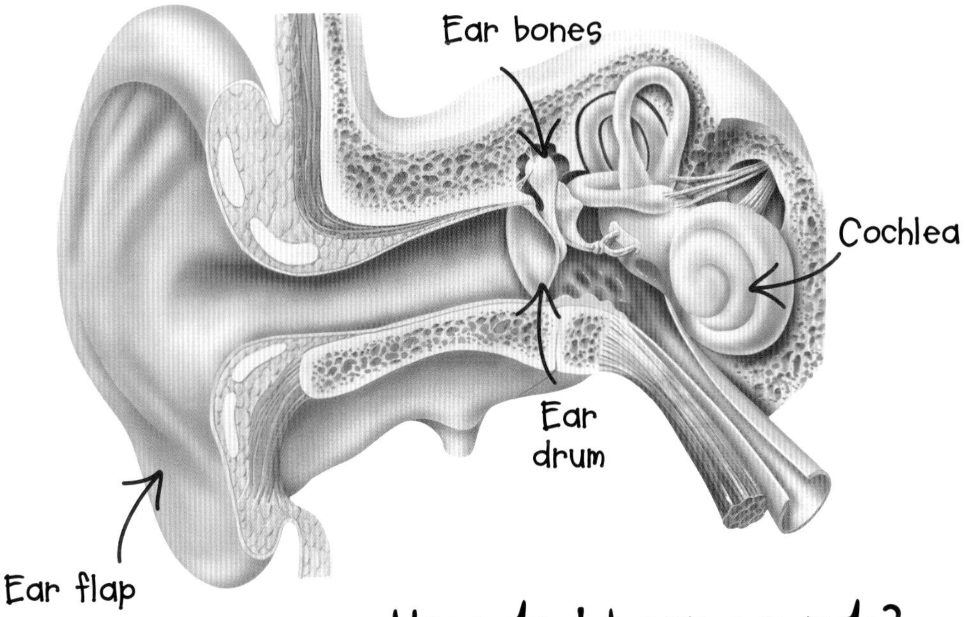

How do I hear sounds?

The cochlea in your ear contains thousands of tiny hairs. It is also is full of liquid. Sounds make the liquid move. This makes the hairs wave about. Tiny sensors pick up the waving, and send messages to your brain so you hear the sound.

Why can't I see smells?

Because they're invisible! Smells are tiny particles that float in the air. Inside the top of your nose are sticky smell sensors. When you sniff something, the sensors collect the smell particles. They send messages to your brain, which tell you what you can smell.

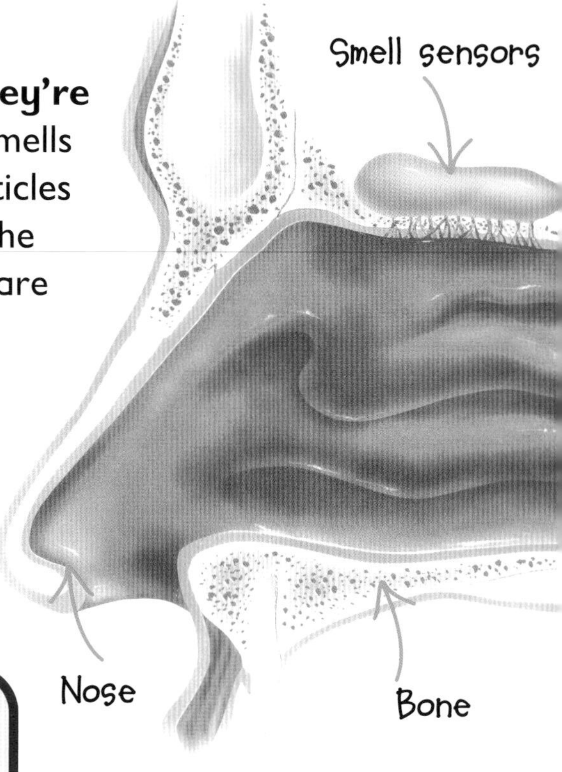

A blocked dose!

Smell and taste work together when you eat. Your sense of smell helps you to taste flavours in food. When you have a cold, your smell sensors get blocked, so you cannot taste, either.

How do I taste things?

With your tongue. Your tongue is covered with tiny taste sensors. These are called taste buds. Buds on different parts of your tongue can sense different tastes, or flavours. Your tongue also moves food around your mouth and helps you to speak.

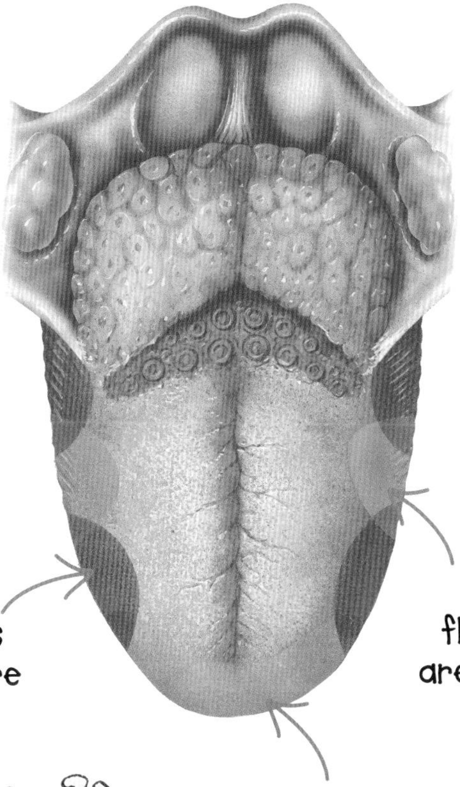
Salty flavours are tasted here
Sour flavours are tasted here
Sweet flavours are tasted here

How many smells can I sense?

Your nose can sense about 3000 different smells. You don't just have a sense of smell so you can smell nice things, such as flowers and perfumes! Your sense of smell warns you if food is rotten before you eat it.

Think

Look at the picture of the tongue. Can you think of three different things that taste sour, sweet and salty?

Is my brain really big?

Your brain is about the same size as your two fists put together. It is the place where you think, remember, feel happy or sad – and dream. Your brain also takes information from your senses and controls your body. The main part is called the cerebrum.

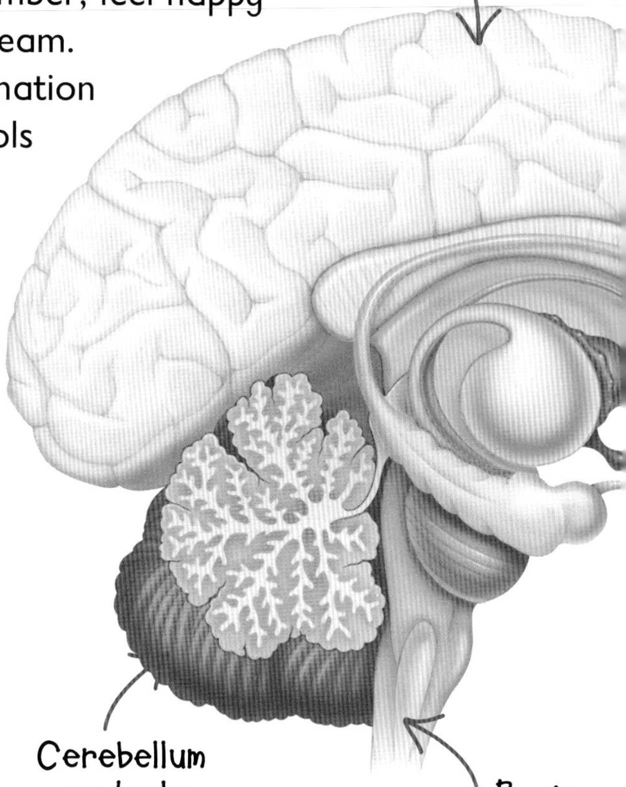

Right and left!

The main part of your brain is divided into two halves. The right half helps you to play music and to draw. The left half is good at thinking.

Can my brain really wave?

Well, sort of! Your brain works using electricity. It has about 10,000 million tiny nerve cells. Tiny bursts of electricity are always jumping around between the cells. Doctors can see your brain working by looking at the electricity with a special machine called an EEG. It shows the electricity as waves on a screen.

Remember

Your brain controls the five senses – smelling, tasting, touching, hearing – can you remember your fifth sense?

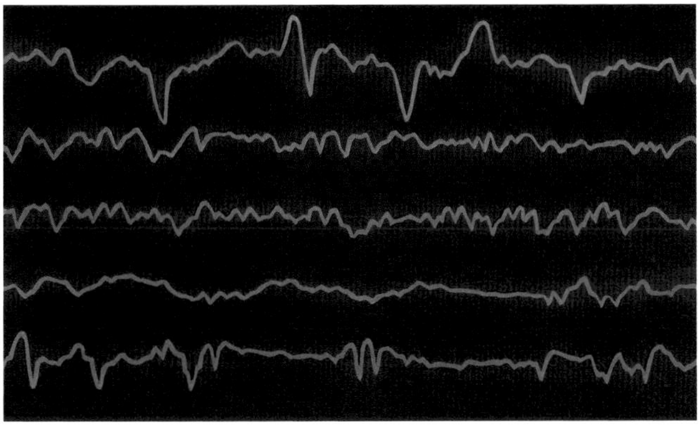

Brain waves from an EEG machine

How does my brain help me to play?

Different parts of your brain do different jobs. One part senses touch. Another part deals with thinking. Speaking is controlled by a different part. The cerebellum controls all your muscles. When you play and run, the cerebellum sends messages to your muscles to make them move.

How can I stay healthy?

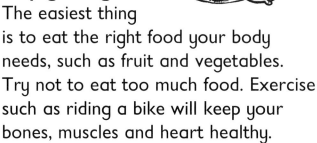

There are things you can do to stop getting ill. The easiest thing is to eat the right food your body needs, such as fruit and vegetables. Try not to eat too much food. Exercise such as riding a bike will keep your bones, muscles and heart healthy.

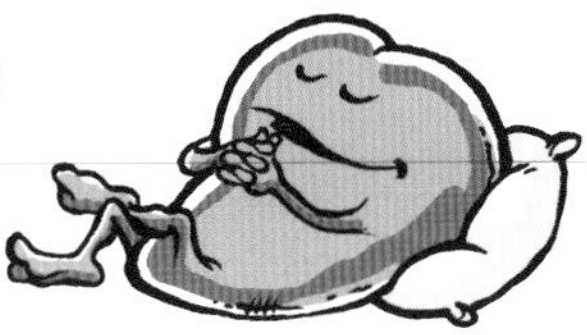

Getting old!

Your body changes as you get old. You get shorter, your skin wrinkles and your hair might go grey. But you could live to be 100!

What can make me sick?

Lots of things can make you sick. Illnesses such as tummy upsets are caused by germs that get into your body. You can help to stop catching germs by washing your hands before eating and after going to the toilet.

Washing your hands kills germs

Why do I have injections?

All children have injections at the doctors every few years. The injections help to stop you catching serious diseases in the future. Doctors also help you to get well again when you are ill. The doctor might give you medicine to make you feel better.

Riding a bike can keep you healthy

Read

Read this page again. What should you do before meal times and after going to the toilet?

Quiz time

Do you remember what you have read about your body? These questions will test your memory. The pictures will help you. If you get stuck, read the pages again.

3. How much hair do I have?

page 194

4. How are bones joined together?

page 197

page 191

1. Am I always learning?

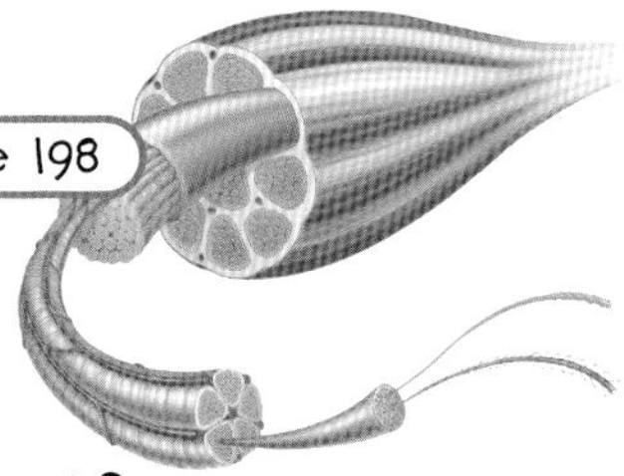

page 198

5. How do muscles work?

2. Why do I sweat when I'm warm?

page 193

page 201

6. What makes air go into my lungs?

7. Why do I need to eat food?

page 203

11. How do I taste things?

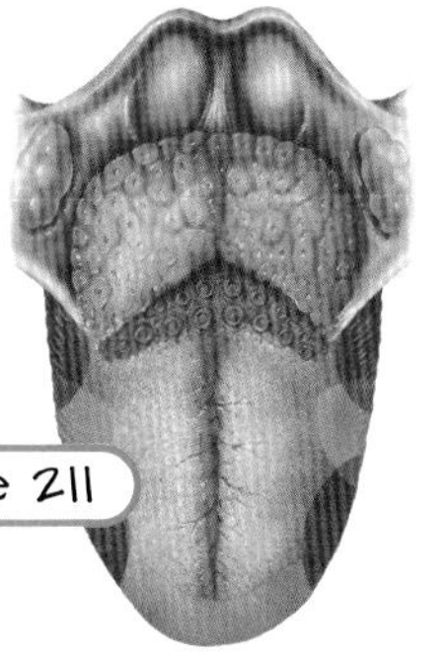

page 211

8. How many sets of teeth do I have?

page 204

12. How does my brain help me to play?

page 213

9. What does blood do?

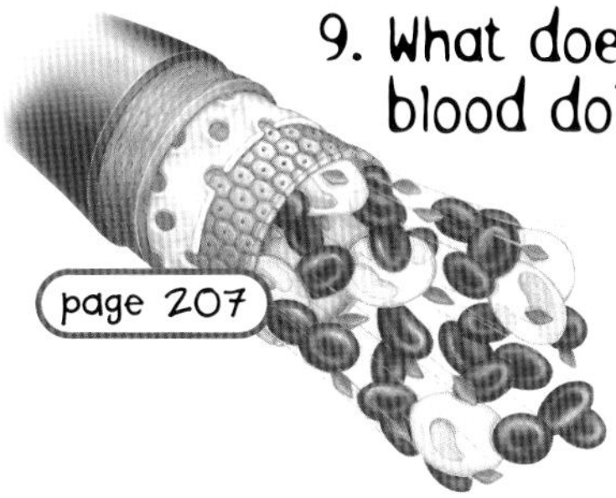

page 207

13. What can make me sick?

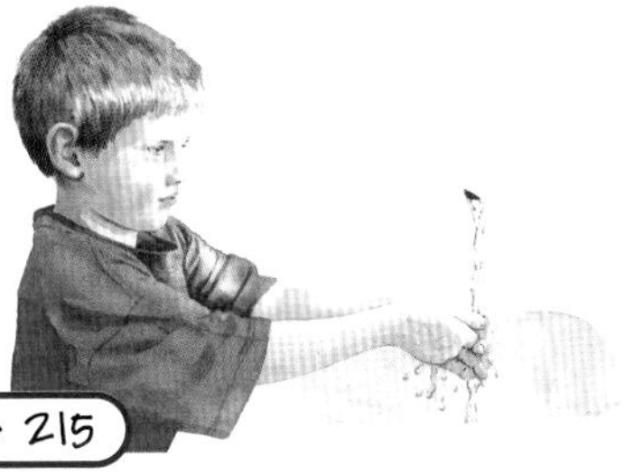

page 215

page 209

10. How do I hear sounds?

Answers

1. Yes, you are
2. To help you cool down again
3. You have five million hairs on your body
4. They are connected by joints
5. The fibres inside get shorter and pull
6. Muscles
7. To keep your body working
8. Two sets
9. Carries oxygen around your body
10. With the parts that are inside your ear
11. With your tongue
12. It tells your muscles to move
13. Germs

Questions about...

Ancient Egypt

Why were the pyramids built?

Pyramids were tombs (burial places) for Egyptian rulers, called pharaohs. The three great pyramids of Khufu, Khafre and Menkaure were built in Giza, Egypt, 4500 years ago.

The Great Pyramid of Khufu is the biggest. It took 20 years and 4000 workers to build it!

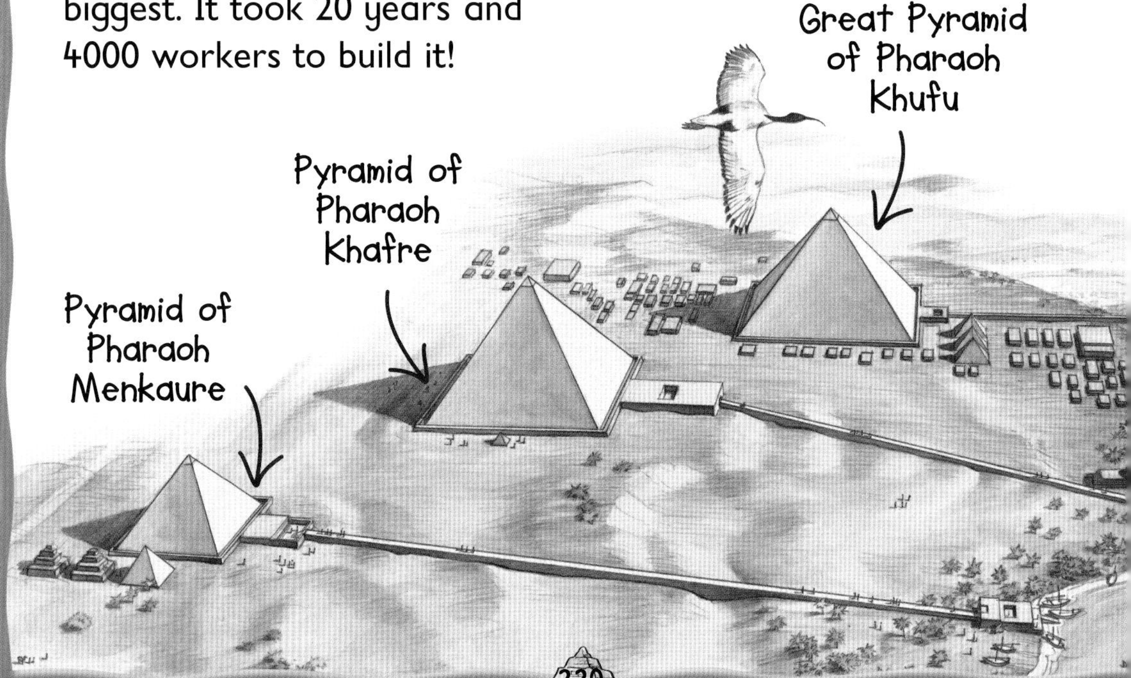

What guards the Great Pyramid?

The pyramids were full of treasures. A stone statue was built to guard the Great Pyramid at Giza. It was carved in the shape of a sphinx. A sphinx has the body of a lion and the head of a man. The sphinx at the Great Pyramid has the face of Pharaoh Khafre.

Tomb robbers!

'The Book of Buried Pearls' told robbers all about the treasures inside the tombs. It also showed them how to get past spirits that guarded the dead.

What was inside the Great Pyramid?

The Great Pyramid had two huge burial chambers. They were built for the pharaoh and his queen. A corridor called the Grand Gallery led to the pharaoh's chamber. The corridor's ceiling was 8 metres tall!

Map

Draw a plan of a pyramid. Include secret tunnels and hidden rooms to stop the robbers.

Who was the top god?

Ancient Egyptians worshipped more than 1000 gods. The most important was Ra, the Sun god. Every evening, Ra was swallowed by Nut, the sky goddess. At night, Ra travelled through the land of the dead. He was born again each morning. Later, Ra became Amun Ra, king of the gods.

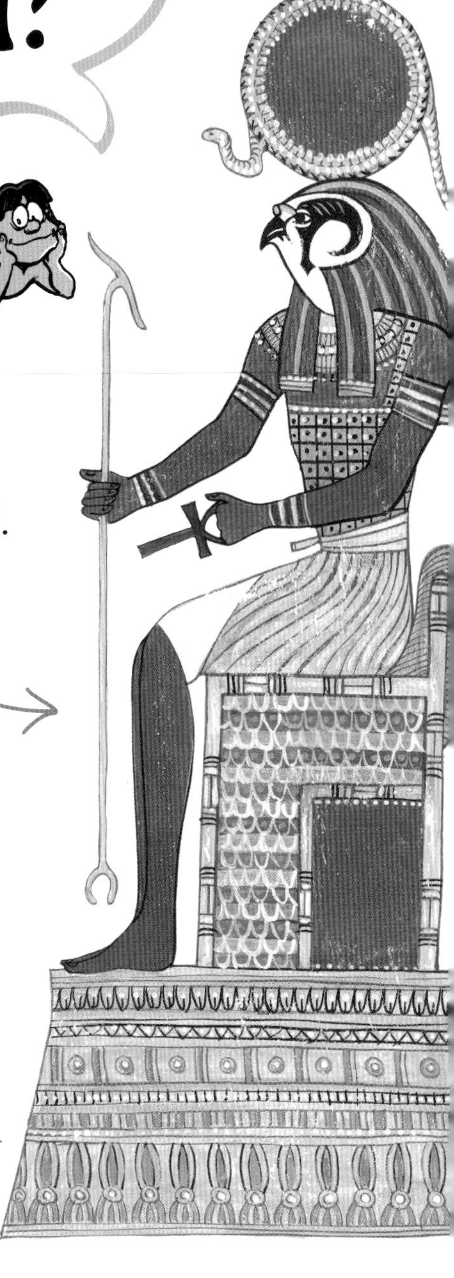

Ra

Dead body god!

Anubis was the god in charge of dead bodies. He looked like a jackal, a kind of dog. People who wrapped bodies for burial often wore Anubis masks!

Why were cats important?

Cats were sacred (holy) animals in ancient Egypt. The goddess for cats, musicians and dancers was called Bastet. When a pet cat died it was wrapped up carefully and placed in a special cat-shaped coffin. Then the cat was buried in a cat cemetery!

Who took care of the temples?

Fabulous temples were built for the gods. Many temples were built for Amun Ra, king of the gods. Priests looked after the temples, their riches and the lands around them. These massive statues of Pharaoh Ramses II guard the temple at Abu Simbel.

Draw

Draw a picture of Ra travelling through the night in the land of the dead. He travelled in a boat.

Temple at Abu Simbel

How were the pyramids built?

Thousands of workers had to cut blocks of stone to the right shape using chisels and saws. Wooden sledges were then used to drag the stones to the pyramid. Each stone weighed more than two and a half big elephants!

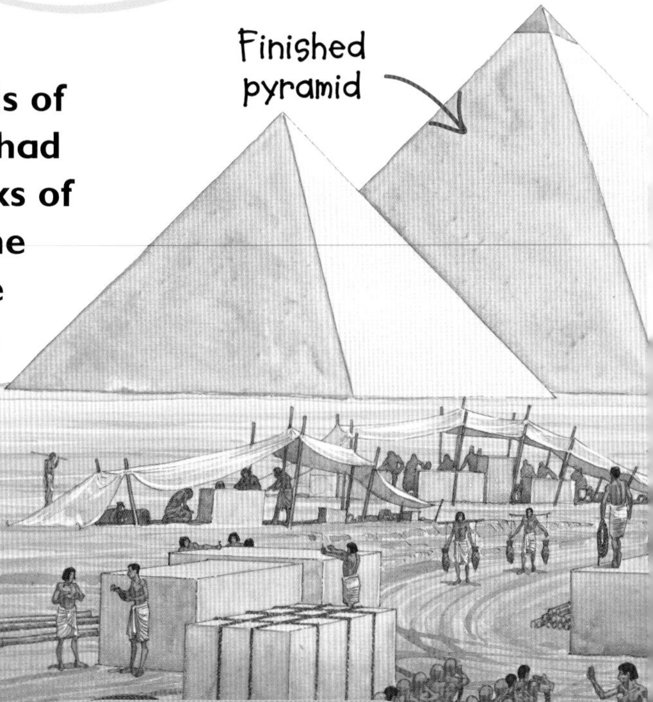

Busy busy!

One ancient Egyptian was a very busy man! Imhotep was a doctor, a priest and a poet. He also designed and built a pyramid!

Were the pyramids painted white?

The finished pyramids had a bright white coating. This wasn't paint, but limestone, which protected the stones beneath. Inner walls were built from clay bricks that were lined with pink granite. White stone covered the floors.

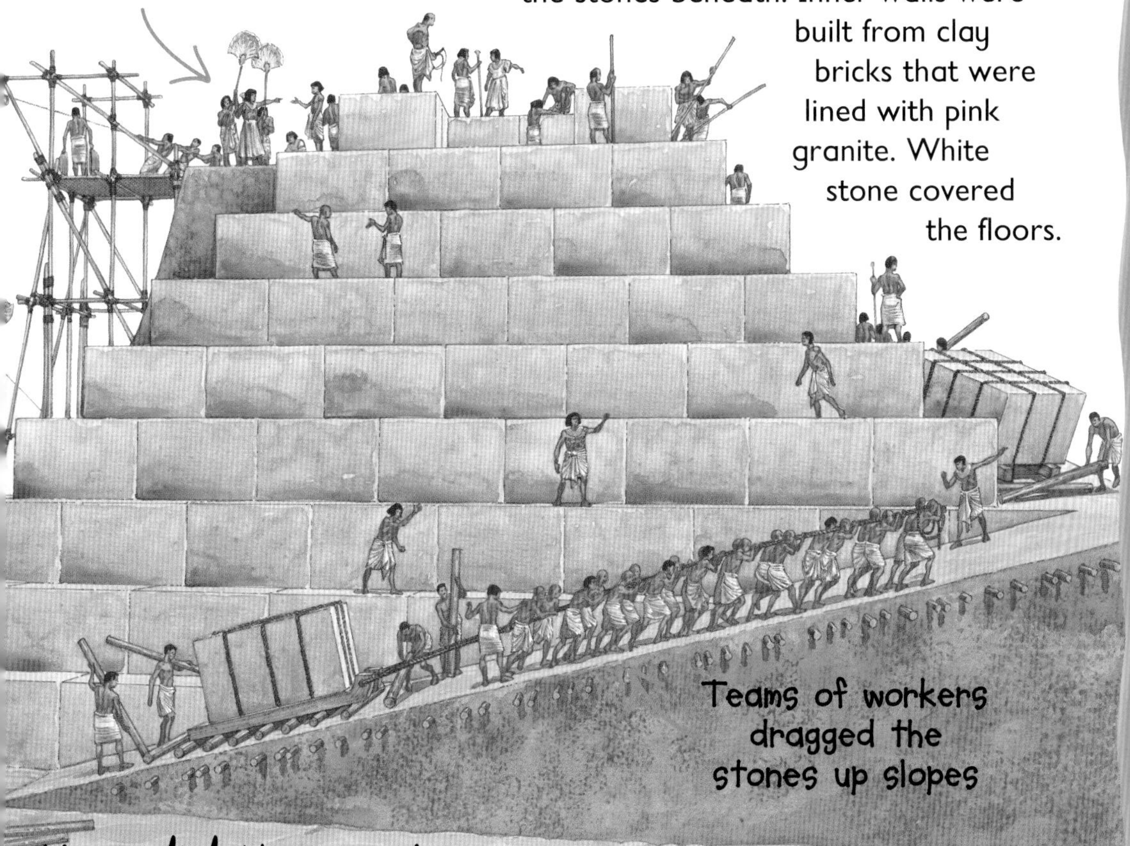
The pharaoh checked the work
Teams of workers dragged the stones up slopes

How did the workers build so high?

The stones were pulled up a ramp to get to each level of the pyramid. The ramp was a steep slope made from baked earth bricks. The pyramid got higher and higher. So the ramp had to be made longer and longer! Sledges were pulled up the ramp on rollers.

Think

Look at the walls and ceilings of your house. What do you think they were built with?

How do you make a mummy?

Ancient Egyptians mummified their dead. First, the inside parts such as the brain, but not the heart, were removed. Then the body was salted and dried. Cloth was stuffed inside the body to help it keep its shape. Then the body was oiled and wrapped in lots of bandages.

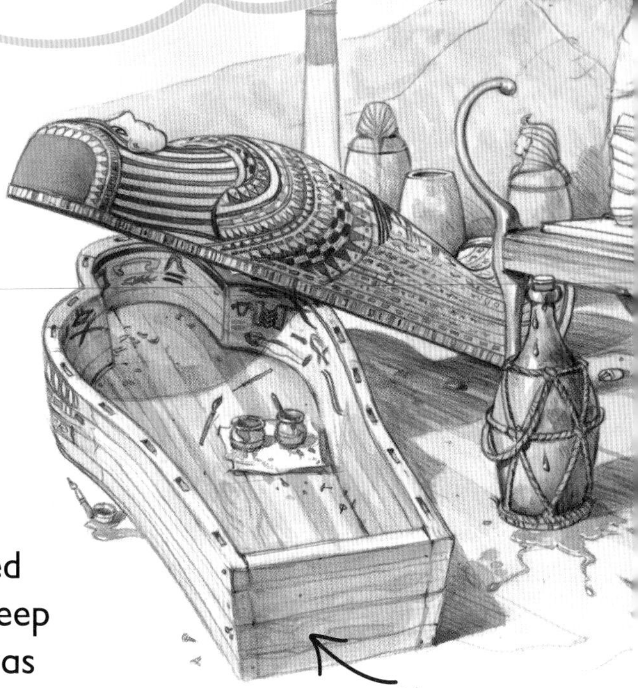

Mummy case

All wrapped up!

The mummy was wrapped in tight bandages. This helped to stop the body from rotting away.

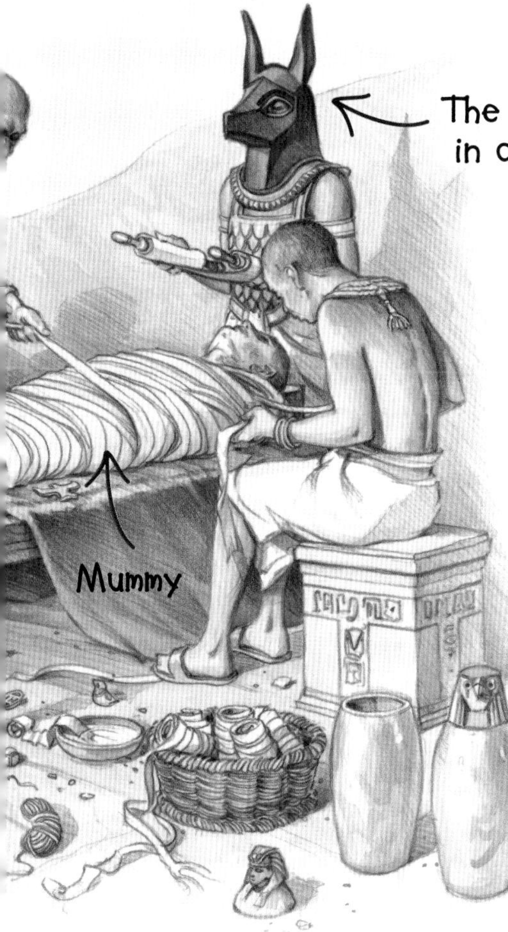

Make

Cut out a mummy mask from card and paint it with a face. It could be the face of an animal.

What did the priest do?

The priest sent the dead person's spirit into the next world. He touched parts of the body with special instruments. This was so that the body could move around in the world of the dead. The mouth could speak and eat in its new life after being touched!

What were mummies kept in?

The mummy was placed in a case. Some cases were just wooden boxes. Others were beautifully decorated. An important person, such as a pharaoh, was placed in a stone coffin called a sarcophagus (sarc-off-a-gus).

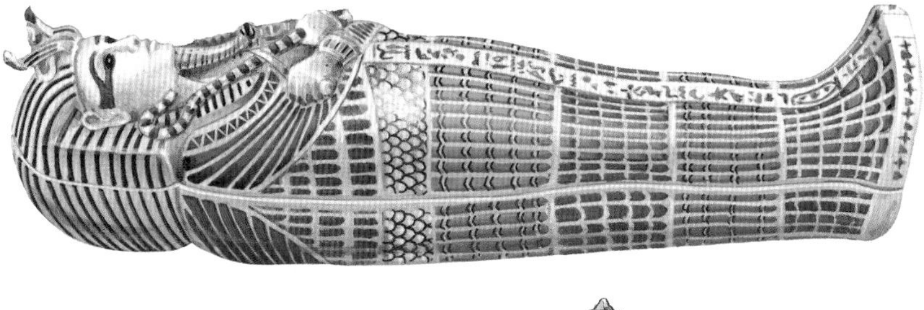

Did food grow in the desert?

Most of Egypt was in the hot desert. However, every year in July, the great river Nile flooded the dry fields. The water brought rich, black soil with it. This soil spread in wide strips on each side of the river. Farmers sowed their seed in this good soil.

How did the Egyptians farm?

Farmers used oxen and wooden ploughs to dig the soil. They weeded and dug channels with hoes. Then they planted seed, mostly by hand. Farmers also kept goats, sheep, ducks and geese. They kept bees to make honey.

Get lost!

Young boys were paid to be scarecrows! They frightened birds with their slingshots and loud shouts!

Farmers' crops

What did farmers grow?

Farmers grew barley for beer and grapes for wine. Dates, figs, melons, cucumbers, onions, leeks and lettuces grew well in the rich soil. Wheat was also grown to make bread.

Draw

Draw a basket full of crops grown by Egyptian farmers. You can see an Egyptian basket in this picture.

Who had the best jobs?

Doctors, high priests or priestesses and government officers had the best jobs.

So did viziers. A vizier helped the pharaoh to rule the land. Next came the traders and craftsmen, such as carpenters and jewellers. Labourers and farmhands had the poorest jobs.

Who was head of the family?

In ancient Egypt the man was the head of the family. The eldest son was given all the land, property and riches when his father died. Women could also own land and property and get good jobs.

Little monkey!

Pet baboons were sometimes trained to climb fig trees and pick the ripe fruit!

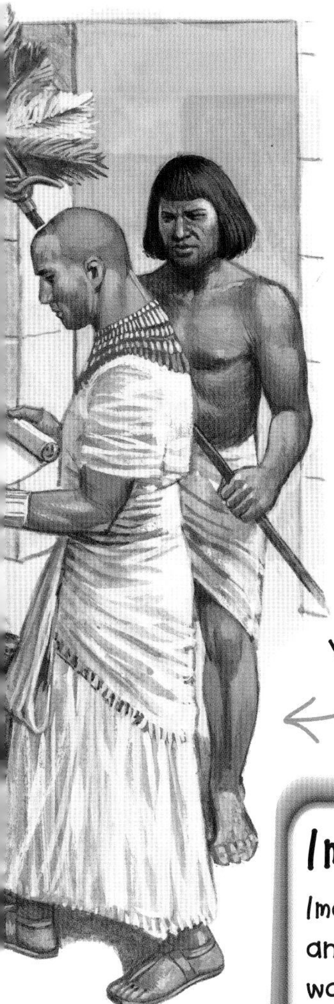

What did children play with?

Children played with toys made from clay and wood. They had carved animals with legs and heads that could move. They also had spinning tops, clay balls, toy horses and dolls. Children played games such as leapfrog and tug-of-war, too.

Imagine

Imagine you are an Egyptian worker. Which job would you choose to do and why?

Who had the biggest houses?

Rich Egyptians lived in large country houses called villas.

Villas often had several storeys. Some had walled gardens with fruit orchards and a fish pond. Poor families often lived in one room. Many lived on crowded streets in the towns and cities.

How did the Egyptians cook?

Some ancient Egyptians cooked their food in a clay oven. Others cooked on an open fire. Clay ovens were made from baked clay bricks. Wood or charcoal were burned as fuel. Cooks used pottery saucepans with two handles.

Mud and straw mixture was poured into a wooden frame
Finished bricks

Were houses built with bricks?

Egyptian houses were built with bricks. Mud from the river Nile was mixed with straw and pebbles. The mixture was shaped into brick shapes and dried in the hot sun. Trunks from palm trees held up the flat roofs. Inside walls were plastered and painted.

Make

Mix clay with dried grass and pebbles. Put the mixture in an ice-cube tray. Let your bricks dry in the sun.

Sticky fingers!

Ancient Egyptians ate with their fingers. Rich people washed their hands between each dish. Their servants brought jugs of washing water for them.

Who shaved their hair off?

Both men and women shaved their hair off. They believed that this kept them clean. Men and women also wore make-up such as black kohl, which lined their eyes.

Fingernail paint and face powder were also used. Red colouring was worn on lips and cheeks.

Egyptian lady

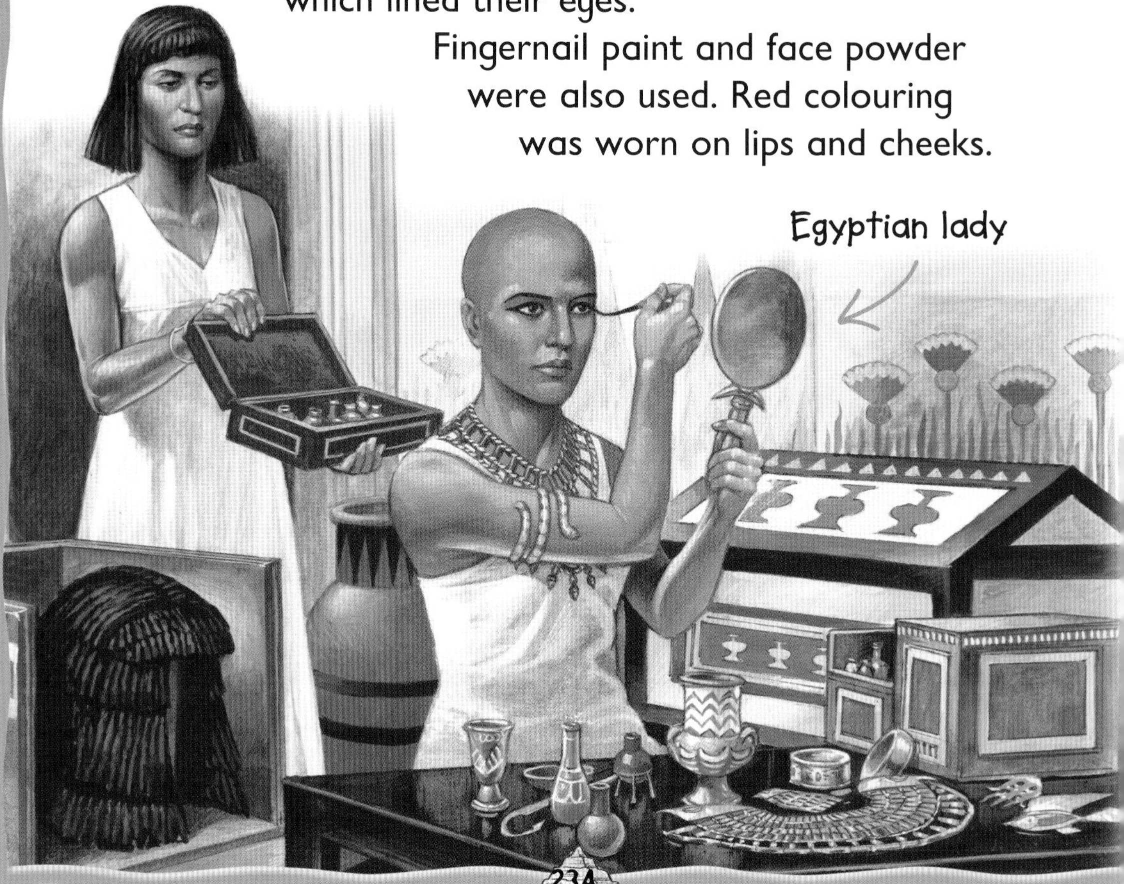

Cosy toes!

Rich people wore shoes made with padded leather. Sandals were made of the grass-like papyrus plant. Poor people went barefoot.

Did Egyptians ever wear wigs?

Rich Egyptians wore wigs made from human hair or sheep's wool. The wigs were kept in boxes held on stands. Egyptians also used hair dye. Girls plaited their hair into pigtails. Some boys wore a pigtail on one side.

Wigs

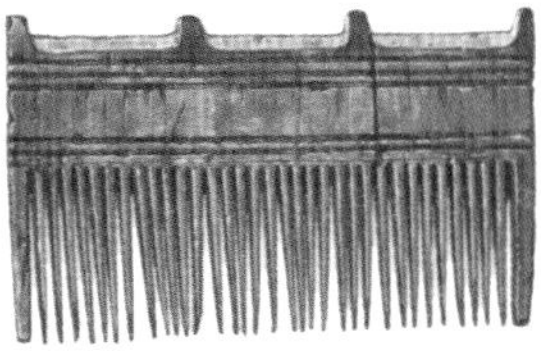

Wooden comb

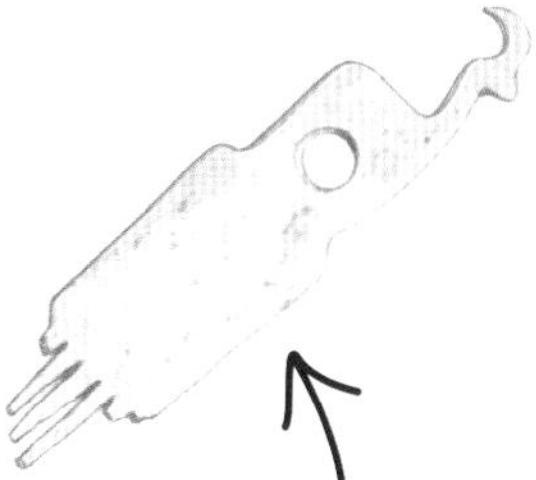

Ivory comb

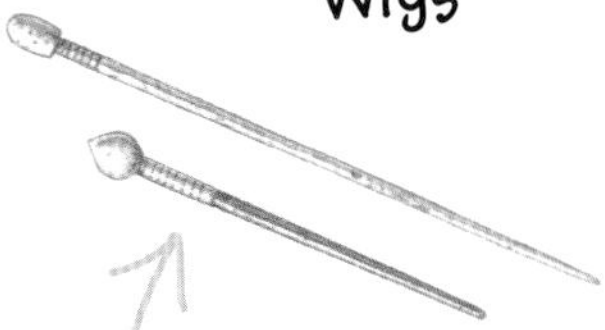

Hair pins

What was the fashion?

Rich women wore the best linen cloth with beads sewn onto it. The cloth was dyed in pale colours. It was made into long dresses and cloaks. Men wore long robes. They also wore cloths wrapped around the waist. These were tied in a knot.

Make

Draw an Egyptian wearing clothes and make-up. Use wool to make a wig. Glue this to the person's head.

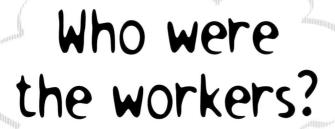

Who were the workers?

Most Egyptians were labourers who worked on farms and building sites. There were also carpenters, potters, jewellers and shoemakers. These people were called craftworkers and they had shops in towns. Some worked for rich people.

Craftworker

Draw

Draw symbols for different jobs. Try a hammer for a carpenter or a ring for a jeweller.

How did Egyptians write?

Egyptians used symbols for writing. These were called hieroglyphs. Some hieroglyphs stood for words. Others stood for sounds. School children had to learn 700 different hieroglyphs!

School children

Did people write on paper?

The Egyptians had no paper. Instead they wrote on papyrus. This was made from reeds that grew next to the river Nile. Papyrus lasts a long time. Sheets of it have survived 3000 years!

Packed lunch!

Workers took bread, onions and a cucumber for their lunch. They washed it down with weak beer.

Quiz time

Do you remember what you have read about Egypt?

These questions will test your memory. The pictures will help you. If you get stuck, read the pages again.

page 221

1. What guards the Great Pyramid?

page 223

2. Why were cats important?

3. What were mummies kept in?

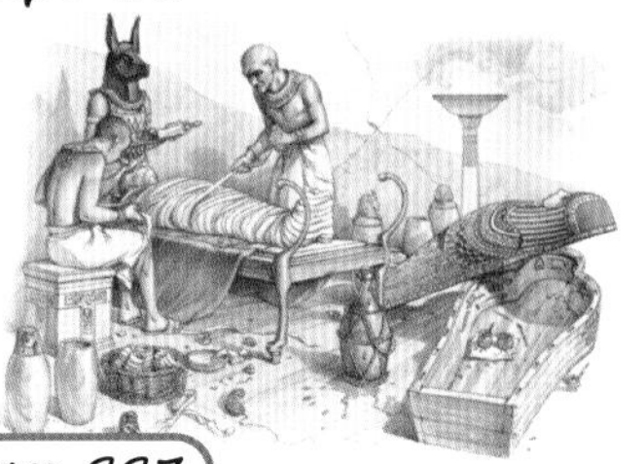

page 227

4. What did the priest do?

page 227

5. What did farmers grow?

page 229

6. Who was head of the family?

page 230

7. What did children play with?

page 231

8. How did the Egyptians cook?

page 232

9. Who shaved their hair off?

page 234

10. What was the fashion?

page 235

11. Did Egyptians ever wear wigs?

page 235

12. Did people write on paper?

page 237

13. How did Egyptians write?

page 237

Answers

1. The sphinx
2. Because they were holy
3. Mummy case or sarcophagus
4. Sent the dead person's spirit into the next world
5. Barley, grapes, dates, figs, melons, cucumbers, onions, leeks and lettuces
6. The man
7. Wooden or clay toys, spinning tops, clay balls, toy horses and dolls
8. With clay ovens or open fires
9. Men and women
10. Dresses, cloaks and long robes
11. Rich Egyptians did
12. No, they wrote on papyrus
13. Egyptians used symbols to write

Questions about...

Ancient Rome

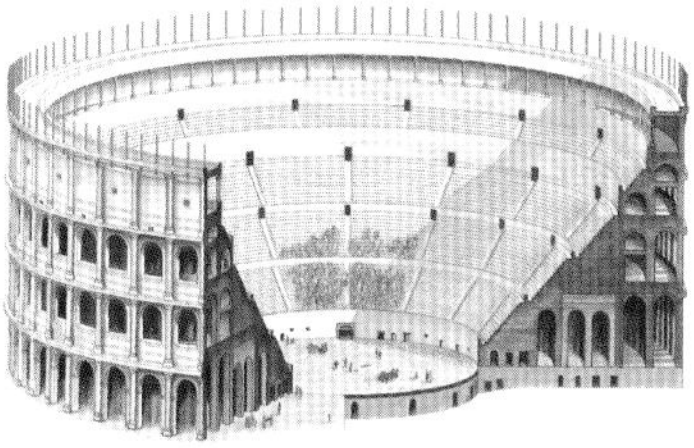

What was the Roman Empire?

Rome is a city in modern-day Italy. About 3000 years ago, it was just a small village. It began to grow into a large, powerful city. About 2000 years ago, Rome ruled many different lands. All of these lands, including Rome itself, were known as the Roman Empire.

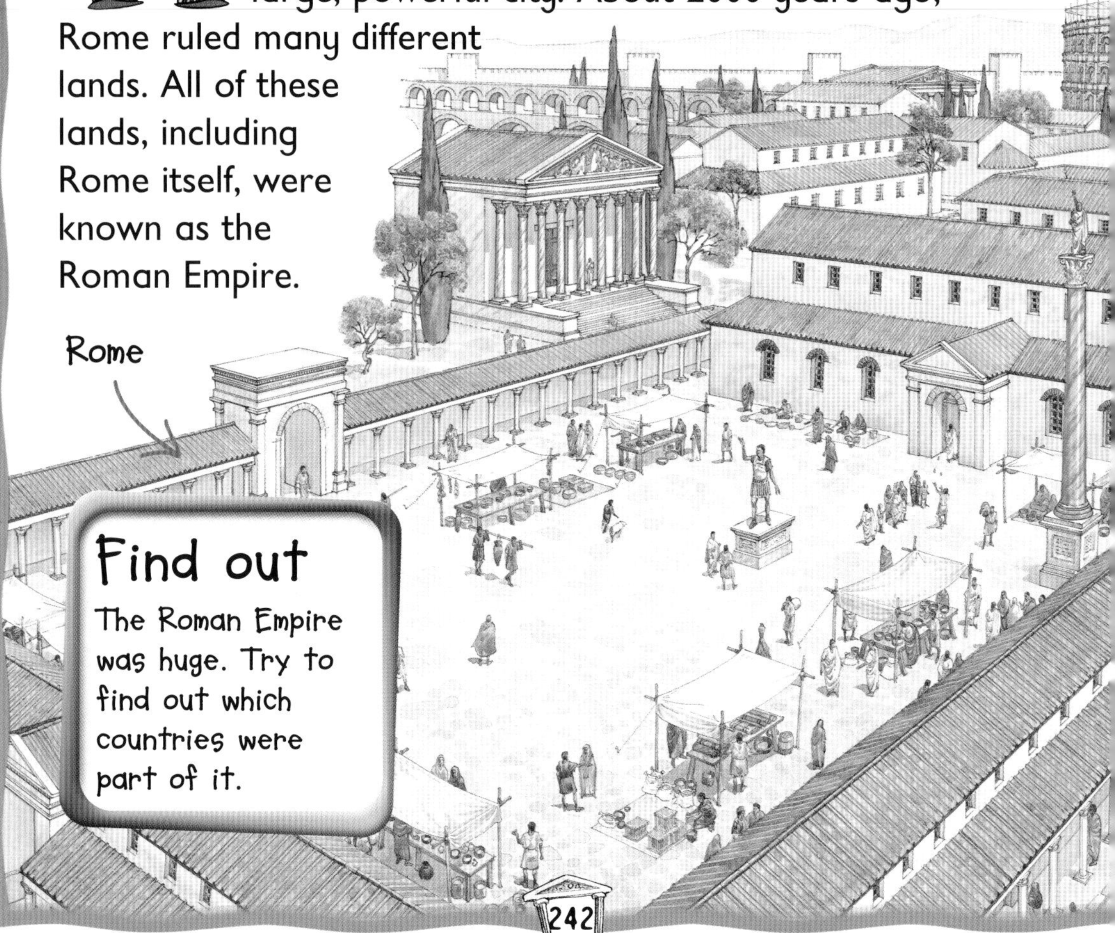

Find out

The Roman Empire was huge. Try to find out which countries were part of it.

Where did people go shopping?

Rome had the world's first shopping centre. It was called Trajan's Market, and was built on five different levels on the slopes of a hill in the centre of Rome. It contained more than 150 shops in a large main hall.

Time to go!

The Romans designed the first public toilets. Users sat next to each other on rows of seats.

Did people live in blocks of flats?

The Romans built the world's first high-rise flats. Most people who lived in Ostia, a busy town close to Rome, lived in blocks of flats known as 'insulae'. Each block had up to 100 small rooms.

What did the Romans eat?

People ate just bread and fruit for breakfast. Lunch might be leftovers from the night before. The main meal was eaten in the evening. It might include meat such as goose or hare, and vegetables and fruit. It took all day to prepare.

Preparing dinner

Plan

Find out what the Romans ate then plan your own Roman menu. Include a starter, main dish and dessert.

Did people have dinner parties?

Yes, they did – and they lay down to eat! People lay on long couches around a table. They often wore crowns of flowers and they took off their sandals before entering the dining room.

Dinner party

Yuk!

Yummy dishes for a Roman banquet might include eel, thrush, dormouse or poached snails. If that upset people's stomachs, pickled cabbage was eaten to make them feel better!

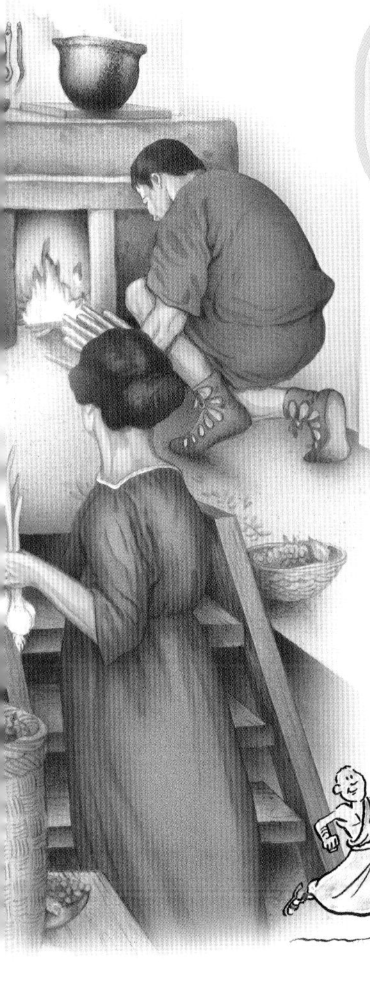

Who ate takeaways?

Ordinary people did. Many went to cheap eating houses for their main meal, or bought ready-cooked snacks from roadside fast-food stalls.

What did children learn at school?

Only boys went to school. At the age of six they began to learn reading, writing, arithmetic, history and sport. They were also taught public speaking.

At school

Inky fingers!

Soot from wood fires was used to make ink. It was mixed with vinegar and sticky gum that oozed from trees. Some Roman writing has survived 2000 years.

Did children use calculators?

Calculators hadn't been invented, so children learned to count with their fingers! A wooden counting frame called an abacus was used to work out sums.

Count

If boys started school aged 6 and left when they were 16, how many years did they study for?

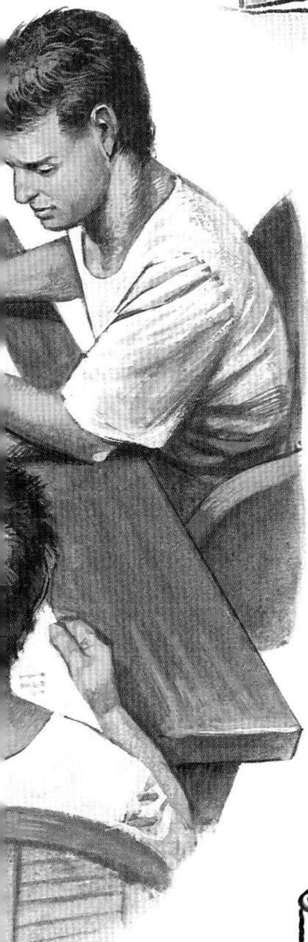

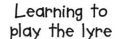

Learning to play the lyre

Why didn't girls go to school?

Roman girls were expected to stay at home and learn how to run a household. This was training for when they were married. Most girls were taught how to play a musical instrument called the lyre.

What was a toga?

Most men wore a long robe called a toga. It looked good, but it was bulky and uncomfortable to wear. Important men wore togas with a purple trim. Most children wore togas, too. Married ladies wore a dress called a 'stola' and a shawl called a 'palla' over the top of it.

Did people wear make-up?

Both men and women wore make-up. The Romans admired pale, smooth skin. Crushed chalk was used as face powder, red ochre (crumbly earth) for blusher and plant juice for lipstick.

'Scare' cut!

Going to the barbers could be very painful. Scissors and razors had not been invented. Barbers used big, sharp shears to trim men's hair and beards!

Find out

What did Julius Caesar wear on his head?

What were Roman hairstyles like?

Hairstyles went in and out of fashion. Women would curl, plait or pin up their hair. Wigs and hair extensions were popular, as were headdresses and hairbands.

Who wore precious jewels?

Men and women wore rings of gold, silver or bronze. Many of these rings were decorated with amber or precious stones. Rich ladies wore necklaces and earrings of gold and pearls, while poorer women made do with beads of glass or ceramics. Cloaks were fastened with fine brooches.

Baby love!

Romans gave a good luck charm called a 'bulla' to their babies to keep them safe from harm.

What was a mosaic?

The Romans liked their homes to look good, too. Beautiful pictures called mosaics decorated floors. Each mosaic was made from thousands of small tiles made from coloured stone or pottery.

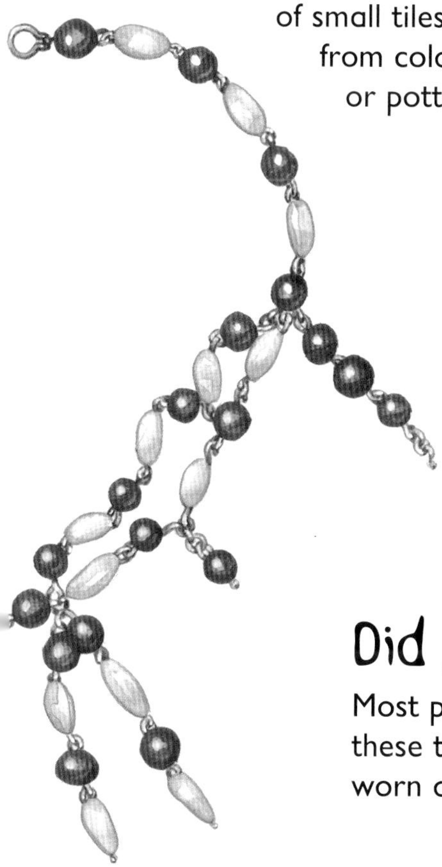

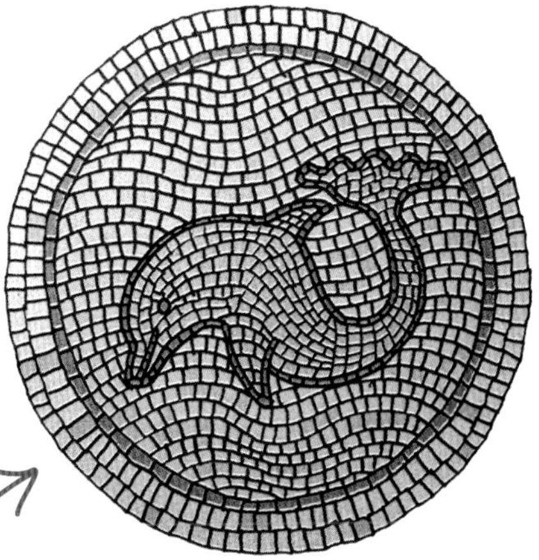

Mosaic

Make

Look at some Roman mosaics in a book then make your own using squares of coloured card.

Did people wear shoes?

Most people wore leather sandals. Soldiers wore these too, but with studded soles so they were not worn out by marching. Boots were worn for riding.

How clean were the Romans?

The Romans were very clean. They often visited the public baths. These huge buildings were also fitness centres and a place to meet friends. Visitors could take part in sports, such as wrestling, have a massage or even get their hair cut.

What a stink!

Although the Romans liked bathing, they only visited the baths once in every nine days.

Did the Romans listen to music?

The Romans liked music and dancing. Ordinary people liked listening to pipes, flutes, cymbals and horns. Rich people preferred the quieter sound of the lyre.

Think

Roman baths were a good place for people to meet their friends. Think about where you go to meet your friends.

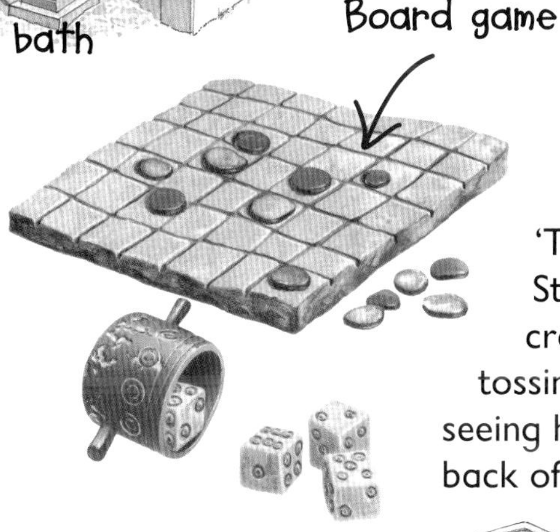

What games did people play?

Popular Roman games were 'Tables', 'Robbers' and 'Three Stones' – a version of noughts-and-crosses. A favourite girls' game was tossing little bones into the air and seeing how many they could catch on the back of the hand.

What was the Colosseum?

The Colosseum was an amazing building. It was a huge oval arena in the centre of Rome, used for fights between men called gladiators, and for pretend sea battles. Up to 50,000 people could sit inside. It was built of stone, concrete and marble and had 80 entrances.

Draw

Romans followed chariot racing like we support football. Draw a poster advertising a chariot race.

Did Romans race to the circus?

The Romans liked a day at the races. Horses pulled chariots around a track, called a 'circus'. The most famous was Circus Maximus. Twelve chariots took part in each race, running seven times round the track.

Chariot racing

Superstars!

Some gladiators became so popular that people wrote graffiti about them on walls.

Was chariot racing dangerous?

Yes it was. Chariots often smashed into each other and overturned. Each driver carried a sharp knife called a 'falx', to cut himself free if this happened. Many horses and drivers were killed.

What was army life like?

Roman soldiers were well paid and well cared for. They were often called upon to defend the Roman Empire from enemies, so the army was very important. Soldiers were trained in battle and often had to march long distances along straight roads.

Brrrr!

Roman soldiers guarding the cold northern frontiers of Britain kept warm by wearing short woollen trousers, like underpants, beneath their tunics!

Testudo

Was a tortoise used in battle?

When soldiers had to defend themselves against enemy attack, they used a 'tortoise'. Their shields made a protective 'shell' around them. It was called a 'testudo', or tortoise. Soldiers carried three main weapons – javelins, swords and daggers.

Did soldiers cook dinner?

Yes they did. Soldiers had to find or make everything they needed to survive. They built camps and forts defended by walls. Soldiers had to be able to cook, build, and be doctors, blacksmiths and engineers – and they all had to fight!

Roman soldiers

Discover

Can you find out which famous British queen the Romans had trouble defeating?

What was a villa?

Villas were large Roman country houses. They were surrounded by orchards, fields, flocks of sheep or herds of cattle. Country villas were owned mainly by the rich. The first villas were small farmhouses, but as Rome became powerful, villas became magnificent mansions.

Pets

Roman villa

Garden

Plan

Plan your own villa. Draw pictures of how it might look.

Did people keep pets?

Roman families liked to keep pets. Statues and paintings show many children playing with their pets. Dogs, cats and doves were all popular. Some families also kept ornamental fish and tame deer.

Love struck!

The Romans invented Valentine's Day, but called it 'Lupercalia'. Boys picked a girl's name from a hat, and she was meant to be their girlfriend for the year!

Where did people go on holiday?

In the summer, Rome became hot, stuffy, smelly and dirty. Rich Romans often had two homes, so they would leave the city and escape to their villa in the countryside.

Why were farms important?

In Roman times, most people lived and worked on farms. Without farms, the people of Rome would starve. Farmers produced food for city people, which was grown on big estates by teams of slaves, and on small peasant farms where single families worked together.

Squeaky clean!

When Romans bathed, they covered their bodies in olive oil and then scraped it off to remove all the dirt and sweat!

Why were olives so special?

Olives grow on trees. The Romans used them as food, or crushed them to make oil. Olive oil was used as medicine, in cooking, for cleansing the skin – and even for burning in lamps.

Imagine

Imagine you are a Roman farm worker, what job would you do and why?

Did grapes grow on trees?

Roman grapes did grow on trees, almost! Vines are climbing plants that produce grapes. The Romans planted them among fruit trees, which supported the vines as they grew.

Who was the top god?

The Romans worshipped many different gods. Jupiter was king of the gods. His wife Juno was worshipped by married women. Mars was the god of war and Venus was the goddess of love. Neptune, god of the sea, sent earthquakes and terrible storms. Messenger of the gods was Mercury.

Jupiter and Juno

Mars and Venus

Find out

School children had their own goddess. Can you find out what she was called? Use a book to help you.

Neptune

Did people go to church?

Temples were beautiful buildings. They were built so that people could worship the gods. At the centre was a shrine. Here, people would leave food and wine as gifts to the gods.

Animal magic!

The Romans believed they could foretell the future by watching animals. For example, bees were sign of riches but a hooting owl meant danger!

Temple

Which god started storms?

Neptune was god of the sea. The Romans believed he could start and stop storms. He was also the god of earthquakes. Sea travel was dangerous in Roman times, so sailors prayed to Neptune to keep them safe on their journeys.

Mercury

Why were roads always straight?

The Romans built thousands of kilometres of roads. They were built to link the rest of the empire to Rome itself. To make travel as fast as possible, roads were built in straight lines taking the shortest route.

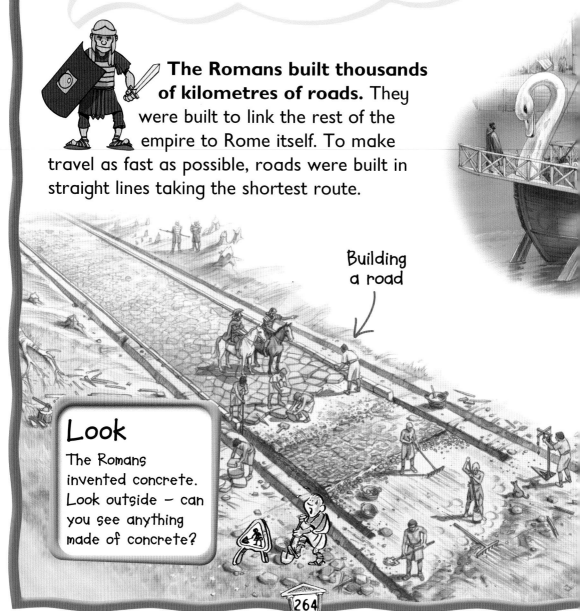

Look

The Romans invented concrete. Look outside – can you see anything made of concrete?

Roman ship

Could ships sail to Rome?

Most ships were too big to sail up the river Tiber to Rome. Instead, they stopped at Rome's main port, Ostia. Here, the ship's cargo was loaded onto smaller barges and taken the final 25 kilometres to Rome.

Crystal ball!

The Romans often consulted a fortune-teller or a priest even before setting out on a long journey.

Did people travel in their beds?

Town streets were crowded and very dirty. Rich people travelled in curtained beds called litters, carried shoulder-high by slaves. Ordinary people used stepping-stones to avoid the mud and rubbish on the streets.

Why was Rome so beautiful?

The Romans built beautiful buildings. They invented concrete, and used clay bricks baked at high temperatures, which lasted longer than unbaked ones. Arches were built to create strong walls and doorways. Huge domes were made for buildings that were too big for wooden roofs.

Pipe up!

Our word 'plumber' comes from 'plumbum', the Latin word for the lead used by Romans to make water pipes. The same word is also used for a 'plumb-line', still in use today.

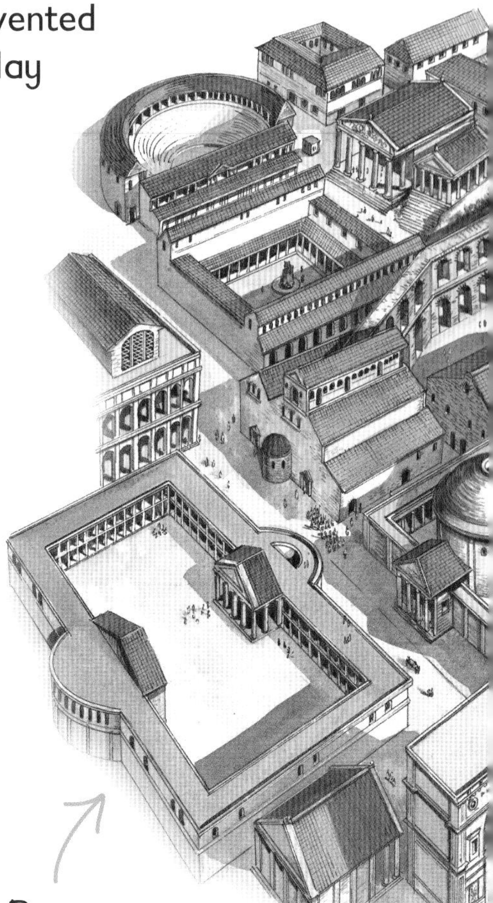

Roman buildings

Were there doctors in Rome?

Yes there were, but the Romans believed that illness was caused by witchcraft. To find a cure, they visited a temple to ask the gods to make them better. They might see a doctor who made medicines from plants or carried out simple operations.

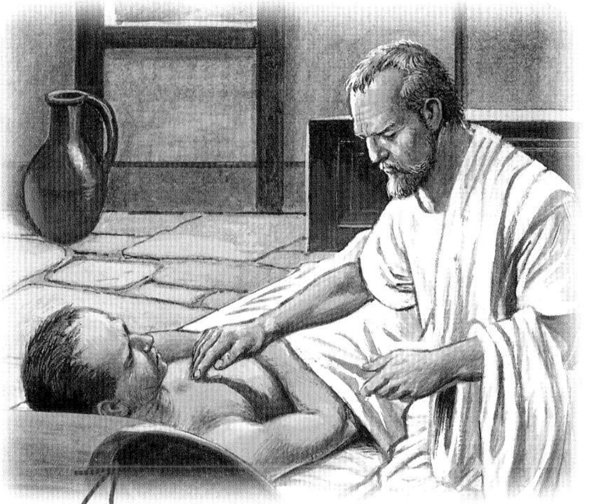

Doctor and patient

Find out

Romans spoke their own language. Can you find out what it was called?

How was Rome supplied with water?

Water from mountain springs was carried on raised stone channels into the city. Once the water reached the city, it flowed through pipes to baths, fountains and toilets.

Quiz time

Do you remember what you have read about ancient Rome? Here are some questions to test your memory. The pictures will help you. If you get stuck, read the pages again.

page 243

1. Did people live in blocks of flats?

page 245

2. Who ate takeaways?

3. What did children learn at school?

page 246

4. What was a mosaic?

page 251

page 252

5. How clean were the Romans?

6. Did the Romans listen to music?

page 253

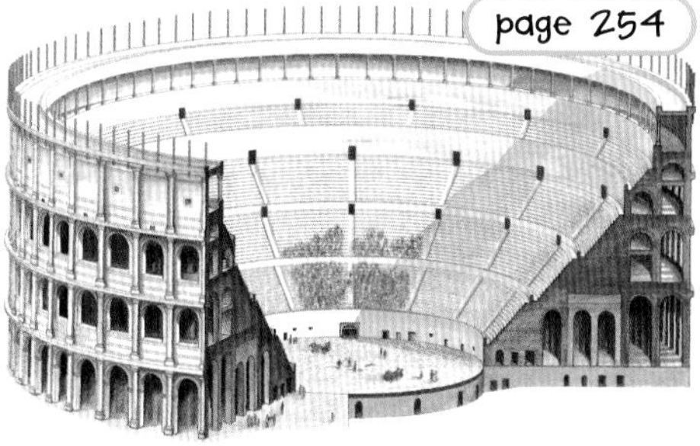

page 254

7. What was the Colosseum?

8. Did people keep pets?

page 259

page 261

9. Why were olives so special?

10. Did grapes grow on trees?

page 261

11. Who was the top god?

page 262

12. Did people travel in their beds?

page 265

13. Why was Rome so beautiful?

page 266

Answers

1. Yes, Rome had the first high-rise flats
2. Poorer people
3. Writing, arithmetic, history, sport, public speaking
4. Pictures made from coloured stone or pottery
5. Very clean, they often visited the baths
6. Yes, they liked music and dancing
7. A huge oval arena used for gladiator fights and pretend sea battles
8. Yes they did
9. Because they were used as food and crushed to make oil that was used for many things
10. Grapes grew on vines that grew around trees
11. Jupiter
12. No, they travelled in litters
13. Because the Romans built beautiful buildings

Questions about...

Vikings

Where did Vikings come from?

The Vikings lived about 2000 years ago. Viking warriors came from Denmark, Sweden and Norway to raid villages and steal treasure. Viking families began to settle in England, Ireland, Scotland and France. They explored Iceland, Greenland and Russia – and even travelled as far as North America.

Who discovered Greenland?

A Viking called Erik the Red discovered Greenland. It was a dark and icy place but Erik wanted people to come and live there. He called it 'Greenland' so they would think it was a warm place full of trees and grass.

Greenland

Imagine

Can you imagine discovering a new country? What would you call it?

Why did Vikings carry their boats?

In winter, Vikings made long overland journeys. In some places, they carried their boats over ground between rivers. The Vikings were brave adventurers, keen to seek new land and treasures. Each journey took several years.

Pirates!

The word 'Viking' means 'pirates', 'port-attackers', or 'people of the bays'. This tells us that Vikings spent their lives close to the sea.

Which king killed his brother?

When a Viking king died, each of his sons had an equal right to his throne. Erik Bloodaxe was famous for his cruelty. He wanted to be king so much, he killed both of his brothers and became King Erik of Norway.

Think

What would your Viking name be? You can make it as funny as you like!

Erik Bloodaxe

My name is...!

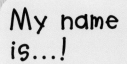

Many Viking rulers had strange names such as Svein Forkbeard, Einar Falsemouth, Magnus Barelegs, and Thorfinn Skullsplitter!

Who tried to stop the waves?

King Cnut was a Viking king of Denmark, Norway and England. He was a cruel ruler. However, Cnut said he was a good Christian. To prove it, he ordered the waves to stop. When they did not he said, "This proves that I am weak. Only God can control the sea."

What was the Jelling Stone?

King Harald Bluetooth built a church at Jelling, in Denmark. Outside the church was a memorial for his dead parents. It was called the Jelling Stone and was decorated with Viking and Christian carvings.

What was a dragon ship?

Vikings built ships called 'drakar', or dragon ships. These ships were designed for war. They were long, speedy and beautifully carved. Because they were so light, they could sail easily onto beaches.

Drakar ship

Did Vikings have maps?

No, they didn't. The Vikings used the positions of the Sun, Moon and stars to guide them on their travels. They also followed the direction the wind was blowing in.

Remember

Can you remember the Viking word for 'dragon ship'?

Gold to go away!

Viking pirates threatened to attack if they were not paid to sail away. This usually worked, and villages paid the gold – again and again!

Who was afraid of the Vikings?

Vikings could be very scary! People living in seaside villages were often afraid of them. Gangs of warriors carried out raids on defenceless villages. They stole valuable treasure and healthy young men and women to sell as slaves.

Viking raid

Why were Vikings so fierce?

To scare their enemies in battle! Viking warriors dressed in animal skins and charged at their enemies, howling and growling like wolves, and chewing at their shields. These warriors were called berserkirs and this is where the word 'berserk' comes from.

Berserkir

Did swords have names?

Viking warriors loved their swords so much, they even gave them names such as 'Sharp Biter'! When a warrior died, he would be buried with his sword by his side.

Design

Draw your own Viking sword and shield. What name would you give to your sword?

Shield

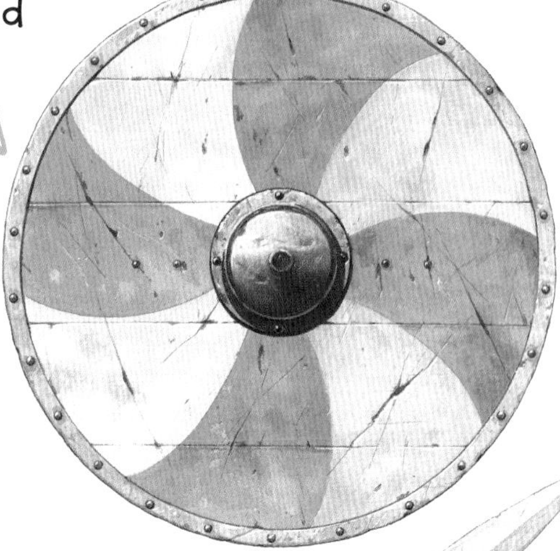

What weapons did Vikings use?

Vikings had to make or buy all of their weapons. Poor soldiers carried knives and spears. Wealthy Vikings had metal helmets and tunics, and fine, sharp swords. They carried a round shield that was made of wood covered with leather.

Sword

Helmet

Soldier women!

Women went to war but they did not fight. Instead, they nursed wounded warriors and cooked meals for hungry soldiers.

Who rode an eight-legged horse?

Odin was king of the Viking gods. He rode an eight-legged horse called Sleipnir and had two ravens called Thought and Memory. Odin sat on a high throne so he could see all of the Universe. Sometimes he liked to dress as a traveller and take a holiday in the human world.

Discover

Can you find out about any other Viking gods or goddesses – which one is your favourite?

Who controlled the thunder?

The storm god Thor controlled thunder. Viking farmers hated thunderstorms because they ruined their crops. They would pray to Thor to stop the thunder and let their crops grow. Thor rode in his chariot through the clouds holding a giant hammer and thunderbolt.

Sea god!

Njord was the god of the sea. He was married to the giantess Skadi, who watched over the mountains.

Why were warriors so brave?

Because they believed they would go to heaven when they died. Vikings thought that dead warriors were remembered forever, and that they went to heaven to feast with the gods.

Why did animals live in houses?

Homes were needed to shelter animals, as well as people. In towns, pigs, goats and horses were kept in sheds. In the countryside, the weather could be cold and wet. Farmers lived in longhouses, with an area for animals at one end. This meant that the people and animals stayed warm and dry.

What were runes?

Runes were the 16 letters of the Viking alphabet. People used them for labelling belongings with the owner's name, recording accounts, keeping calendars and sending messages. There was no paper, so runes were carved onto wood.

Runes

Make

With a cardboard box, make your own Viking house. You could even glue some grass to the roof.

Why did Vikings get ill?

Vikings suffered from chest diseases. This was because their houses did not have windows and were often damp and full of smoke from the fire burning on the stove.

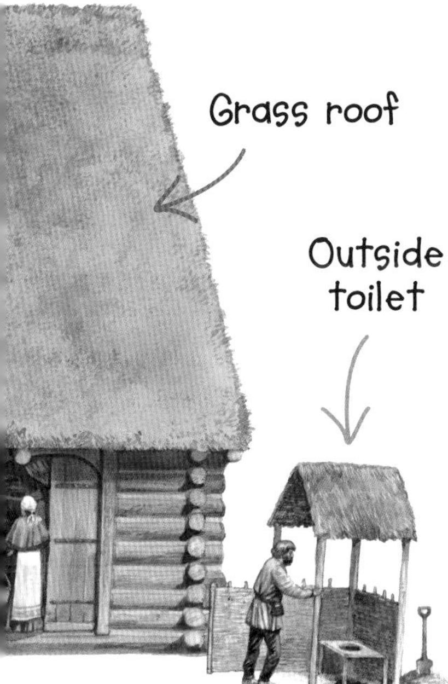

Precious cow!

Viking farmers loved cows! A cow was precious because it gave milk, clothing and meat, and its droppings were spread on the fields to help crops grow.

How did grass provide food?

Grassy fields provided food for animals and people. Sheep and cows needed fresh grass to eat. These animals then provided milk and meat for people to eat. Farmers also cut the grass and dried it out to make hay to feed the animals in the winter.

Discover

Have a look at the labels inside your clothes. What are your clothes made of?

Did Vikings have factories?

No! Vikings had no machines, so all work was done by hand. Families had to make or grow everything they needed. They built their own houses and furniture and they made their own clothes and toys. Blacksmiths made weapons and tools for people to work with.

Blacksmiths

Why was the sea so important?

Because people could catch fish to eat. People also gathered shellfish from the seashore for dinner. Vikings built their villages close to the sea in case they needed to travel to new places.

Itchy clothes!

Clothes were made of wool and could be very itchy. Women made smoother, finer cloth to wear as underwear.

What was sold at markets?

Vikings held markets on the beach. Farmers would sell meat, milk and fur to travellers. Some Vikings travelled a long way to buy different things to sell. They would buy woollen cloth from Britain, wine from France, glass from Germany, jewellery from Russia and spices from the Middle East.

How were quarrels settled?

Many quarrels were settled by fighting. Quarrels between families could continue for months. This lead to people on both sides being killed, until each family was prepared to seek peace.

Settling an argument

Bone comb!

Animal bones that were left over from mealtimes were used to carve combs, beads and pins. Deer antlers were used to make finer combs.

Pretend

With a friend, pretend to be a pirate and Viking. Who is more scared of who?

Who were the Vikings scared of?

Pirates from Russia! They sailed across the sea to steal treasure from Viking towns. So Vikings defended their towns with wooden walls and troops of warriors.

Did girls go to school?

No, they didn't. Instead of going to school, girls helped their mothers with cooking and cleaning, fed farm animals, fetched water, gathered wood, nuts and berries and learned how to spin, weave and sew.

Think

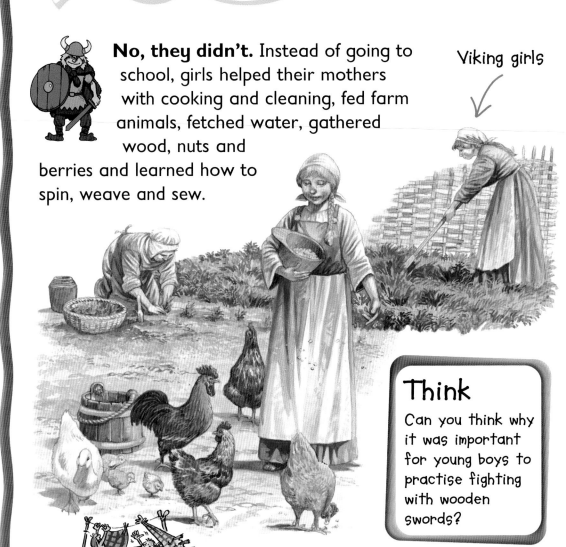

Can you think why it was important for young boys to practise fighting with wooden swords?

Were wives expensive?

If a Viking man wanted to marry, he had to ask the woman's father for permission and pay him a bride price. If the father accepted this, the marriage went ahead, even if the woman did not agree.

Who used wooden swords?

Viking boys practised fighting with wooden swords and small, lightweight shields. They also learned how to ride horses and use real weapons. They had to be ready to fight by the time they were 15 or 16 years old.

Viking boys

Wise women!

Many young women died having a baby. This meant there were fewer older women. Older women were thought to be very wise and people respected them for their knowledge and experience.

What did people wear?

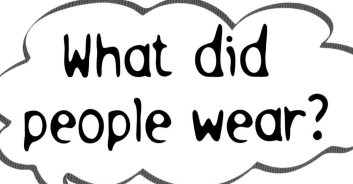

Vikings wore lots of layers to keep out the cold. Women wore long dresses of linen or wool with a woollen over-dress. Men dressed in wool tunics over linen shirts and woollen trousers. Men also wore fur or sheepskin caps while women wore headscarves and shawls.

Clothing

Dress up

Have a look through your wardrobe and see if you can dress up as a Viking!

Glass jewels!

The Vikings imported broken glass from Germany, to melt and recycle into beautiful glass beads.

Did people wear jewellery?

Both men and women liked to wear lots of jewellery. They thought it made them look good and it also showed how rich they were. Rings and arm braclets were given to warriors as rewards for fighting bravely in battle.

Gold ring

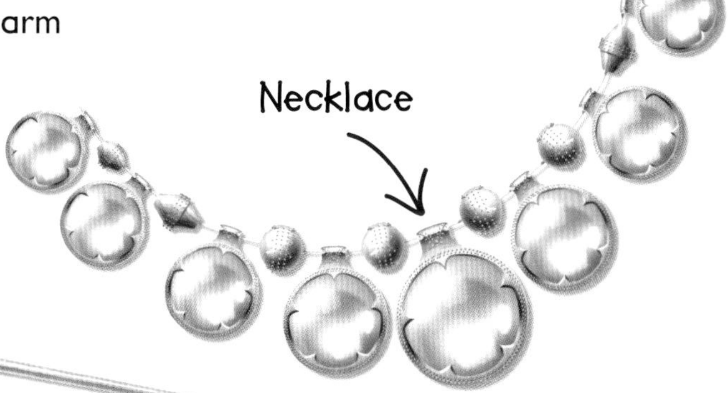

Necklace

Brooch

Did Vikings wear make up?

Viking men wore make-up! They particularly liked to wear make up around their eyes – probably made from soot or crushed berries. They thought it made them look more handsome.

How did people get clean?

Vikings bathed by pouring water over red-hot stones to create clouds of steam. They sat in the steam to make themselves sweat, then rubbed their skin with birch twigs to help loosen the dirt. Then they jumped into a pool of cold water to rinse off.

Keeping clean

Did Vikings have toilets?

Yes they did. Houses had an outside toilet that was simply a bucket, or a hole in the ground with a wooden seat on top. Panels of woven twigs were set up around the toilet. Dried moss or grass was used as toilet paper.

Sloping house!

Longhouses were built on a slope. Then waste from the animals ran downhill – away from people living inside!

Hairstyles

How did Vikings wear their hair?

Men let their fringes grow long, and plaited the strands that hung down either side of their face. Women also kept their hair long. They left it flowing loose until they married, then tied it in a beautiful knot at the nape of their neck.

Try

Is your hair long enough to plait like a Viking? Ask an adult to help you.

How did Vikings prepare for battle?

Viking sports were good training for war. Spear-throwing, sword-fighting and archery – shooting at targets with bows and arrows – were all popular. They helped boys and young men to become fit and strong and prepared them for using weapons.

Archer

Drinking horns

Vikings liked to drink ale from cups carved from cattle horns. Warriors would carry these drinking horns on their long journeys.

What was a saga?

A saga was a story that Vikings told to honour heroes who died in battle. The sagas were told to ensure that heroes' names and fame never died. These stories were passed on by word of mouth for many years.

Saga

What did people do for fun?

Vikings liked music and dancing. Kings would hire dancers, clowns, jugglers and singers to entertain their guests at feasts. Vikings also enjoyed playing practical jokes and listening to stories about gods and heroes.

Write

What is your favourite story? Maybe you could try and write one of your own.

Who defeated the Vikings?

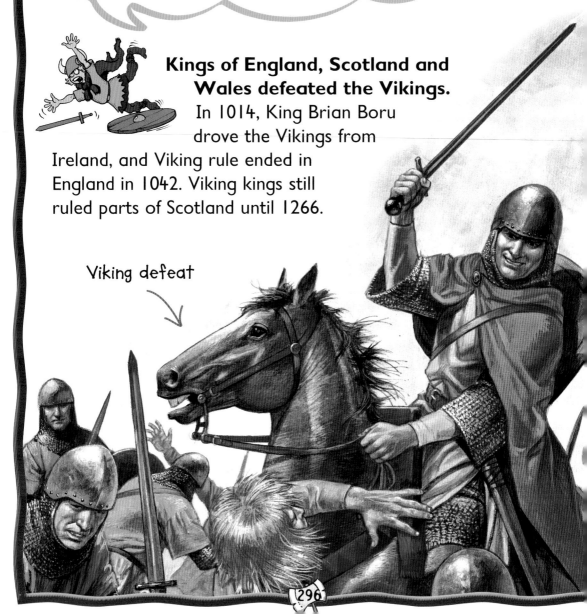

Kings of England, Scotland and Wales defeated the Vikings. In 1014, King Brian Boru drove the Vikings from Ireland, and Viking rule ended in England in 1042. Viking kings still ruled parts of Scotland until 1266.

Find out

Try to find any other Viking words that we still use today. Ask an adult to help you.

Festival

How do we remember the Vikings?

Today, people still celebrate Viking festivals. In the Shetland Isles, people dress up as Vikings then burn a lifesize model of a Viking warship. They do this to remember the Viking festival of Yule, held every January.

Was Santa a Viking?

Santa was a Viking god! Yule (mid-winter) was an important Viking festival. Vikings held feasts and exchanged gifts. They also believed that Viking gods travelled across the sky, bringing good things – just like Santa!

Do you speak Viking?

Many Viking words for everyday things still survive such as 'sister', 'knife' and 'egg'.

Quiz time

Do you remember what you have read about the Vikings? These questions will test your memory. The pictures will help you. If you get stuck, read the pages again.

page 273

1. Why did Vikings carry their boats?

2. Which king killed his brother?

page 274

3. Who was afraid of the Vikings?

page 277

4. Did swords have names?

page 278

5. Who controlled the thunder?

page 281

6. Why did animals live in houses?

page 282

7. Why was the sea so important?

page 285

page 292

11. Did Vikings have toilets?

8. Who used wooden swords?

page 289

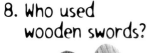

12. Who defeated the Vikings?

page 296

9. Were wives expensive?

page 289

page 297

13. Was Santa a Viking?

10. How did people get clean?

page 292

Answers

1. To transport them between rivers
2. Erik Bloodaxe
3. People living in seaside villages
4. Viking warriors gave their swords names
5. Thor, the storm god
6. To keep them warm and dry
7. So people could catch fish to eat
8. Viking boys
9. Viking men had to pay money to their bride's father
10. They steamed themselves
11. Yes, they did
12. Kings of England, Scotland and Wales
13. Yes, Santa was a Viking god

Questions about...

Knights & Castles

Why were castles built on hills?

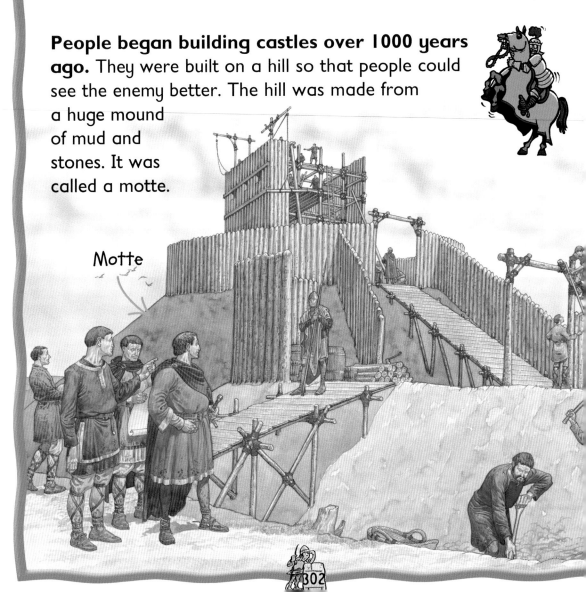

People began building castles over 1000 years ago. They were built on a hill so that people could see the enemy better. The hill was made from a huge mound of mud and stones. It was called a motte.

Were all castles made from wood?

Early castles were made from wood. They were not very strong and they caught fire easily. People began to build stone castles. These were much stronger. They lasted longer and did not burn.

Stone castle

Slimy walls!

Builders often covered wooden castles with wet, slippery leather. This stopped them from burning so easily.

What was a moat?

Builders dug a big ditch around the castle. Then they filled it with water. This watery ditch was called a moat. Enemy soldiers got wet and cold if they attacked the castle from the moat. It was hard to fight from the bottom of it, too!

Think

Stone castles were a lot warmer in winter than wooden ones. Why do you think this was so?

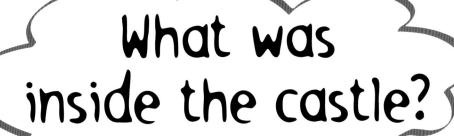

What was inside the castle?

A big courtyard was inside the castle. This was called a bailey. A thick wall was built all around it. Smaller buildings were put up inside the bailey.

Sometimes there were gardens. There were often animals and chickens, too!

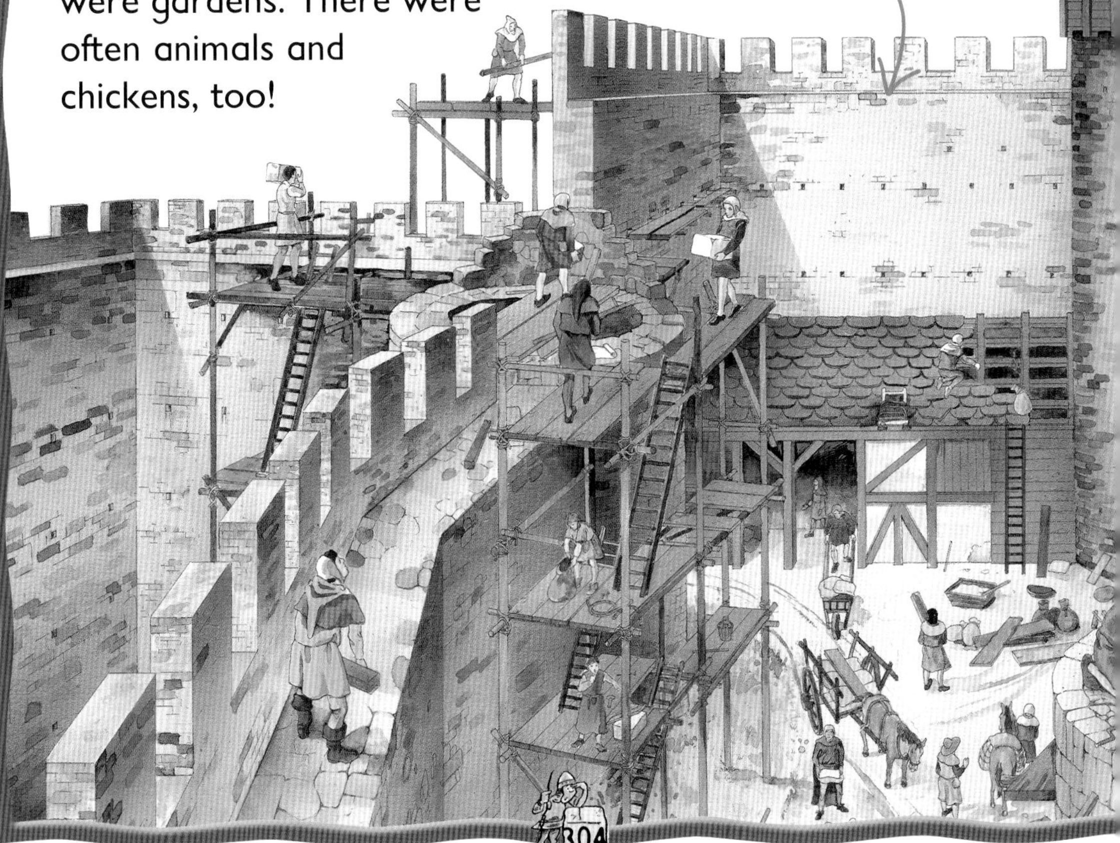

Where was the safest place?

The safest place in the castle was a tall, strong tower. This tower was called a keep. The lord of the castle lived there with his family. In later times they slept on the top floor. There were big rooms downstairs to hold feasts for visitors.

Thick walls!

The walls of the keep were at least 3.5 metres thick! This meant that building a castle took a long time. It was also a very expensive job.

How did people get bread and water?

A castle often had its own mill and bakery. Many castles got water from a well. The well was dug inside the bailey. A massive wheel drew water up into the castle. Later castles had piped water with taps.

Measure

The keep walls were 3.5 metres thick. Use a tape measure to see how thick this is.

What happened at knight school?

A knight had to train for 14 years! First, he went to a lord's house when he was seven years old. There, he was taught how to ride and to shoot with a bow. Then he became a squire and was taught how to fight with a sword.

Count

A nobleman's son went to knight school when he was seven. He studied for 14 years. How old was he when he became a knight?

Who had the best horses?

Rich knights owned three horses. The heaviest horse was used for fighting and in tournaments. The quickest was used for long journeys. The third carried the bags!

Dying for love!

Jaufre Rudel was a French knight. He sent love letters to the beautiful Countess of Tripoli, even though had never seen her! When he finally met her he fell into her arms and died!

What was dubbing?

A new knight was given a special ceremony called a dubbing. First, he had to spend a whole night in church, praying on his knees. Then the new knight was tapped on the shoulder with a sword.

Did knights fight with a ball?

Knights hit the enemy with a spiked ball on a long chain. This was called a 'morning star'.

Knights used swords, too. Foot knights from Switzerland used a halberd. This was an axe with a hook on the back. It was good for getting a knight off his horse!

Get to the point!

Soldiers called 'retrievers' fetched all the fallen arrows. They had to run through the battle to get them!

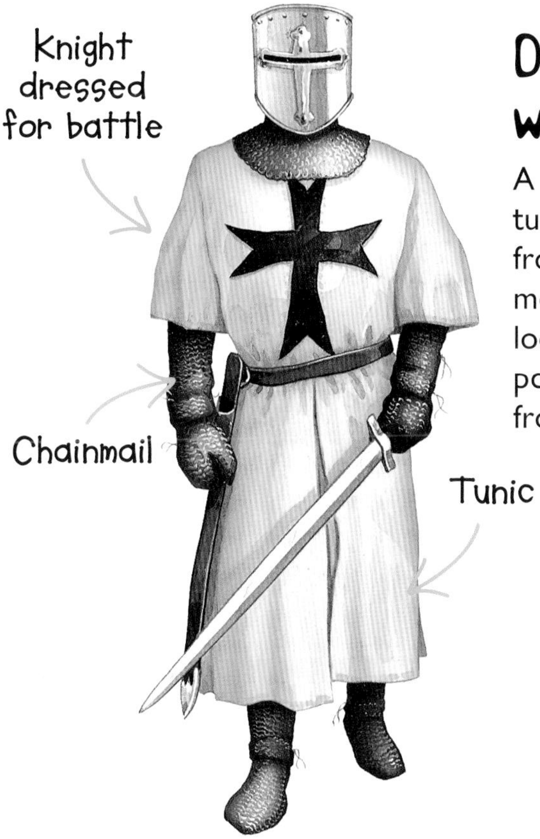

Did knights wear woolly jumpers?

A knight in early times wore a bright tunic with long sleeves. It was made from wool or linen. He also wore metal armour called chainmail. It looked and felt like knitted wire! A padded jacket stopped the chainmail from scratching the skin.

Design

In later times, knights wore steel armour. They even wore metal shoes! Design your own suit of armour to protect a knight.

How long was the Hundred Years War?

The Hundred Years War was fought between the English and the French. It actually lasted for 116 years, between 1337 and 1453. English and Welsh soldiers used longbows against the French. The bowmen could fire 12 arrows every minute!

How were knights told apart?

Knight wearing coat of arms

A knight wore a helmet that covered his head. Even his soldiers could not recognize him! Each knight put a special symbol on his shield and robes. The symbols and colours were called a 'coat of arms'.

Don't shoot the messenger!

Using a coat of arms was called 'heraldry'. This is because the lord's messenger was called a 'herald'. The herald wore his lord's coat of arms as he crossed the battlefield.

What was a herald?

A herald was a messenger. He carried messages for knights during battles. The herald had to be able recognize each knight by his coat of arms. The heralds were very good at recognizing coats of arms. This eventually came to be known as heraldry.

Herald

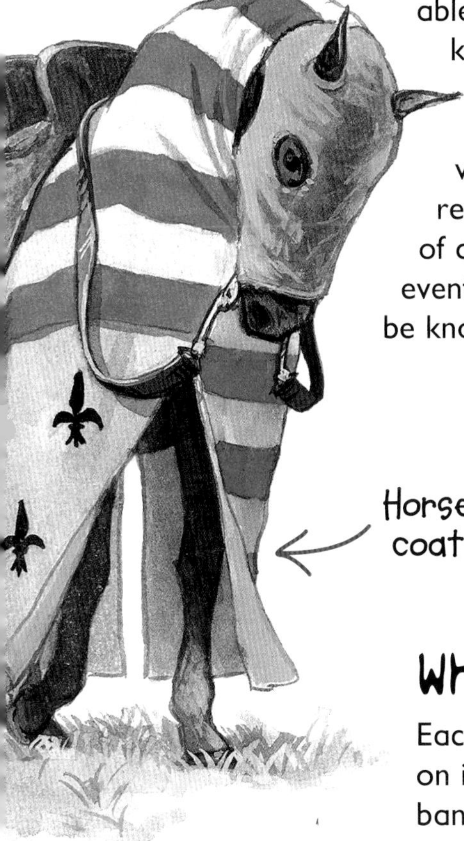

Horse wearing coat of arms

Where did soldiers meet?

Each lord had a banner with his coat of arms on it. Knights and soldiers gathered around the banner on the battlefield. The lord could then explain his battle plans. The winner of a battle often stole the enemy's banner from him.

Make

Draw and cut out a shield from cardboard. Paint your own symbol on it.

Did knights have fun?

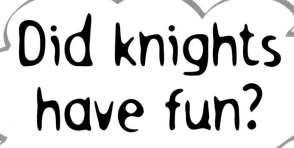

Yes they did! Knights took part in competitions called tournaments. These helped them to improve their fighting. The knights formed two teams that fought each other in pretend battles.

Did knights only fight on horseback?

At a tournament, knights also fought on the ground. They wore heavy armour. Skill and speed were much more important than strength.

Make

Write and design a programme for a tournament. You can include fighting competitions and entertainment.

Rotten cheat!

Some knights tried to cheat in a jousting competition. They wore special armour that was fixed to the horse's saddle!

Knight taking part in a tournament

How did knights find a wife?

Ladies from the king's court went to tournaments. The knights showed off their bravery to their favourite lady. Each knight tried to push another knight off his horse with a long pole called a lance. This was called jousting.

Jousting knight

What was a siege?

People sometimes became trapped inside a castle if the enemy surrounded it. This was called a siege. The people inside could not get food supplies. So they had a terrible choice. They could either starve to death or surrender to the enemy.

Think

Try to think of ways to get into a castle without being seen. Look at pictures of castles to help you. Draw a map of your route into a castle.

How did the castle crumble?

Sometimes the enemy bashed down the castle gates with battering rams. These were thick tree trunks capped with iron. The enemy also tried to climb the walls with giant ladders. Huge catapults hurled burning wood and stones.

Hairy weapons!

Giant catapults were wound up with ropes made of human hair! The hair was made into plaits and was very strong.

How did enemies get inside a castle?

Sometimes enemy soldiers dug tunnels underneath the castle. They then popped up inside the castle walls. The enemy also pushed wooden towers against the castle walls. Soldiers hiding in the towers leapt out and climbed into the castle.

Quiz time

Do you remember what you have read about knights and castles? These questions will test your memory. The pictures will help you. If you get stuck, read the pages again.

1. Why were castles built on hills?

page 302

2. What was a moat?

page 303

3. Where was the safest place?

page 305

4. What happened at knight school?

page 306

5. What was dubbing?

page 307

6. Did knights fight with a ball?

page 308

7. Did knights wear woolly jumpers?

page 309

11. How did a knight find a wife?

page 313

8. How were knights told apart?

page 310

12. How did the castle crumble?

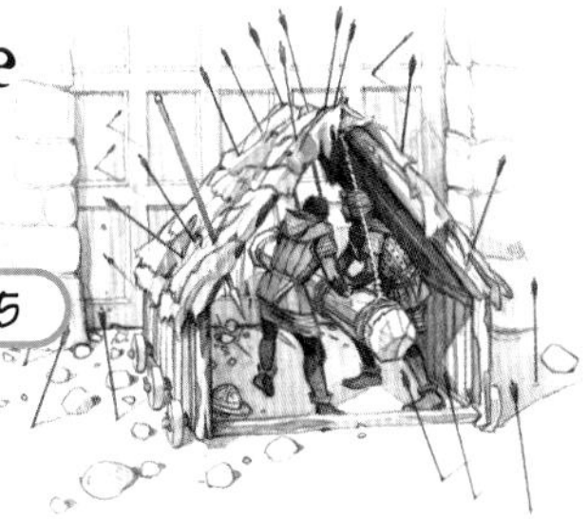

page 315

13. How did enemies get inside a castle?

page 315

9. Where did soldiers meet?

page 311

10. Did knights only fight on horseback?

page 312

Answers

1. So people could see the enemy
2. A watery ditch around a castle
3. The keep
4. Boys were trained to be knights
5. A special ceremony for a new knight
6. They fought with a spiked ball on a chain
7. No, they wore chainmail and tunics
8. By coats of arms
9. Around the banner on the battlefield
10. No, they also fought on the ground
11. When he was jousting
12. The walls were bashed with battering rams
13. They dug tunnels under the castle

Questions about...

Pirates

What is a pirate?

Pirates are people who steal from ships and ports. As soon as the first ships began to carry goods, pirates began to attack them. About 600 years ago, there were many pirates sailing on the seas and oceans around the world.

A pirate attack

Hairy pirates!

'Barbarossa' was a nickname for two pirate brothers. 'Barbarossa' means 'Redbeard' – because they both had red beards!

Who was afraid of the Barbarossas?

Every sailor was afraid of the two Barbarossa brothers! They were pirates who attacked ships about 500 years ago. One of the brothers captured the town of Algiers in North Africa. The other attacked ships that belonged to the Pope, who was the leader of the Christian church.

Make

Make your own Barbarossa mask. Draw your pirate's face on card. Use red wool to make a big red beard.

Did all pirates want treasure?

Pirates from the Mediterranean were called corsairs. They didn't want treasure. Instead, they took people from ships and ports and sold them as slaves. Corsairs also captured rich people. They were paid a lot of money to release them.

Corsairs and their ships

Who stole the Spanish gold?

About 500 years ago, Spanish captains sailed to the Americas. There they found gold, silver and jewels. The Spanish stole it from the American people and took it back to Spain. Pirates often attacked the Spanish ships before they got home and took the treasure from them.

Act

Try to act out your own story about Spanish and English captains. One is trying to steal treasure from the other.

When were pirates not pirates?

English captains such as John Hawkins raided Spanish treasure ships. England and Spain were enemies at this time, so the English thought it was okay to steal from the Spanish. The captains wanted to be called 'privateers' instead of 'pirates'.

Pirate queen!

Queen Elizabeth I of England encouraged her sea captains to be privateers. However, the privateers were often robbed before they reached England!

Can you be a pirate with one leg?

Francois Le Clerc

Yes! Francois Le Clerc was a dangerous pirate with just one leg. In the 1550s, he raided Caribbean islands owned by Spain. He captured the port of Havana on the island of Cuba. No one would pay Le Clerc to give up the port, so he burned it to the ground.

Did sailors fight the pirates?

Sailors fought hard against pirates when they were attacked.

But they didn't try to fight Francis L'Ollonais in the 1660s. He was very cruel and tortured his prisoners. When Francis attacked a ship, the captain and sailors usually gave up without a fight.

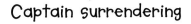

Captain surrendering

What did pirates do with their money?

Pirates sold their treasure to people at the docks. They usually made lots of money. Most of the money was spent in public houses!

Spend! Spend! Spend!

Pirates could spent 3000 pieces of silver in one night. That's about £45,000 in today's money!

Francis L'Ollonais

Where was there a pirate paradise?

Port Royal was a harbour on the island of Jamaica. A strong fort guarded the harbour. Pirates could even mend their ships in the docks. Jamaica was ruled by the English, who left the pirates alone.

Paint

Paint a pirate scene with ships and a port. There might be lots of ships, with the pirates carrying their treasure onto dry land.

Pirates in Port Royal

Could women be pirates?

Yes, they could! Mary Read dressed up as a man and became a sailor in the 1700s. Her ship was raided by pirates and Mary decided to join them. Her ship was raided by 'Calico Jack' and his wife, Anne Bonney. Mary made friends with Anne and they fought against the navy.

Mary Read and Anne Bonney

Make

Make a plate of food for a pirate's prisoner! Take a paper plate and stick on cut-out food – such as caterpillars!

Whose prisoners ate caterpillars?

Ching Shih was a Chinese pirate. In 1807, she controlled many ships that raided China's coast. Ching Shih was a great leader. She had very strict rules for her sailors. Her prisoners had to eat caterpillars in boiled rice!

Baldy!

Grace O'Malley shaved her head to look more like her sailors. She was given the nickname 'Baldy'!

Who said she was sorry?

Grace O'Malley went to sea when she was a young girl. She ended up controlling pirate ships off the coast of Ireland. Grace had 20 ships under her command. In 1593 Grace asked Queen Elizabeth I of England to forgive her for being a pirate.

What were the best ships?

Pirate ships had to be very fast! Many were small and easy to sail. Schooners were ships that had two masts. Corsairs sailed in galleys – ships that had oars as well as sails. The captain had a cabin in the stern (back of the ship). Treasure, gunpowder and food were stored in the hold, beneath the deck.

Where did pirates sleep?

Most pirates slept on the deck unless the weather was bad. Some put up hammocks below deck in the middle of the ship. It was cramped, smelly and noisy. This made some pirates ill. So did their food. They didn't eat enough fruit and vegetables!

Recycling!

Pirates even stole their prisoners' clothes! They usually sold them, but sometimes kept the best items for themselves.

Write

Look at the picture of the galley. Write a guided tour of the ship. Describe how the pirates lived on it, too.

What did pirates eat?

Pirates mostly ate dry biscuits and pickled meat when on board ship. They hunted for fresh meat when they landed on islands. They also collected fresh water and fruit. Pirate cooks often had only one arm or leg. They couldn't fight, so they cooked!

Who was afraid of a flag?

Merchant seamen were terrified when they saw the flag of a pirate ship. Early flags were bright red. By the 1700s, pirates flew black flags. Each pirate captain added his or her own symbol. Sometimes this was the famous white skull-and-crossbones.

Were buccaneers heroes?

Buccaneers were violent thieves. Some people thought they were heroes. Bartholomew Roberts was a buccaneer. His nickname was Black Bart. He was handsome and bold, yet he never drank anything stronger than tea! In the 1720s, he captured 400 ships.

Duck!

When pirates attacked a ship, they shot at sailors working on the sails. They also shot at the helm, the steering area of the ship.

Pirate flag

Where was the treasure?

Sailors often hid their treasure. Pirates had to break down walls and doors to find it. They threatened their prisoners until they revealed the treasure. Pirates had frightening weapons such as knives, daggers and pistols.

Pirates looking for treasure

Design

Design your own pirate flag. Choose a bold colour. You could draw your own frightening symbol on it.

What was the best treasure?

Gold and silver was the best pirate treasure. It could be gold or silver coins, plain bars or made into fine ornaments. Silk cloth and hardwoods such as ebony were also valuable. So was ivory. But pirates were not so happy with cotton, coal or iron.

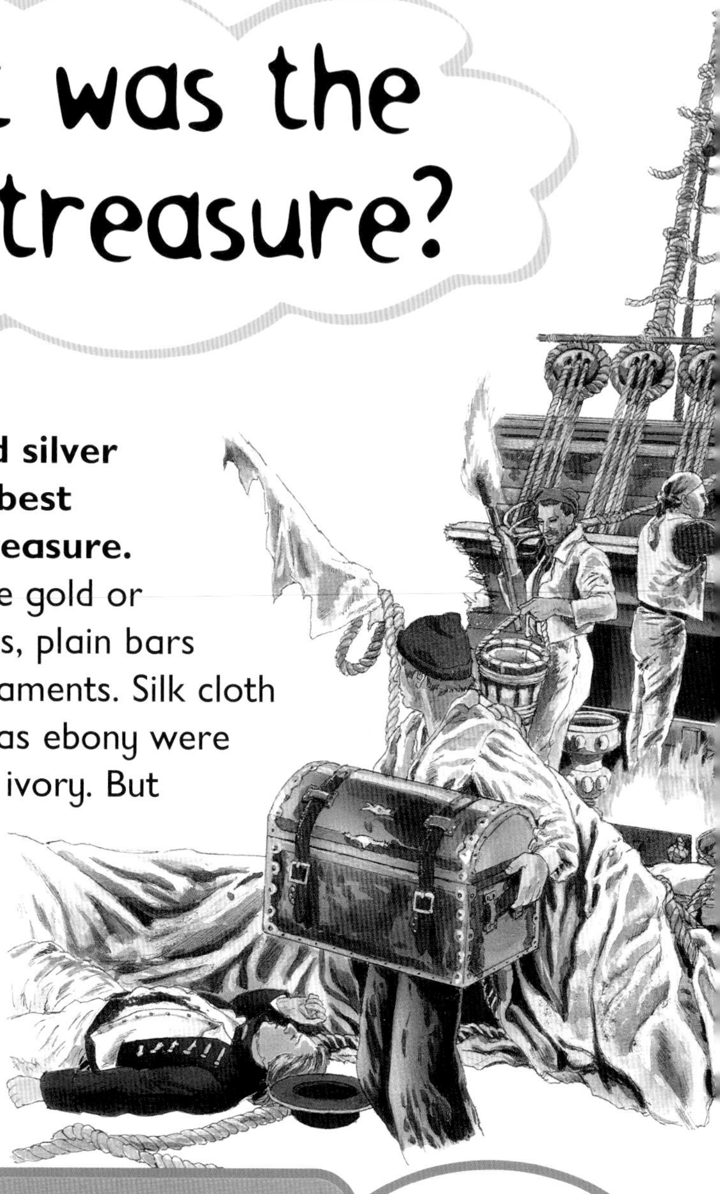

Pirates and their stolen treasure

Spicy sands!

Spices from India and Sri Lanka were very valuable, but they were difficult to sell. Pirates often dumped them overboard. These spices piled up on the beaches.

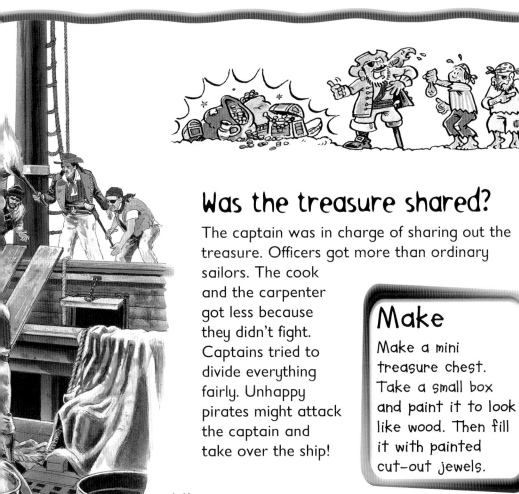

Was the treasure shared?

The captain was in charge of sharing out the treasure. Officers got more than ordinary sailors. The cook and the carpenter got less because they didn't fight. Captains tried to divide everything fairly. Unhappy pirates might attack the captain and take over the ship!

Make

Make a mini treasure chest. Take a small box and paint it to look like wood. Then fill it with painted cut-out jewels.

Where were all the jewels?

Pirates stole jewels from ships all over the world. Diamonds came from Africa. Red rubies and blue sapphires came from Burma. Green emeralds were mined in Colombia. Divers scooped up shiny pearls from the Persian Gulf.

Treasure chest

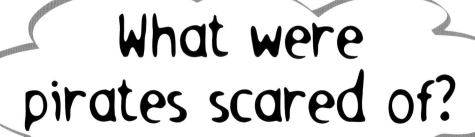

What were pirates scared of?

Shipwreck was a pirate's greatest fear. Terrible storms could blow up in the warm waters around the Caribbean, the Indian Ocean and the Far East. In 1712, a storm blasted Port Royal in Jamaica. Winds smashed ships to pieces.

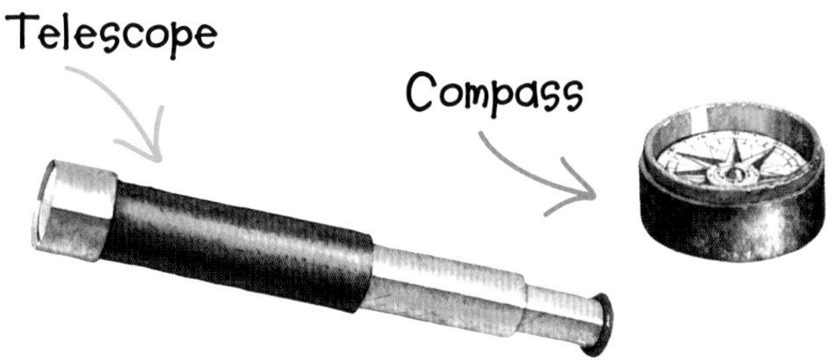

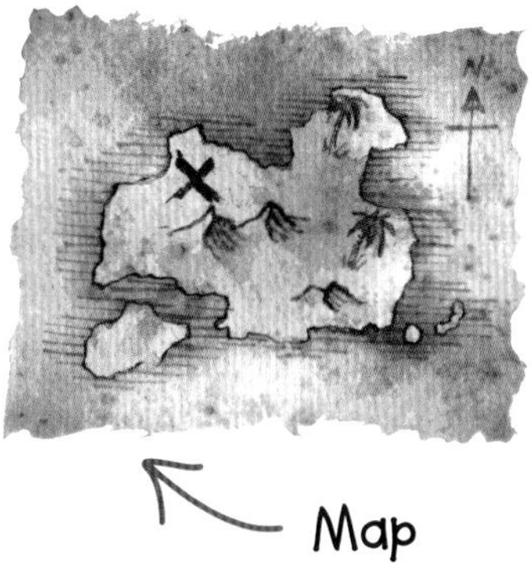

How did pirates find their way?

Pirates used the position of the Sun and stars to guide them in the right direction. They also used a compass to help them. A telescope helped pirates to see landmarks and work out their position. Pirates used maps to find their way on land.

Write

Pretend you are captain of a pirate ship. Write down all the jobs that are carried out on board every day.

Round and round!

Captain William Dampier was a brilliant navigator. This means he knew where he was going! In the 1680s he sailed around the world three times.

How did pirates save a sinking ship?

Pirates tried to pump out water if the ship was leaking. Sometimes ships ‘ran aground’. This means they got stuck in shallow water. The pirates had to throw out anything heavy. This helped the ship to refloat. Sometimes they threw out food barrels and cannons.

Who is Long John Silver?

Long John Silver is a one-legged pirate. But he isn't real! He appears in a book called *Treasure Island*. This adventure story is all about pirates and buried treasure. It was written by Robert Louis Stevenson in 1883.

Dancing pirates!

Blackbeard was a real and dangerous pirate. In 1798, his story was made into a ballet!

Long John Silver

What ate Captain Hook's hand?

Captain Hook is a fierce pirate in a story called *Peter Pan*. It was written as a book and a play by J.M. Barrie in 1904. Peter Pan is the hero. He cut off Captain Hook's hand and fed it to a crocodile. That's why the Captain needed a hook.

Captain Hook

Did pirates sing?

Gilbert and Sullivan were famous songwriters. They wrote a musical about pirates in 1879, called *Pirates of Penzance*. But the pirates were softies! They wouldn't steal from orphans – children who had no parents – so everyone pretended to be an orphan!

Write

Write your own pirate story. Your pirates can be kind or cruel. They could be modern pirates. What would treasure be like today?

Quiz time

Do you remember what you have read about pirates?
These questions will test your memory. The pictures will help you. If you get stuck, read the pages again.

1. What is a pirate?

page 320

2. Who was afraid of the Barbarossas?

page 321

3. When were pirates not pirates?

page 323

4. Did sailors fight the pirates?

page 324

5. What did pirates do with their money?

page 324

6. Could women be pirates?

page 326

7. Whose prisoners ate caterpillars?

page 327

8. Where did pirates sleep?

page 328

9. What did pirates eat?

page 329

page 330

10. Who was afraid of a flag?

11. Where were all the jewels?

page 333

12. How did pirates find their way?

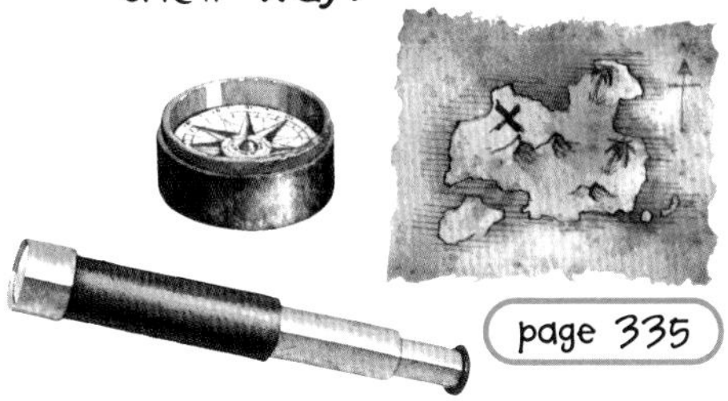

page 335

13. What ate Captain Hook's hand?

page 337

Answers

1. A person who steals from ships and ports
2. All sailors
3. When they were privateers
4. Yes, sailors fought hard against pirates
5. They spent it in public houses
6. Yes, they could
7. Ching Shih's prisoners
8. On the deck, or below deck in hammocks
9. Dry biscuits and pickled meat
10. Merchant seamen
11. Jewels came from all over the world
12. With a compass, telescope and map
13. A crocodile

Questions about...

Explorers

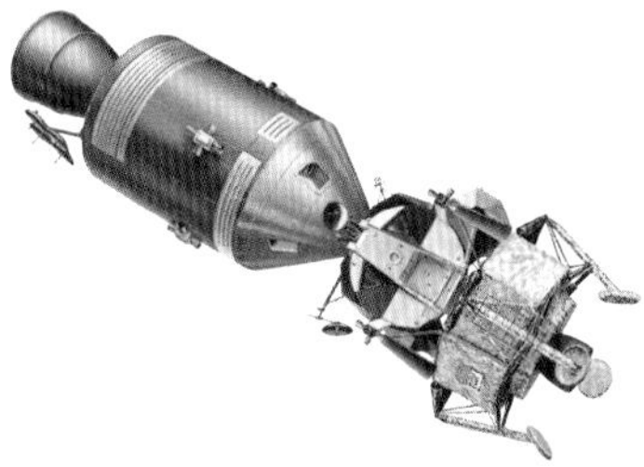

Who wanted to find a magical land?

In ancient times, Egyptian queen Hatshepsut sent explorers to look for a magical land. The land, called Punt, was full of treasure and beautiful animals. Hatshepsut's sailors brought back gold, ivory, monkeys and perfumes for the queen.

Queen Hatshepsut

Flat world!

The ancient Egyptians thought the world was flat and rectangular, with the sea running around the edge.

Who crossed the Alps with elephants?

In 22 BC Hannibal Barca, a famous military leader, invaded Italy. To get to Rome, and avoid being attacked, he took 46,000 soldiers and 37 war elephants across the Alps. It was one of the greatest military operations ever carried out in ancient times.

Make

Draw a map of your own magical land and colour it in. Don't forget to name it.

Who were the best sailors?

The best sailors in ancient times were the Phoenicians (say 'fuh-nee-shuns'). They came from what is now Syria and Lebanon and sailed all over the Mediterranean Sea. The Phoenicians used ships that had sails and oars.

Who was Marco Polo?

Marco Polo was a famous explorer who lived in Italy in the 1200s. He travelled to Asia at a time when most people in Europe never went far from their homes. Altogether, Marco travelled over 40,000 kilometres.

Marco Polo

Think

Imagine that you are a famous explorer. Write a list of everything you would need to take on your travels.

What did Marco Polo discover?

Marco Polo discovered lots of amazing inventions on his travels through Asia. He saw fireworks, paper money, ice-cream and eyeglasses for the first time. He also discovered that the Chinese had a postage system and could post each other letters.

Empty deserts!

On the way to China, Marco Polo crossed the vast, empty Desert of Lop, now called the Gobi Desert.

Who searched for a gold city?

In the 1500s, Spanish explorers searched for a mysterious city called El Dorado. Everything in the city was said to be made of gold. However, they never found the city, and people believed that the gold had been melted down and sent abroad.

Which explorer was very unlucky?

In the 1300s, Moroccan explorer Ibn Battuta, dreamt that a giant bird picked him up and carried him away. Battuta thought that the dream was a sign from God, telling him to go exploring. During his travels he did not have much luck. He was kept prisoner, chased by pirates, attacked by thieves and shipwrecked.

Why did explorers travel in junk?

A junk was a giant Chinese sailing ship. In ancient times, Zheng He, a Chinese explorer, had the largest sailing junks on Earth. The biggest was 130 metres long and 60 metres wide.

Discover

Where did you last go on holiday? How did you get there? How long did it take you?

Who was not allowed to explore?

Xuan-Zang, an ancient explorer, was banned from exploring by the Chinese emperor. He sneaked out of China and returned 16 years later with holy books and statues. The emperor was so pleased, he gave him a royal welcome.

Family values!

In many of the places Ibn Battuta visited, he got married. He had several wives and children in different parts of the world!

Who brought back a giraffe?

The Chinese sailor, Zheng He Zheng, was one of the world's best explorers. In the 1400s, he sailed to Africa. On his travels he collected precious stones, plants and animals to take back to the emperor. The emperor's favourite present was a giraffe from east Africa.

Zheng He Zheng

Star sailing!

Before the compass was invented, the first explorers had to rely on their observations of the Moon and stars to find their way.

Discover

Can you name any spices? Do you know any foods that have spices in them?

Vasco da Gama

Who found the route to Asia?

In the 1400s, Portugese sailor Vasco da Gama sailed to Calicut in India to find spices. The rajah, Calicut's ruler, did not let da Gama take any spices, so he went home empty-handed. However, the King of Portugal was very happy that da Gama had found the sea route to Asia.

Why were spices like gold?

In the 1400s, spices such as cinnamon and nutmeg were as valuable as gold. Spices came from Asia and were carried to Europe on the backs of camels. This took a long time and made them very expensive to buy.

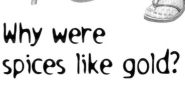

Who found the Americas?

Christopher Columbus found the Americas by mistake! He wanted to sail around the world to Asia in his ship the *Santa Maria*. When Columbus spotted land in 1492, he thought he had sailed to Japan. In fact, he had found the Bahamas, just off the American mainland.

Discover

Which sea is closest to where you live? Look in an atlas or on a map to find out.

Why did Columbus make a mistake?

Because he had travelled to the wrong place! As Columbus thought he had arrived in Asia, he called the lands he found the West Indies, and the people he met, Indians. They are still called this today – even though the West Indies are thousands of miles from India.

Hot stuff!

Sailors were afraid to sail around Africa. This was because of a myth that said if people went too far south in the Atlantic Ocean, the Sun would burn them to ashes.

Where was Vinland?

Five hundred years before Columbus, the Vikings found a new land and called it Vinland. They left after they kept getting into fights with the local people. Today, Vinland is known as America.

Who played a nasty trick?

The Spanish explorer Francisco Pizarro captured the Inca leader Atahuallpa in 1532. Atahuallpa said that if Pizarro set him free, he would give him a room filled with gold. Pizarro agreed. Once Atahuallpa had handed over the gold, Pizarro killed him and took over the Inca capital city, Cuzco.

Why did a dog get paid?

Spanish explorer Vasco Nuñez de Balboa sailed to America in 1500 looking for treasure. He took his beloved dog, Leoncico, with him. Leoncico never left his master's side and Balboa even paid him his own wage.

Whale of a time!

When sailing past Scotland, Greek explorer Pytheas was amazed to see fish as big as boats. In fact they weren't fish – they were whales.

Vasco Nuñez de Balboa

How did explorers tell the time?

Explorers could not tell the time at sea because clocks didn't work on ships. John Harrison, an inventor, created a new clock (called the chronometer) that could measure the time precisely, even at sea.

Look

Next time you go on a journey, write down how many different kinds of animals you see.

Which city was hiding?

In the 1400s, the Inca people of South America built a city called Machu Picchu on top of a mountain. Built from large stones and watered by a spring at the top of the mountain, the city was so well-hidden, that Spanish invaders never found it. An American explorer re-discovered the city in 1911.

Play

With your friends, play a game of hide and seek. Take it in turns to be the hider and the seeker.

Who founded the New World?

In 1607, 100 British people arrived in what is now called the United States of America. They founded the first permanent settlement and others soon followed. The continent was named the New World, and Europe, Asia and Africa became known as the Old World.

Ferdinand Magellan

Rich pickings!

In the 1500s, Francis Drake captured a Spanish treasure ship. It was carrying a cargo that was worth more than £12 million in today's money.

Who tried to sail around the world?

Portuguese explorer, Ferdinand Magellan, wanted to sail around the world during the 1500s. Magellan thought he could get to Asia and buy spices. Many of his crew died from a disease called scurvy and Magellan himself was killed in war. Only one of his five ships sailed home safely.

Who went on an important mission?

In 1768, Captain James Cook was sent on an important mission by the British navy. He went to the island of Tahiti and made observations of the planet Venus passing in front of the Sun. He also explored Australia, New Zealand and the Pacific Islands and made new maps.

What was scurvy?

Scurvy is a serious disease that is caused by not eating enough fresh fruit and vegetables. Many explorers and sailors suffered from the disease when on long voyages, as they had no access to fruit and vegetables.

Try it

How much fruit do you eat? You should eat five pieces of different fruit and vegetables every day to stay healthy.

Dr Livingstone

Captain Cook

Which explorer went missing?

In 1869, the explorer Dr Livingstone went missing. He'd gone exploring in east Africa and no one had heard from him. Everyone thought he had died. An American writer, Henry Stanley, found him in Tanzania. He greeted him with the words, "Dr Livingstone, I presume?"

Tasty trip!

Captain Cook was the first European to discover Hawaii, in 1778. He called it the Sandwich Island.

Who first crossed America?

Meriwether Lewis and William Clark travelled across America in 1803. They sailed down rivers on a boat. When the rivers grew too narrow, Lewis and Clark used canoes. Local Native American guides helped them paddle their canoe and find their way across America.

Brotherly love!

Lewis and Clark met some fierce native warriors whilst exploring. By amazing chance, the warrior leader turned out to be the brother of their guide.

Rene Caillie

Who went exploring in disguise?

The French explorer Rene Caillie wanted to visit the ancient city of Timbuktu, but only Muslims were allowed in. He dressed up as an Arab trader and sneaked into the city in 1828. He was the first European to go there and return home alive.

Make it

Create a disguise for yourself using hats, sunglasses and old clothes. Does anyone recognize you?

Who was scared by bears?

American explorer Meriwether Lewis was chased by a bear whilst out hunting. Lewis tried to shoot the bear, but he ran out of bullets. The bear chased Lewis into a river, then walked away and left him alone.

Who tried to get to the North Pole?

Norwegian explorer, Fridtjof Nansen did. He built a ship called *Fram*, which was designed to get stuck in the ice without being damaged. It was the strongest wooden ship of its time. As the iced moved, it carried the *Fram* nearer to the North Pole. Nansen almost reached the Pole in 1895, but not quite.

Pole position!

In 1911, the explorer Roald Amundsen and his team were the first people to reach the South Pole.

Who crossed Australia?

The middle of Australia is so hot, it is very hard to travel across. In 1860, Robert Burke and William Wills entered a competition set by the government to cross the middle of Australia. Both explorers starved to death and only one member of their team survived.

Burke and Wills

Who were the first Australians?

Aborigines were the first people to live in Australia. They arrived from Asia over 70,000 years ago. Many Aborigines lived in the Australian outback. Here, it is very hot and dry, and a long way from any big towns.

The *Fram*

Discover

Write a list of all the different animals you would expect to find in Australia.

Did explorers travel by sled?

In 1910, an explorer called Roald Amundsen used dog sleds to travel to the South Pole. Husky dogs pulled the sleds, and if a dog died, it was fed to the other dogs. This reduced the amount of food the men had to carry. Amundsen reached the South Pole in 1911.

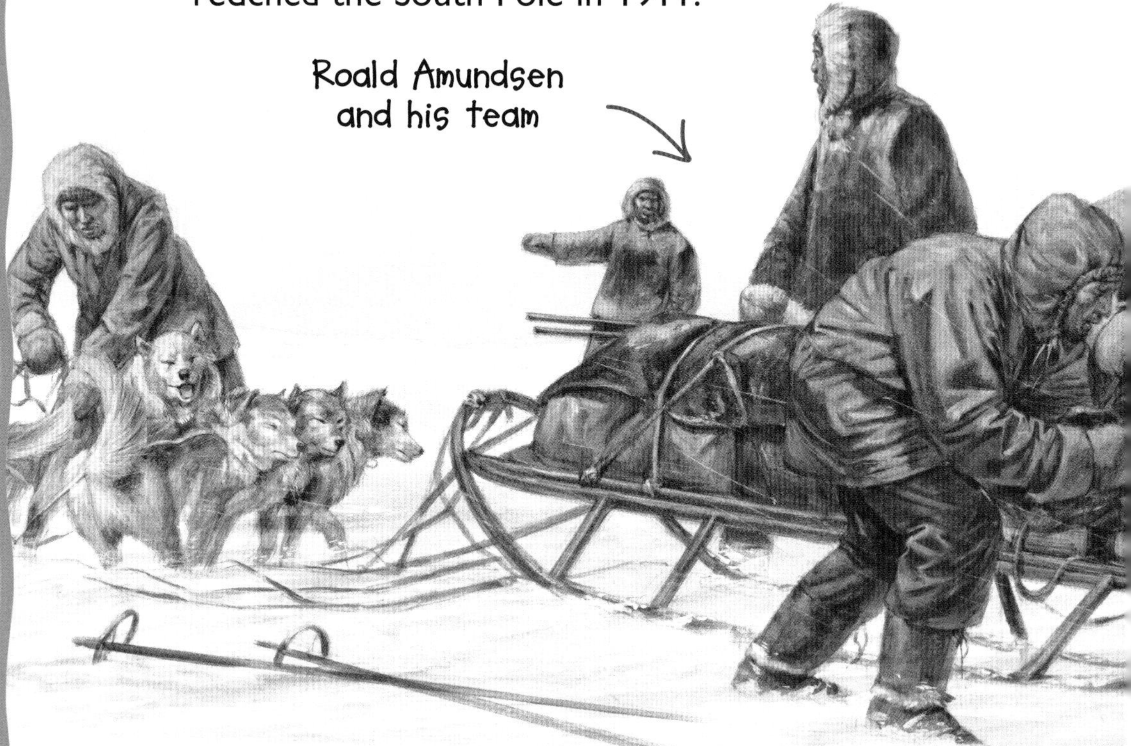

Roald Amundsen and his team

Who conquered Everest?

On 29 May, 1953, Tenzing and Hillary, were the first people to reach the top of Mount Everest, the highest mountain in the world. Since then, many other people have climbed the mountain.

Think

What sports can you play in the ice and snow? Have you tried doing any?

Peary and Henson

How did explorers keep warm at the North Pole?

By wearing sealskins! American explorer Robert Peary and his assistant Matthew Henson wore sealskin clothes when they travelled to the North Pole in 1909. The skins were light, waterproof and very warm. Peary paid local people to make his clothes and equipment.

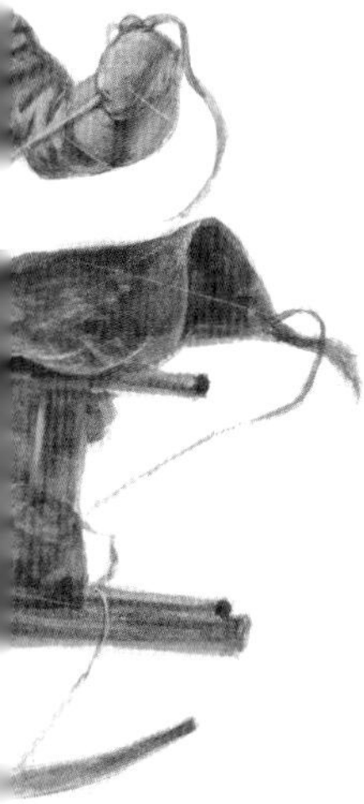

A mountain of rubbish!

Today Mount Everest is covered in litter and old oxygen tanks left behind by climbers.

Who explored the natural world?

Charles Darwin went on a round-the-world voyage on a ship called the *Beagle*. Darwin was a nature expert and found many new birds, plants, insects and other living things. Once back in England, Darwin wrote important books about the natural world.

Charles Darwin

Who discovered nine cities?

In 1870, a German called Heinrich Schliemann travelled to Turkey to see if he could find the ancient city of Troy. He discovered the ruins of nine cities, and also dug up piles of beautiful gold jewellery.

Going ape!

In 1871, Darwin wrote a book called The Descent of Man. In the book, Darwin said that the very first humans were related to apes.

Which ship explored the seabed?

In 1872, a ship called *HMS Challenger* set out to explore a new world – the bottom of the sea. The ship measured the seabed, using ropes to find out the depth of the ocean. On its round-the-world voyage, *Challenger's* crew also found many new kinds of sea creatures.

HMS Challenger

Draw

You have discovered a new type animal. Draw a picture of it and give it a name.

How did people get to the Moon?

In 1969, astronauts travelled to the Moon in a spacecraft called *Apollo 11*. It was launched into space by a huge rocket. It took three days to get to the Moon. Once there, the astronauts spent two hours exploring before flying back to Earth.

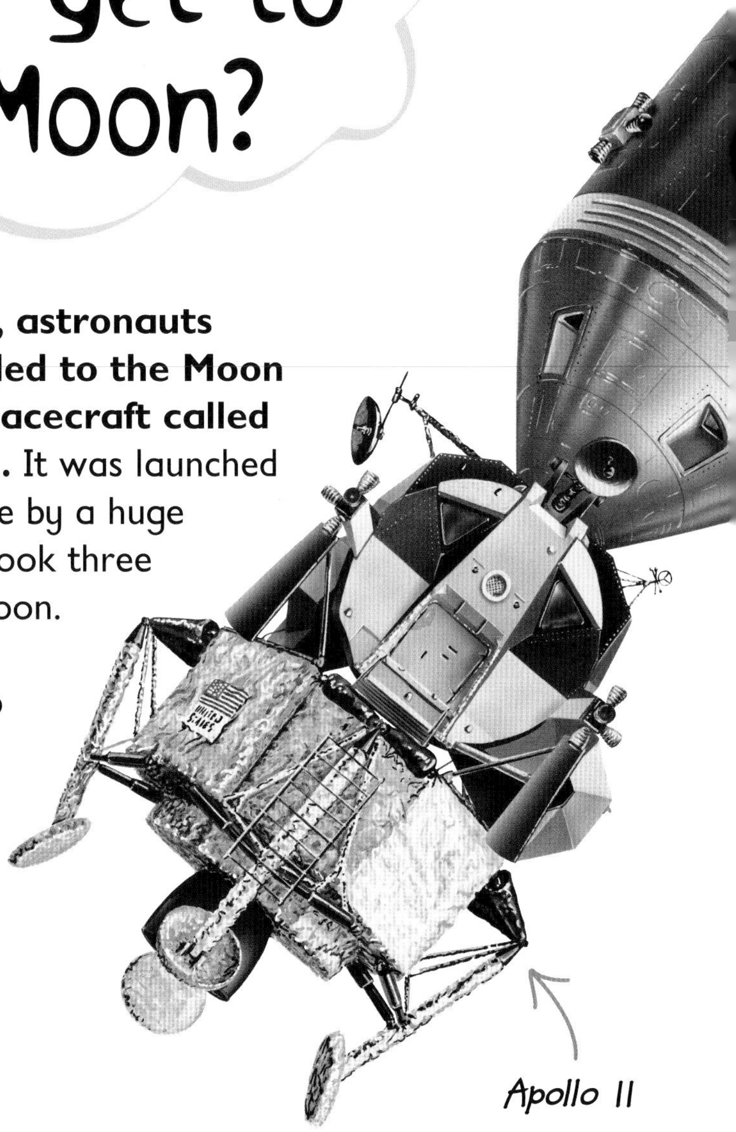

Apollo 11

Look

Can you see the Moon and stars when you look at the night sky?

Space animals!

The first astronaut in space wasn't a human, but a dog named Laika. Sadly, Laika died during the voyage, but she led the way for more space exploration.

Who was the first man on the Moon?

The first person to stand on the Moon's surface was American astronaut Neil Armstrong, followed by Buzz Aldrin. They were part of the crew of *Apollo 11*. Both men collected rocks to take back to Earth.

Yuri Gagarin

Who was the first human in space?

In 1961, Yuri Gagarin became the first human to go into space. Gagarin flew around the Earth once in his spacecraft called *Vostok 1*. This took nearly two hours. He then travelled back to Earth and landed safely.

Quiz time

Do you remember what you have read about explorers? These questions will test your memory. The pictures will help you. If you get stuck, read the pages again.

page 345

1. Who searched for a gold city?

page 346

2. Which explorer was very unlucky?

3. Who brought back a giraffe?

page 348

4. Why were spices like gold?

page 349

5. Who played a nasty trick?

page 352

6. How did explorers tell the time?

page 353

page 356

7. Who went on an important mission?

8. Who was scared by bears?

page 359

9. Who tried to get to the North Pole?

page 360

10. Who were the first Australians?

page 361

11. Who conquered Everest?

page 363

12. Who explored the natural world?

page 364

page 367

13. Who was the first man on the Moon?

Answers

1. Spanish explorers
2. Ibn Battuta
3. Zheng He Zheng
4. Because they were very valuable
5. The Spanish explorer Francisco Pizarro
6. Using a chronometer
7. Captain James Cook
8. Meriwether Lewis
9. Fridtjof Nansen
10. The Aborigines
11. Tenzing and Hillary
12. Charles Darwin
13. Neil Armstrong

Index

C

H

I

J

K

L

N

O

P

R

S

T

U

V

W